Covert Hypnosis
2020
Revised and Expanded

GW00771728

An Operator's Manual for Influential Unconscious Communication

Kevin Hogan

Kevin Hogan
www.kevinhogan.com
Copyright 2011
Kevin Hogan
All Rights Reserved

**Covert Hypnosis 2020 (Revised and Expanded):
An Operator's Manual**

Includes Bibliographic References

ISBN: 1-934266-21-3

ISBN: 978-1-934266-21-2

Psychology
Self-Help Techniques

Printed in the United States of America
Network 3000 Publishing
3432 Denmark Ave. #108
Eagan, Minnesota 55123
USA
(612) 616-0732

Rights inquiries should be directed to the email: meta@ix.netcom.com
www.network3000publishing.com

4

Table of Contents

Foreword

Why I created Covert Hypnosis

The Social Engineer,

The PUA,

The Salesperson,

The Therapist,

The Leader,

The Online Marketer,

The Advertising Agency,

The Cult.

All are performing the same actions. Why? They all want to persuade others to their way of thinking.

If you have control in any situation, you will never be at a loss of job, work, success. If you have no control in most of life's situations, then your life is out of control.

In 1997 I was researching Thought Control, Behavior Modification and everything known to date about Mind Control.

I came upon two unique books, *Covert Conditioning* and it's partner, *Covert Conditioning Casebook* by Joseph Cautela and Albert Kearney.

In a nutshell, **Covert Conditioning is a POWERFUL psychological tool utilizing the imagining of behaviors being performed, then either reinforced or extinguished.**

The tool is equally as effective for all of the above individuals mentioned.

This is different from traditional hypnosis in that hypnosis doesn't use behavioral reinforcers or extinguishers in imagery work. And it needs to do so to have a higher level of effectiveness.

Covert Conditioning differed from other psychological tools in use in behavior modification for much the same reason.

An example.

In the past one might want to encourage someone to quit smoking. A therapist would have the person imagine behaviors they would do in place of smoking.

They would have the person see themselves in all kinds of situations.

They wouldn't see or experience the reinforcement.

There was no audience applauding.

There was no one in the imagery that was telling the person how proud they were of the individual.

There was no check up at the doctor where the doctor said, "You probably just saved your life..."

There was no reinforcement.

To this day, almost all hypnotic interventions neglect covert conditioning.

I assure you it is a mistake.

The difference between adding reinforcers and extinguishers into imagery, hypnosis and behavioral modification is a game changer. It often doubles or triples the results.

No matter how effective, most people don't change the use of their favorite form of therapy, intervention or modality. They become religious about what they were taught. They become victims of their own mind control and that of those that are in their environment.

I encourage you to read *Covert Conditioning* as well as the companion volume *Casebook*.

In the late 1990's I was very active in the "hypnosis community." For a decade I was the President of a State Licensed School for Hypnotherapy and Hypnosis in Minnesota.

I spent much of that time researching hypnotic techniques, NLP strategies and techniques and the approaches of other related fields.

Some of what we researched provided shocking results.

Example: I found that what I had learned about eye accessing cues (NLP), for example, was totally unfounded. A three state study showed undeniable results.

I had been wrong.

Embarrassingly wrong.

I had a popular book on the book shelves (*The Psychology of Persuasion: How to Persuade Others to Your Way of Thinking*) with "The NLP Eye Accessing Cue Chart" proudly displayed on one of the pages.

The chart was simply what I "was taught in NLP."

I had convinced myself it was "real" and that "it worked."

It didn't.

I had developed an absolute blindness so that I saw what I wanted to see.

I had been in a contextual trance.

Constant research helped find other errors, inferior processes, impotent tools.

And we learned often by complete luck, different behavioral modification techniques and experiences that actually did work.

The first edition of *Covert Hypnosis* represented what I wanted to be the foundation of a new field of research. It was released in 1999.

And Covert Hypnosis was born.

It was exciting to be the founder of a field of study.

For three years it was the only work in the field. It needed to grow.

And it did.

Unfortunately, voids where research was needed became filled by typically unproven NLP Techniques and, typically marginal Conversational Hypnosis approaches to change work.

Most of this material was tested in the 90's and early 2000's and found to be impotent.

Most, but not all.

In the last decade, we've seen many of the techniques of Covert Hypnosis that I developed in the 1990's go "mainstream", and that is exciting.

Much of the language of Covert Hypnosis spread into public use, in addition to language used at Universities.

It's exciting to see terms I coined from 1991-2002 now in use.

- Covert Hypnosis
- Covert Persuasion
- Law of Reciprocity
- Law of Expectancy
- Master Persuader

And over 20 other terms or phrases that were part of this body of work are now used in everyday language around the world.

But the work is far from complete.

Covert Hypnosis, as I developed it, is still incomplete.

This manual has been revised. It is updated.

Much of the material was well researched, validated and reliable. It needed no change.

My continuing study and fascination is what works in persuading, influencing, and changing minds.

Short term.

Long term.

What's effective.

What is rapid in nature.

What is brief, subliminal, supraliminal, biologically/evolutionarily "wired."

Much, like the origins of Covert Hypnosis, found its roots in Covert Conditioning, some of Milton Erickson's work, and the absolutely breakthrough findings of Dr. Stephen Reiss at Ohio State University...Covert Hypnosis is not the complete brainchild of Kevin Hogan.

It is an eclectic field that needs to return to its origin.

What is proven to work in silent influence...

This book brings you up to date.

Enjoy!

Kevin Hogan
Minnesota, 2011

Introduction: What This Book will DO for YOU

If you want the girl to say "Yes", you are in the right place.

Don't think this is a strictly for PUA book. It's not. It's far more broad in scope than that.

This book will show you not only how to get the girl (or guy) to say "yes", but you will find out how to:

- Gain control of almost any social situation.
- Increase sales.
- Get the raise you want.
- Manage for maximum compliance with elegance and brilliance.
- Get the best deal on anything you buy.
- Get to agreement quickly in relationships.
- Get anyone to do just about anything you want them to do.

This book does require a reader with average or above intelligence. This is not Covert Hypnosis for Dummies.

I'll give lots of examples from sales because most people of influence tend to earn their livelihood as salespeople, marketers or entrepreneurs. I attempt to stay away from examples from most other obvious uses for this knowledge.

Why?

You want to be able to learn a CONCEPT and apply it to ANY SITUATION. If I give you a script, it will work for one person, one time, and it won't work again. I know, I've written scripts for companies. They burn their customers out.

Imagine I had a great "line" to pick up the cute girl over there.

Imagine someone reads a book with that line in the book.

They use the line with the cute girl.

She says "No!" The guy was an idiot.

You approach the girl the next day.

You aren't an idiot but you used the same words as the guy who was....yesterday.

This is exactly what happened with "Sales Techniques" in the 1970's.

Salespeople burned out customers and created great suspicion of the field in general.

Don't turn "Yes", into "No."

Scripts are for the weak.

Concept is your strength.

Using the tools you learn in this book, you will eventually be able to almost "read" people's minds.

Let's go back to the guy wanting to ask the girl out and combine that with the concept of "reading minds" for a moment.

If you are at the bar or club and you have a trick or psychic cold reading effect you happen to be drop dead perfect at executing, there is almost NOTHING that impresses a woman more than being able to read her mind. Because cold reading is almost foolproof in execution, that is an excellent opener. That means you could do a Palm Reading (a very good idea as you incorporate touch with the compelling belief that you are linked with the girl) by example.

But here's the thing.

If you are this tightly scripted (You only know how to ask a girl out if you do a Palm Reading) you will fail far more often than you will succeed.

Understanding CONCEPT means that you have more intelligence than being a script reader.

You have 10 ways to approach the girl, the prospect, the client, the employee, the child.

And more importantly, you learn to understand WHY these approaches work so you can easily construct equally as effective approaches.

Covert Hypnosis opens the door for giving you the most flexible communication known to man.

You will be able to know what program is running at each given moment and easily "see" what strings are "in play" and ready to be pulled. *You will be in control of each communication you participate in.* Your confidence will soar. People will literally beg you to sell them your products.

Mastering covert hypnosis means that you will be able to move people to the point where they seemingly cannot control themselves. They will demand to be with you, to want your input or buy from you.

Zig Ziglar once said, "They don't care about how much you know until they know how much you care." That is a Mind Access Point, and that is our philosophy in teaching you. (A M.A.P. is a stimulus response trigger rooted in behavioral conditioning or neurobiological response.)

> *If you truly care about people, they will demand to be with YOU, buy your services and they will be loyal to you for a lifetime.*

Napoleon Hill, the great success philosopher, said to "go the extra mile" for people.
Are You READY?
Say "Yes", or "YES!"

What else will you learn as you turn the pages in this book?

- You will learn how to predict human behavior with accuracy.

- You will learn how to cause her to desire...you.

- You will learn specifically what to do to create demand for your products or services.

- You will find out how the simplest hidden elements of an environment or even a touch at the right moment can turn "no" into "yes."

- You will learn exactly what the motivating forces are within each individual and among groups as wholes.

- Discover how to alter your products or services so people insist that you allow them to buy from you, NOW.

- Learn how genes influence other's behavior, so you can pull their genetic-strings.

- Find out all the keys to writing powerful copy that backs up verbal claims and makes for great personal presentations.

- Realize the limitless potential of unconscious communication.

Unconscious Communication:
Reaching The Only Decision Maker You Will Ever Need To Talk To

What is unconscious communication? Before we define it, let's see if we can give you two vivid examples to prime your mind to understand the concept before putting it into words.

1) Have you ever met someone with whom you had instant chemistry?

2) Have you ever met someone whom you knew you didn't like, before they ever uttered a word?

In both cases, unconscious communication was occurring long before anyone spoke.

Unconscious communication includes the sending and receiving of verbal and non-verbal communication as it is perceived by the unconscious mind. The unconscious mind is that part of our thinking that we are not aware of at any one moment. It's always there and it's always paying attention. In fact, it's always communicating.

What are some other examples of unconscious communication?

- The way a person smells may or may not register at the conscious level of thought but it "speaks volumes" at the unconscious level. The scent you wear or whether you wear none at all alters the entire perception of any selling situation you enter into.

- The exact body posture and gestures you have can trigger positive or negative emotions in anyone you meet. People aren't aware of these triggers at the conscious level, but the unconscious mind immediately detects them.

- For example: If the person you are speaking with was physically struck by a parent as a child, just viewing a hand raised above the head can create fear. At the conscious level the buyer doesn't know that he rejected you on the basis of something that happened to him as a child, but the unconscious mind knew instantly that it didn't like the other person.

- Where you sit at a table will increase or decrease your chances of "hearing yes", depending on what chair you select and how you sit in that chair.

- When making a presentation, whether you use a podium, and/or how you use a podium can make or break a successful communication attempt before you utter a word.

- Wearing contact lenses will make some attempts at using covert hypnosis more likely to succeed and others less likely. This book will teach you how to know whether to wear glasses or contacts.

- Jewelry sends messages at both the conscious and unconscious level. You'll learn all of the correct types of jewelry to wear and when to wear jewelry. Each person you meet will be different and you will need to make adjustments.

- Your physical appearance will make and break communication. This book will show you when casual is a must, when an expensive coat and tie are demanded, what skirt lengths a female should wear and how the unconscious mind perceives differences in dress.

- The unconscious mind processes the tonality of words and phrases while the conscious mind processes the language. The tonality will normally overcome the actual words and phrases. Do you know when to change your tonality?

- There are words that the unconscious mind almost always says "yes" to. The conscious mind finds them irrelevant but the unconscious mind makes the decisions. Read on and you will learn what they are.

- How close you stand to a person will determine whether or not he is instantly turned off to you and your products and services.

This book brings to your fingertips, (which by the way also send unconscious signals to everyone you meet) the secrets of Covert Hypnosis . We all have coded into our brains thousands of stimulus-response experiences. Any person can knowingly or unknowingly pull your strings and you react immediately without conscious thought. Each of these is a Covert Hypnosis "Technique." If you master only 20 of the hundreds of techniques to gently touch other people's nonconscious mind, you will get pretty much everything you want in life.

Every communication you have from this day forward is going to be much easier. As you find yourself becoming more skilled at unconscious communication, you will find that you rarely ask for a sale. "Closing the sale" will quickly become a thing of the past or, at worst, a mere formality. Your clients will literally *demand* that you sell them your products and then they will develop loyalty to you in a such a way that makes future selling a mere formality.

That isn't a promise, it is a guarantee. Utilizing unconscious communication is a skill that takes some time to master.

As you practice one technique each day, you will find yourself in control of every persuasive situation you enter into. You're on your way to being in charge from this day on.

Turn the pages and learn how these triggers developed in each of us. Then learn how to pull the right strings and push the right buttons with each of your clients. Let's get to it...

Trance Action

Chapter One

Remember When You Forgot This?

You're driving your car to the office or work. Somehow you arrive safely even though you are a bit surprised that you don't remember much of anything that happened from the time you left your driveway to the time you pulled into your parking space. How is that possible?

You got in the car and you drove. You should be able to remember the turns you made, the signs along the way, and the exits you took to get to work, but you don't.

The reason?

You were in trance.

You may have always wanted to ask a hypnotist if he could make you forget what happened while you were in trance. Now you don't have to wonder because you do it every day on your own!

There are several "types of trance" (what some people mistakenly call hypnosis). One kind of trance is what we call the *dissociated trance.*

The implication here is that **you have at least two very distinct "tracks" going on in your mind at the same time.** In the case of driving your car to work and not remembering the commute, you don't remember it because you were partially dissociated from the driving experience. The nonconscious part of your mind was pretty much driving the car and the conscious part of your mind was "sitting in the passenger seat," maybe having an imaginary conversation with your boss, your spouse, a customer or your kids. Whatever the conscious part of your mind was doing, it wasn't driving the car or you would remember the signs, the roads, the commute and the other cars, but you don't.

The reason you don't remember is because your conscious mind was distracted by thinking about other things it considered more important than driving.

When someone asks you what *a hypnotic trance is like* you can tell them, "it's like when you are driving a car and you can't remember how you got where you were going to."

The nonconscious mind drove the car to work and your conscious mind sat in the passenger seat having conversations with others or maybe watching movies of what the day would be like. The conscious mind was in deep thought. The unconscious mind was driving the car. We call this experience "dissociation" or *"divided consciousness."* This is a common everyday trance experience that nearly everyone is familiar with. It's that simple!

What is very interesting is that if someone had pricked you (once) with a pin, or pinched you, while you were driving, you almost certainly wouldn't have consciously felt a thing! Most people experience these dissociated states of mind each and every day.

Now, I want to be absolutely certain you completely understand trance and dissociation.

What are some other examples of the dissociated trance state?

- Have you ever read a book or an article and at some point you realized that you didn't remember what you had just read and had to go back and read it again...and again? (Your conscious mind was focused on something other than the book and your unconscious mind was trying to read the book!)

- Can you recall a time when you were listening to someone talk to you but you were really involved inside with your own thoughts and weren't able to keep up with the person talking to you? (Your conscious mind was busy at work and your unconscious mind was nodding your head but your attention wasn't really "all there.")

- Have you ever cut the lawn or made dinner, only to barely remember the experience as you were busy "inside" thinking or talking to yourself? (This is like driving to work and not remembering how you got there. Two very distinct tracks going at the same time and you did a good job at both.)

It is worth noting, by the way, that in some cases, the unconscious mind does a good job when the conscious mind is busy doing something else. When does this happen? When the unconscious mind is guiding an activity that is primarily physical in nature or an activity that has been done many times, the conscious mind can attend to other more thoughtful projects on the "inside."

Unfortunately when most people *try* to do two different "thinking" activities at the same time, the results are usually not as good. It is very difficult to keep track of two conversations at the same time. It's also difficult to be "inside" talking to yourself while listening to someone talk with you and then attempt to process both sets of communication. In fact, it just doesn't work.

So far so good...

The Power Trance and Other Everyday Trances

The Everyday Trance of divided consciousness is the ideal trance for managing pain and reducing the effects of symptoms. It's necessary to experience divided consciousness if you are going to ride a bike and think about other things at the same time.

The Flow State...The Power Trance

There is another kind of trance that is experienced by many people every day and that is called the *"Flow State"* of mind or the *Associated Trance*. You might also call it the *Power Trance* because of the remarkable things that people accomplish in this state of mind.

The Power Trance occurs when you are thoroughly engrossed in some activity that you obviously are challenged by, or you are completely absorbed and engaged, or you simply and completely love to partake in. Maybe you remember a time when you were watching your favorite TV show and found yourself crying because of the reality of the fictional drama. You watched a horror movie and were completely terrified even though you "knew" it was "just a movie." Perhaps you have played a game and lost track of everything outside of the game to the point where the rest of the world just "disappeared."

During these kind of experiences you become completely wrapped up in whatever you are doing. What's going on in the outside world just becomes unimportant. You lose track of anything outside of your desired experience. *These periods of everyday trance remind us how easy it is to associate to, or step into, a different reality other than our own.* Remember this as you read on!

Have you ever played a game or done some activity where everything else around you just seemed to disappear?

An excellent chess player will play an entire game of chess and not think of anything but that game of chess. We call this being associated. The chess player

18

has no other thoughts, no other distractions. The chess player's mind is only in the chess game.

A great tennis player is completely "in the zone" when playing the game. There are no thoughts of what to make for dinner, the trip home or paying taxes. Her thoughts are completely involved in the game and when the tennis player is really good, the thoughts almost seem to disappear and she is simply playing the game as if she is a part of the game.

Two things happen when you are completely in the moment in this type of everyday trance. The first is that the world dissolves around you and you become part of the experience. You don't experience the game, *you are the game*. The other thing that happens is that you are completely focused. You don't worry about what other people think of you, you don't think anything that isn't relevant to your actions, you simply experience the moment as you are.

This "flow state" is the optimal state for peak performance and one we will return to over and over again throughout this book. When you are in flow, everything you experience in flow is like making love. It could go on forever and you would be happy and successful, never wanting to leave.

The Flow State (Power Trance) occurs when a person is..

a) challenged but not overwhelmed by the environment
b) has a strong desire to engage the challenge

In other words, the person wants to play baseball but because they've only been playing for a few years they don't want to face a Major League Baseball Pitcher because they will simply strikeout every time they come to the plate. It becomes pointless, uninteresting. The challenge is too great.

Similarly, the adult doesn't want to play baseball against 10 year olds because there is no challenge and thus no desire, even though the person loves baseball.

All of The States and Trances that we have discussed to this point are trance-related,, but they are not "hypnosis."

Trance is not hypnosis, though hypnosis can occur while in trance. Hypnosis can also occur outside of trance!

The mystery deepens...

Optimal Trance Moments and Your Real Biorhythms

Oddly enough, there are moments or periods when trance is most easily "achieved." There are moments where trance is easy to induce in another person.

To capture this idea you want to understand "biorhythms."

Many years ago, the idea of biorhythms became popular. There were supposedly three cycles of time that everyone experienced, beginning at birth. These cycles would give you various high and low points, say, emotionally and intellectually, every few weeks. Over time, it became obvious that these specific multi-week period biorhythms simply didn't exist.

However, there are biorhythms that *do* exist.

Most women, for example, have a periodic menstrual cycle, though it is by no means perfectly predictable from month to month.

There are also daily rhythms that almost everyone experiences called **Ultradian Rhythms.** These cycles begin about every 90-120 minutes and they vary from person to person in both when they begin and how long they last. These periods of "spacing out" happen to just about everyone, every day, several times per day. Almost everyone experiences these cycles. Using these cycles can benefit your health, happiness and can completely change your life! The Ultradian Rhythm phenomenon is important to practitioners of hypnosis because, as Milton Erickson knew, there was a specific time to do change work and that time was when someone entered that period of "spacing out."

The ideal moment to utilize many of the tools of Covert Hypnosis is this moment.

What IS Hypnosis?

Hypnosis comes from the root word "hypnos" which means sleep.

Sleep, however, has nothing to do with what hypnosis is. ("Psychology," by analogy, literally means study of the soul, and of course, psychology is nothing of the kind. Similarly the word "hypnosis" is a misnomer, meaning nothing like what it's literal origin is!)

Hypnosis is best and most simply defined as bypassing the critical faculty of the mind.

Some people would submit that hypnosis is the ability to access specific every day trance states of mind at will, both dissociated (divided) and associated (possible flow state). I wouldn't argue that.

Others will tell you that Hypnosis is the umbrella field of study of altering states of mind and consciousness to create change in your mind which will ultimately create change in your body and your life.

That works as well.

Hypnosis can help you heal, create change and help you pursue your life's dream. Hypnosis is influence.

For the purpose of this book, to begin to learn to master Covert Hypnosis, hypnosis is bypassing the critical faculty of the mind in the most rapid and efficient manner possible.

Now what does THAT mean?

The Critical Faculty of the mind is a metaphor that is best thought of as the B.S. Detector. It raises red flags when "it sees something it doesn't like."

Turn off the Critical Faculty of the mind and there is an open door waiting for you.

This book shows you how to "do hypnosis" on purpose instead of the experience happening randomly, if at all.

Going Deeper

Chapter Two

Hypnosis and Trance Phenomena are Everyday Experiences

So just what is a trance?

A trance is a narrowing state of attention. Trance experiences include a simple every day daydream, "spacing out," being completely "into" an erotic experience, or being worried about something that might happen. In each of these cases, your attention is focused in a specific area and you are not consciously thinking about everything else that is going on around you.

Each and every day, you experience many trances. On any given day you may live through trances of frustration, annoyance, depression, anxiety, and a host of other unwanted experiences. All of these trance states can be changed through hypnosis or self hypnosis.

Self hypnosis is a process whereby you take control of the trances you experience on an hour by hour and day by day basis.

For yourself, you can learn how to de-hypnotize yourself from the trances (states of mind) you no longer wish to experience. You can also learn how to hypnotize yourself so you can experience those states of mind you do want to enjoy. Your mind is for you to take control of.

But what of controlling the mind of others?

That's an experience.

But first I want you to take control of *your* mind.

For this specific experience, allow yourself to be calm in a quiet environment, if possible.

Clear your mind. You can imagine all of the worries and problems of the day getting smaller and eventually becoming granules of sand that slip from your hands as you try and hold them...ever tighter...with less success...

Go out into the future...10 years...and imagine a specific day that you will be living...living a life that makes a difference...and experiencing the rewards of that living.

Imagine clearly who is with you and how they look. Notice what others in this vision are wearing and how they see you. Look around in this vision and in your mind's eye, see how positively people respond to you. Notice what you hear. Notice what you feel...the air temperature.

Relish these moments.

Notice how you feel inside.

Now, bring these feelings back with you, to today...and realize that this is your future and that your future is now in part, in your present.

How does this make you feel inside?

When you are ready, take a deep breath in...and then out...and then focus on the words that come next on the following page....

...

...

...

...

...

...

...

...

...

...

...

...

...

...

...

...

...

...

...

...

This experience *uses a hypnosis technique you will use a great deal and ultimately master in Covert Hypnosis. It is known as "pseudo-orientation in time."*

Pseudo-orientation in time is a common trance experience that includes clearly seeing a future scene or event. You may see yourself getting married or divorced. You may see yourself getting audited by the IRS or making a big sale. Whatever you are seeing, you are not experiencing something in this moment or from the past. You are in the future. If you were going to direct your mind to focus on a desirable future event, you would be using this experience on purpose and then you would experience one kind of self hypnosis.

Each day, you can go out into your future and bring back to the present, the pleasant feelings and experiences that you expect to happen there. The more rich and real they become, the more your unconscious mind will seek out specific life patterns to achieve your desired future. The unconscious mind, though childlike, is very much the goal-seeking part of you. Therefore when you regularly experience sensory rich (everything you can see, feel, hear, touch and taste) experiences in your imagination, your mind will become directed toward making those creations a reality. The unconscious mind has a tendency of finding ways to make the pictures and images it experiences real, for better or for worse. *This is the first lesson of hypnosis and self hypnosis.*

The simple images of going 10 years into the future can help you make dramatic changes in your life. The reason is simple. The unconscious mind accepts these images as virtually-real. The unconscious mind then begins to seek out paths that will ultimately lead to the experiences you set forth in your mind. It isn't quite magic but it comes very close!

Imagine what would happen if you could learn the power of hypnosis and use it in your everyday life. What would you do? How would you act? Would you change yourself in some way? Would you think about changing others around you?

Never underestimate the power of hypnosis. You will find that you can improve your health, your happiness, your intelligence and even your income...all through the power of hypnosis.

And while we are defining terms....

What is Self Hypnosis?

Self hypnosis includes a variety of experiences that involve shifting your state of mind from one state to another. Self hypnosis encompasses the creation of inner reality and fantasy using the power of the imagination for purposes as wide ranging as simple relaxation to killing cancer cells. Self hypnosis can include experiencing one, two or all of the "senses" in the mind's eye. Self hypnosis can be experienced with your eyes open or closed. There is no single definition of self hypnosis because the varieties of methods of altering states of consciousness, the depths of the changes in conscious experience and the intention of the changing of states make the simple term "self hypnosis" too limiting to describe all that can be done with the power of your mind.

Self hypnosis by implication is directed by the self and therefore we predict that a part of the self is always in consciousness even when a large part of the self is active at the unconscious level.

The Power of the Mind

Your mind can do some pretty remarkable things.

Your mind can control your Self.

Once you can control your Self...for periods of time, you can control Others.

Controlling Your Self is not as instantly simple as it might sound.

Your "Self"?

Your nonconscious brain can "decide" on some answers to problems at speeds only exceeded by the guy in the car behind you hitting his horn when the light turns green for you. (The brain cranks out rapid- fire answers to questions like these: Should you hit the brakes? Should you pick up the stranded motorist? Should you donate to the person collecting at the front door? Do you buy Dove or Ivory?) The unconscious mind decides all of the answers to these questions so you don't have to think about it at the conscious level.

If you had to consciously decide what to do in every single situation in life you would be completely overwhelmed and never get anything done. The wonderful thing about the unconscious mind is that once it understands something it will take care of it for you without asking for further advice from the conscious mind. Your unconscious mind automatically brakes when necessary and drives by the motorist as you call 911 on your cell phone to call for police help for the person.

The unconscious mind has learned over the years what to do, and it continues to do those same things over and over again until intentionally taught to do something differently.

Using the power of your mind, you can learn how to lengthen your life, perform better at work, lose weight, stop procrastinating, learn faster, physically look better, be happier and create virtually any kind of lifestyle you can imagine for yourself. Your mind is the control panel of your life and it is also completely in charge of altering the overall health and function of your body.

Most of the experiences we have, our character, our habits, our choices can all be improved or changed with self hypnosis. Your character is partially predisposed by genetics. There are genes that predispose some people to being a criminal or getting divorced.

However, we can take control of these aspects of our life with hypnosis. We can also take charge of our health with self hypnosis even though many of the diseases and disorders people experience are genetically predisposed. Our genes definitely bring us life and they bring us many of the challenges that we must overcome as well!

Self hypnosis has been shown to improve the longevity of some people with breast cancer. Self hypnosis can improve health in people with both chronic and psychosomatic illnesses. That said, be certain it is clear that just because hypnosis can help improve the health of the chronically ill individual, it doesn't follow that psychosomatic or chronic illnesses aren't "real." Psychosomatic illnesses are very real and often deadly. There is good news, though! Hypnosis can often completely "unplug" psychosomatic illnesses and can sometimes give new life to the sick or dying people who suffer from these terrible illnesses.

People who suffer from tinnitus, environmental illness, fibromyalgia, chronic fatigue syndrome, multiple chemical sensitivity and numerous other disorders can make great long-term gains with hypnosis. Many of these illnesses are not just physical or psychosomatic, but they are indeed both of organic and emotional origin.

In situations of great stress and distress, a hormone called cortisol is released into the body. Cortisol release is directly related to reduced effectiveness in the immune system. Even though an immune system that is too strong can be dangerous, most people can use a bit of an immune boost.

When Should You Do Self Hypnosis?

One interesting recent discovery in the field of hypnosis is that almost every human needs about a 20 minute break every 90 minutes or so.

After working or being active for about 90 minutes, research reveals that people should take a break and mentally rest. These cycles appear to happen across all cultures and are evident in men, women and children. Recognizing just when we need to take a break can help us use that time most effectively. The best way to utilize that time appears to be with hypnosis.

If we work through these break times we are actually creating stress that is completely un-necessary for our lives. You can learn how to take 15-20 minute breaks that will help you heal and excel in your personal life. Certain activities are good for you during these break times while others are not. One of the world's greatest hypnotherapists (Milton Erickson) used to wait until the beginning of his client's mental break times before putting his clients into trance.

He knew something at an intuitive level that we now know to be a fact: There is a best time to do hypnosis and that is at the beginning of this important break called the common every day trance.

If you are reading a book, you will know when you come to this part of your cycle because your eyes will get "fuzzy" and "gloss over." If you have ever read a paragraph or a sentence and then re-read it several times and didn't understand what you read, then you have read into a break time that your body is demanding. The left brain is essentially shutting down and is not interested in taking in any more information until it has taken a mental rest. Erickson used this moment to do his best and most important work.

These rhythms have been evident for centuries but recently Ernest Rossi, Ph.D., author of *The Twenty Minute Break*, has championed the optimizing of the natural experience of these Ultradian rhythms in everyday life. When people go into these short periods of being "spaced out" they could maximize these moments by listening to self hypnosis tapes or just taking a 15-20 minute break.

I won't be returning to this notion as it relates to your Self, in this book, so be certain that you RECOGNIZE this moment in yourself and others. Much of your success in using what is in this book will depend on your learning to spot these specific moments.

A Thumbnail Sketch of the Mind and Brain

One simple (over) generalization you are probably ready to make about the brain is that it is divided into two parts. The thinking part of the brain we will refer to as the cortex. That's a generalization, of course. It's not perfectly true or right, but for the sake of discussion.

The emotional part of the brain, we will refer to as the limbic system.

The cortex is the part of the brain that helps us act rationally in the face of emotionally charged circumstances. The thinking part of the brain keeps us out of trouble by stopping us from doing harm to others when we get angry. It is also the part of the brain that helps us make good decisions for ourselves when the emotional part of our brain would have us do otherwise!

The emotional part of the brain is called the limbic system. The emotional part of our brain plays an important role in psychosomatic illnesses. The negative emotions are important to experience but also equally as important to discharge when the time is right. Hypnosis helps us do this as well.

The limbic system is where the emotional/irrational part of us lies. It is where the flight/fight response is generated from. We want this part of our brain to make only the decisions that are absolutely necessary.

The limbic system, for example, is the part of you that makes you run faster than you normally can when a dog is chasing you. It is the part of you that recognizes that "thing" crawling across the floor might be a snake. It doesn't know that it's a snake but it knows that it might be a snake and so it makes you act swiftly. The emotional part of your brain is very important to your survival but it can also cause us all kinds of problems.

Phobias (often single trial and always fear-based learning) are created in the limbic system from incorrectly associating a trigger to a fear response. For example: Claustrophobia (a fear of being in tight quarters or closed in places) might start when someone is physically punished in their bedroom and then told to stay there for the rest of the night. The person then unconsciously associates being in the room with feelings of sadness, pain and hurt. A phobia has been created.

When we talk about the conscious mind, we are talking about everything that you are completely aware of at this moment.

When we talk about the unconscious mind, we are talking about everything that you have "stored" in memory or are currently experiencing, but are not aware of at this moment.

All of your memories, experiences, and emotions that you are not experiencing now, make up your unconscious mind.

For example: You are reading the words on this page. You see the black and the white on the page. You are sitting or lying down and know that. You are aware of any sounds around you and these are all conscious thoughts. Whatever you are focusing on right now, is in consciousness. Your conscious mind is where you put your attention.

As we change what we pay attention to, we change what is in our conscious awareness. As we focus more intently on what we are paying attention to, we automatically reduce our awareness of other things that are happening around us.

Our conscious mind generally can hold about seven bits of information at any given moment in time. A phone number is usually about the maximum that most people can hold in consciousness at any given time. Everything else that is going on out there is not going to be coded into our conscious awareness without our forgetting the phone number we were thinking about. Try this experiment. My phone number is 612-616-0732. 612-616-0732 . Got it? Now listen to all the other sounds that are going on around you. Feel how you feel inside. Look up at the environment around you.

It is very hard to remember new information without "coding" it into your brain. Coding means that some kind of association or rehearsal of information takes place. Some people code phone numbers by saying them over and over again. Other people use mnemonic devices to remember them. Most people write them down and put them in a phone book! The reason this is so is that it's hard to remember new information without having something to associate it to. That phone number that you read really is my phone number but you probably won't remember it because numbers are very difficult to remember.

People don't have much to associate numbers to.

Now, what was my phone number?

Now you have an idea of what the conscious mind is and what I mean when I say those words. The conscious mind changes from moment to moment and it is what you are aware of, now.

The unconscious mind is very different from the conscious mind.

The unconscious mind is the repository for every piece of information you have ever learned and experienced. Some information that you have learned or experienced is very difficult to recall.

Did you go to college?

Can you quickly name four of your professors that you had in college?

Most people over 30 cannot even name two of their professors from college.

Most people over 25 cannot remember the names of all of their teachers from elementary school. Can you? Who was your first grade teacher? Can you remember your second grade teacher? What was the name of your third grade teacher? Fourth grade? Fifth grade? Sixth grade?

If you can't remember, don't worry about it. Most people don't recall all of their teachers. After all you only spent every single day for a year with this person and then saw them in the hallway for years after that...

We've defined almost everything except...

What is "Covert"?

Covert means "covered" or "hidden." "Stealth" or "secret."
Covert doesn't connote "good" or "evil."
Covert is simply... invisible.

Covert Hypnosis is bypassing the critical faculty of the mind through invisible, secret or hidden means.

Covert Hypnosis should not be confused with Conversational Hypnosis which relies on "Hypnotic Language Patterns" and similar tools. Some of these patterns have some value and I will point out a few of them later in the book, but generally speaking, conversational hypnosis has been completely marginalized by the work I began creating and developed in Covert Hypnosis in 1996.

No longer do we rely (solely) on words. More often the tools of Covert Hypnosis are far more subtle and silent. Body Language nuances, The Core Drives of Human Behavior, the ability to ask a question to generate a state or response you want to receive, and more.

Covert Hypnosis takes predictable responses and reactions to minimal stimulus/factors and helps you reverse engineer the situation so you can cause almost any reaction you choose in a group or with individuals.

These are elements of Covert Hypnosis. These...and more...

As you will see...Covert Hypnosis is pure power.

Even Deeper into Them...and You

Chapter Three

You now understand a little bit about just how divided consciousness is all but necessary for trance. But that's only trance.

What's the next crucial question you need to be able to answer in order to utilize Covert Hypnosis?

Does divided consciousness mean that you are two people?

Are you really two personalities woven into one person?

I confess, it's a funny thing- the personality of the unconscious mind correlates to a person's behavior and the person's conscious mind correlates to a person's behavior...but *the conscious mind and unconscious mind of one individual don't correlate to each other!*

In other words, you are indeed two "different people", or perhaps you might say you have two different "parts" or "Ego States."

And so are they.

They are what they "think" and they are what they "do," and the overlap between the two is not as big as you, or they, would like.

THE KEY TO COVERT HYPNOSIS...One of the Great Secrets of the World

CORE CONCEPT: People typically look to make sense of themselves and the world around them. Because all people do and say things that truly surprise, individuals must construct (fabricate) a narrative (story) that makes sense of those behaviors that conflict with one's intentions. The rationales and explanations help put the inconsistencies behind and move on to other things.

Without rationalization, both to yourself and others, you'd go nuts. And so would they.

If you had to stop reading right now and just understood that CORE CONCEPT, you would have enough to develop something similar to Covert Hypnosis yourself!

"What were you thinking?!"

The question has no real answer because the person wasn't thinking ANYTHING.

They simply acted, behaved.

There was no thought.

There was no consideration.

They didn't think about it, or consider it, or wonder, or ponder, or anything. There WAS a STIMULUS and THEIR NONCONSCIOUS REACTED TO IT. That caused a behavior.

The result was perhaps strange or even outrageous. Completely unexpected.

And neither the person who performed the action or anyone watching it would have a REAL ANSWER to the question, "What were you thinking?"

The fact is if they could answer literally it would sound something like this...

"I was thinking about something else and my body and brain behaved by taking actions that were completely nonconscious in nature for which I had no control over as I was doing a math problem in my mind."

Sounds like a bad excuse. And it might be a poor excuse, but it's how humans function.

Why are people conflicted so often?

Why can't they make up "their mind"?

Why can't they "decide"?

Why can't they get past, "part of me says yes and part of me says no?"

It's because there...are...two.

Memory Distortion

What makes understanding your Self and others even more difficult is the painfully distorted memories you carry in that three-pound universe.

The brain simply isn't a video recorder that records events.

The brain is a vast array of storehouses and interpreting functions that constantly *store, re-store, interpret and reinterpret* our memories and beliefs.

False memories are so common that almost every conversation of any length includes reference to at least one memory that never happened.

One of the most powerful "tools" of Covert Hypnosis is "installing" a false memory.

Obviously, this could be done for the purpose of great harm, but I would encourage you to do so only for good. I will explain why...and how... later in this book.

Think of it this way. You order a chocolate dip cone. That first dip is going to be the experience. That dip is when the memory gets coded into the neural net in the brain. You ask the guy to dip it again in the chocolate. That is the same as reviewing the memory.

Reviewing the memory changes the memory and the content in the memory as well as future interpretation of that memory.

KEY POINT: Recognizing these two defective elements of the human experience (our suspect memory and the dual nature of our personality), one can understand the arguments, the fights, and butting of heads that take place in relationships and communication in general between people who have lived through the same events and remembered and interpreted them so differently.

At this point in every conversation, in every relationship of every kind and type, YOU now have a MASSIVE EDGE of CONTROL.

People tend to believe that others should be "responsible for what they say and do", and of course there is truth to that.

But now YOU KNOW that there is a question that must be asked and answered:

WHICH YOU?

By understanding to just ASK that question you now have more knowledge about a person's Self(s) than *they* ever will.

The conscious mind that is engaged in conversation that requires thought and consideration is one part of the human. The Unconscious Mind, which is the sum of all those memories and interpretations and the reactions put in place, is another part of the same human.

Take that Unconscious Mind and break it down a bit and you learn even more...

Five Parts of the Unconscious Mind

There appear to be five specific "parts" or facets of the unconscious mind that establish the RULES for YOUR behavior.

- how people construct themselves and others
- expectations about themselves and the social world
- goals and values
- emotions
- competencies and self-regulatory plans

What's interesting is that people do not have access to these elements of their unconscious experience, therefore they are poor at "knowing who their unconscious mind is...and how it will cause them to behave in a given situation."

32

Recent research does show that there is some predictability in how you will respond to other people. If, for example, you are fond of your sister, you will tend to be fond of people who exhibit similar behaviors as your sister.

This is because humans are "Recognition Creatures." We tend to respond or react in a similar way to things that look/sound/feel like other things that we respond and react to.

When the thing slithers on the floor, you don't think about it...you simply "know" it is a snake, even if it isn't. Your brain recognizes it as a snake even if it is a piece of rope or string.

If you take a gun and shoot the snake only to find out that it was a piece of string, you'll probably wonder...what...you were thinking.

And you weren't.

You just reacted in a very predictable fashion.

That predictability is another critical piece of the Covert Hypnosis Code.

But how do you know what you or ANYONE would do in a given circumstance?

You learn which of The 16 Core Drivers or Desires have shaped your behavior. Once you know which 2 -4 drivers are driving your Brain Bus, it's really fairly simple to predict your behavior. Find out what drivers are driving someone else's bus, and you can predict their behavioral reactions.

Probably nothing is more important to Covert Hypnosis than understanding - knowing, what a person will do and consciously think in most situations. The Unconscious Self is much easier to predict and understand than you'd ever guess once you know those drivers.

And once you know the Core Desires, you can change behavior, cause people to do specific behaviors.

You can't change behavior if you don't know how what the person perceives to be reality or truth.

Without knowing the drivers, you are guessing, playing with "Hypnotic Language Patterns" and often making yourself look bad.

Example? Imagine you see the girl. She's beautiful.

You pull out your book of Hypnotic Language Patterns and attempt to dazzle her with your Syntactic Ambiguity. You attempt to get her to say "yes" and she says, "no."

And then she looks at her friend and says, "What an idiot."

That all transpired because you have no idea what drives her. You don't even know what drives YOU.

Learn her core drivers and everything changes. NOW you know how to frame communication. The charts in this book show you PRECISELY what people think about you and what they think about other people in general. You can KNOW what they are thinking as long as you identify their drivers.

It's that simple. Once you know what someone is thinking, you can all but read their mind and NOTHING is more impressive than that.

When someone believes you have "special knowledge" or "incredible insight," they ascribe almost diety-like traits to you.

And that isn't so unreasonable because almost no one has the ability to see these core desires and drivers.

It wasn't but 15 years ago that Dr. Stephen Reiss finally catalogued the Core Desires and identified the perceptions an individual experiences when they are driven by a specific driver. Reiss's book "Who Am I" is brilliant and should be on your book shelf.

All it takes is a few questions and being attentive to capture the information you need. I've included many, many questions in this book. Most of those questions relate to selling situations. But obviously, all you do is change the context as needed, as the intent of the questions stay the same from context to context.

Until you know the drivers, you are simply playing a random game with people. Sometimes you win, sometimes you lose.

People who engage hypnotic language patterns (an example among many "tools" that are generally impotent, thought there are exceptions) are like cute children who often get their way by their simple level of being obnoxious. But that provides no lasting or predictable success.

Allow yourself to learn and KNOW people and what they think.

So who are YOU? WHO are THEY?

Understand your Self first, and then it is much easier to understand others.

How do you find out what your own Core Desires Are?

1) Go to the Chapters that reveal the Core Desires and learn first what drives YOU.

2) Then look at each of those drivers and match yourself up with the perceptions of Self vs. Perception of Other People. When you strongly resonate with a Desire or its Polar Opposite, you have found one of your strong drivers.

3) Do that for all 16 Core Desires.

Do not skip this exercise or you will NOT understand the rest of what follows in this book.

I promise you will never learn more about your Self and what makes you tick.

Once you've found your drivers, think about your best friend or someone in your family you know well, and do the same exercise for them. Find out what makes them tick.

So, how do you actually come to know your "Unconscious Self"?

It's not instantly easy to KNOW your Self. You'll need to study those 16 drivers, their polar opposites and then assess yourself. You'll be able to identify you by going through each driver and finding which perceptions of Self and Others most resonate with you. In a few hours, you'll know your Self a lot better than you ever have.

To actually know yourself, you need to observe the drivers in action in life situations. Be aware when they are "triggered" to defend you or aggressively pursue something.

First, learn which Core Desires (Drivers) move you and understand how you SEE OTHERS and YOUR SELF.

Then begin to pay attention to your behavior in light of what you discover about your Self.

Pay attention to your behavioral IMPULSES in any given situation and you begin to learn "who you are."

And of course, even that is suspect because you don't see your Self as clearly as you will see others.

Research reveals that you are a better judge of others' future behavior than you are our own. You tend to see your Self in a much better light than you see others and that light creates a halo effect that most people believe about themselves.

You tend to see others more accurately.

Real estate agents observe the lack of sense of self-knowledge in others every day. They listen while their clients describe the exact house they want and then show them several houses which their clients love and one which they eventually buy that has little in common with what the individual detailed just hours or days before!

And when you do see your Self behave in some fashion, you often have no idea why you did what you did.

Even when you know the 16 drivers and their polar opposites?

Yes...

Why?

Danger and Arousal

A research project had an attractive woman approach men on a somewhat dangerous footbridge and start a conversation.

The same women later approached men seated on a bench away from the footbridge.

65% of the men who were approached on the footbridge asked the woman for a date.

30% of those on the bench asked the woman for a date.

Arousal was attributed incorrectly to the woman on the bridge instead of the actual anxiety provoking feelings that the person felt on the bridge.

UNDERSTANDING WHY is just as important as understanding the behavior itself.

People want to drive the behavior of others before they understand their own. And of course, they fail.

Unfortunately we don't have the ability to access the "reasons" we do these kinds of things and observation only helps to some degree. Of course, our need to find a reason for behavior, any reason, helps us make sense of our world and make us happy, even if it isn't accurate.

You'll need to do better than that, of course.

And, what about those faced with difficult decisions in life? Beginning or ending a relationship? Buying a business or not?

To Ponder or Not to Ponder

If you can't get your Self to make a decision, you certainly must be able to realize that you aren't likely to be persuasive with others, either.

How do you know if your decision making skills show your ability to control your own mind, thus making you ready for the next Quantum Leap?

Rule of Thumb: Is your financial net worth enough to take care of you/your family for at least 5 years if you quit working today?

Why a financial yardstick?

Because it's the ultimate signpost of Self Control. Either you control your behavior or your behavior causes you to justify it.

Prefer a different yardstick?

Is your Credit Rating over 750?

If so, you have self-discipline, if not self-control.

Using Covert Hypnosis to control The Self begins with the awareness of those drivers and how they shape who you are, what you do and how you perceive others.

And how does Control of the Self play into self persuasion?

The research is compelling. After initially analyzing the problem once, the individual stands a far better opportunity of having made a good determination than the other individual who ponders the same singular event for days, weeks, or months.

Key Point: Once you have the data, crunch the numbers and make a decision.

This is true even when people write out their reasons for their decisions on paper or on computer. In comparison studies, individuals seem to make better decisions when gathering enough information, thinking about it then deciding vs. writing all the reasons for and against an idea. (Ben Franklin is rolling over in his grave...and I'm sure I will, too!)

So, with this rather bleak picture of how poorly we make decisions and how poorly we know each other, what is the answer?!

What is the Answer to understanding the Self?

If you really want the girl to say "yes" and you really want to know what to do with your life...

Going out into the future, and speculating on what events and experiences might take place is the best option for creating the changes necessary when conflicted. **To be sure, we can't accurately predict how we will feel in the future.** This has been shown in volumes of studies. However, we can gain foresight by specifically seeing ourselves in future situations and determining what course(s) of action will ensure the success of those determined course(s).

For years it was thought that journaling was a grand way to determine insight and learn about ourselves. And this is true as long as we do not journal after particularly negative or traumatic experiences which will later taint the story of our life into being something it was/is not.

Instead, it's best to journal on a consistent basis and describe events and experiences with the realization that negative emotions happen daily in everyone and that, in itself, is not necessarily a bad thing as long as action is taken on those states to improve the quality of life each and every day.

Numerous studies have shown that people who think about the negative emotions that have been recorded actually end up far worse than had they not reviewed the emotions of the past. Such is the nature of writing history then re-writing it without the benefit of all the other experiences that occurred that day/week/month/year. Result: These people tend to predict a more negative future for themselves than those who do not ruminate.

Timothy Wilson, Ph.D., says it this way: "Unhappiness and ruminating about your unhappiness is a bad combination that leads to more depression."

In the final analysis, the road to changing the self is about creating behavioral change first which will almost always lead to attitudinal change and thus change feelings from sadness and depression to feelings of contentment and perhaps even happiness.

And what of understanding others?

Begin with the 16 Core Desires.

The same tools you use to get your Self to decide whether to go left or right or pick A or B are the tools you'll use to get others to say "yes" or "no."

Evolution of Hypnosis

Chapter Four

Hypnosis has been known to man for thousands of years. Historically, the practice of making shifts in man's consciousness has been carried out by Shamans, Wiccans, spirit mediums, and spiritual doctors, for various reasons. Ancient civilizations of Egypt and Greece recorded that the fastest way to get in touch with the spiritual realm is through rituals that are similar to what are now called hypnosis, meditation, visualization, and experiences that are often mimicked by drugs.

Experiences common to deep sleep, anesthesia and the power of the nonconscious have been noted in different religious documents, such as in the Old Testament of Christianity and in the Talmud of Judaism.

Taking the cue from their ancient traditions, indigenous cultures even in the present day still take benefit from mind control and suggestion and its ability to heal – or harm.

Mesmerizing Magnetism

In the modern world, hypnotism's first brush with science was known in the late 1700s, through Austrian physician Dr. Franz Anton Mesmer and the "phenomenon" that was called **animal magnetism**. Mesmer believed that through a mystical force channeled through water tubs and magnetic wands flowing from him to his subjects, he can make people and animals go under trances. He claimed this mystical power was due to magnetic waves. He lulled his subjects into submission through fixating them on a certain object, and through monotonous repetition of certain words. This is where the word "mesmerize," which we still use today to pertain to the act of being in awe and dumbstruck to a certain figure, was coined.

But after further scientific study of hypnotism, the concept of animal magnetism was eventually dismissed by none other than Benjamin Franklin.

Abbe Faria, a scientist in the 19th century, declared that the hypnotism practiced by Mesmer was not because of animal magnetism – but through the power of suggestion.

The Pendulum

More studies and experiments in **mind control** followed through the years, but it was a research launched in 1842 that was considered the turning point in the study of Mesmer's ideas. Scottish surgeon James Braid was one of the first scientists to attribute the process of going under a trance to a *physiological* process. He believed that the state of trance was not due to the magnetic power of the hypnotist; but through hard, rapt attention on a striking, moving object over time, as in that iconic clock necklace. "Protracted ocular fixation," Braid believed, will make the brain tired and will cause the subject to be under what he called "nervous sleep." Thus Braid coined the term "hypnotism" and "hypnosis," based on the Greek word "sleep."

Braid, with his contemporaries such as Ambroise-Auguste Liebeault, Hippolyte Bernheim and J.M. Charcot, later focused more on the impact of psychological motivation in hypnosis rather that their early concept of fatigue and nervous sleep.

They were also the first ones to tread upon medical hypnosis, wherein they used hypnotism to treat different psychological and physical conditions.

Following the paths taken by Braid et al., more studies on the use of hypnosis in medicine followed – with better results this time. Mirroring (though perhaps unconsciously) the practices of ancient doctors, modern medicine started to cautiously tread upon the use of hypnosis as anesthesia or pain killers. The medicine world then had a strong disbelief in this method; as in a case in 1842, when there was a report of a successful and painless amputation procedure through hypnotism. But it was quickly dismissed.

Still, pro-hypnotism medical professionals persisted with their studies. Dr. James Esdaille, a British physician who practiced in India, performed almost 400 pain-controlled operations with patients under hypnosis. Known as the "Father of Hypno-anesthesia," Esdaille also integrated his Western education with the culture in India. Hand-in hand with his medical practice, he also performed a drugless trance therapy traditionally from Bengal, India. Esdaille's cases listed eye, ear, and throat operations, amputations, and tumors and cancerous growth removals. Esdaille reported no pain and zero mortality under his so-called "mental anesthesia."

What's more astonishing is that after the surgeries, Esdaille further hypnotically suggested to his patients that their wounds would not result in any kind of infection or side effect. True enough, no one among his patients was reported to have caught any post-operation side effects. Many believed the subconscious aspects of Esdaille's subjects responded well to hypnotism. When Esdaille suggested they would not be infected, their bodily functions acted accordingly and launched antibodies that would fight infection.

Soon, the death of Braid, Esdaille and other kindred colleagues, plus the advancement of anesthetics though chemicals, waned the interest in hypnotism.

Hypnotically Hysterical

Hysteria and hypnosis? Strange bedfellows at first glance maybe; but after hypnosis kept a relatively low profile after Braid, hypnotism made a comeback in the 1880s as new versions of his work were circulated. The revival also came with new experimentations, particularly in the use of hypnosis in treating hysteria led by neurologist Jean Martin Charcot.

Charcot, and later his pupil Pierre Janet, treated various cases of mental conditions, but most particularly hysteria, through what they called *dissociation*. This technique, utilized in a big number of patients, compartmentalizes some of the data stored in the mind, so that aspects such as a particular skill or an information from the past can be hidden or retrieved.

Considered landmark experiments at that time, these findings impressed and inspired later works of French psychologist Alfred Biet and the father of psychoanalysis, Sigmund Frued.

In fact, Freud used the works of Charot and another French doctor, Hippolyte Bernheim, to strengthen the framework of his initial studies on the unconscious and hypnotism.

Meanwhile, science has enriched the layman's dictionary once again since it was in this time that Ambroise-Auguste Liebault coined the term *rapport* – meaning that critical and required consensus between the hypnotist and the subject for a successful hypnosis session. Today, we still use the word rapport to mean that pleasant communication connection between two parties, a certain similarity in wavelength.

Hypnotism and War

A powerful weapon, a strategic device, an intelligence technique and a medical tool – all these roles were said to have been taken by hypnosis during World Wars I and II.

War trauma is common to soldiers who have faced the horrors of war. Hypnotism was used by physicians to help patients in letting go of their "repressed memories", and to eventually treat amnesia or other resulting conditions. This kind of therapy also helps the patient alleviate emotional and mental tensions resulting from the trauma.

John G. Watkins is a United States psychologist best known for his work in the areas of hypnosis, dissociation, and multiple personalities. With his wife, Helen Watkins, he developed ego-state therapy, which uses analysis of underlying personalities rather than traditional talk therapy to find the causes of psychological problems.

The most famous example of the use of ego-state therapy was the interrogation of the Hillside Strangler, in which Watkins solicited a confession by revealing the killer's multiple personalities.

Watkins is a graduate of the University of Idaho and holds a Ph.D. from Columbia University. He is professor emeritus at the University of Montana, where he taught for many years.

Watkins' work continues to be the most influential of all figures in my work both when I was a therapist and now as the creator and developer of Covert Hypnosis.

The powerful suggestion invoked by hypnosis was also used as a tool for military intelligence. For example, extremely confidential information that has to be passed personally can be protected through the power of suggestion. In this case, the information will be given to a soldier under hypnosis. After the information has been relayed successfully, the hypnotist then suggests to the courier that he will never remember a single detail about the message, thus ensuring that it remains a secret forever.

Since hypnosis can also be effective in altering the behavior of a person, it was used as a strategy to infiltrate the enemy's ranks. G.H. Estabrooks, a physician who has worked with United States Authorities in World War II, divulges in a medical journal that the behavior modification properties of hypnosis were useful in sending a deep penetration agent inside a communist territory. He also narrated: "I worked this technique with a vulnerable Marine lieutenant I'll call Jones. Under the watchful eye of Marine Intelligence, I spilt his personality into Jones A and Jones B. Jones A, once a 'normal' working Marine, became entirely different. He talked communist doctrine and meant it. He was welcomed enthusiastically by communist cells, was deliberately given a dishonorable discharge by the Corps (which was in on the plot) and became a card-carrying party member."

Estabrooks work also greatly influenced your author....

And today, 70 years after Estabrooks, we have the most subtle powerful form of bypassing the critical factor of the mind yet, Covert Hypnosis....

Covert Hypnosis

Chapter Five

The phrase alone draws up images of the clandestine and secretive. And perhaps it should. My first goal for the balance of this manual is to show you how to utilize covert hypnosis in any setting: dating, relationships, clinical or corporate, communication or selling.

There is a certain amount of "control" that is implied, and often real, in the term "Covert Hypnosis."

With all that we have discussed to this point, it might be useful to set the stage for the rest of this book.

---

100 years ago, hypnotists would say, "sleep" when they wanted someone to go into trance. They simply misunderstood what was taking place in the subject's mind.

The first definition of hypnosis I want to use is that hypnosis is "a narrowing focus of attention." We will also consider hypnosis as "dissociation" or complete "association."

For example, we may have someone dissociate themselves from their current state of mind and maneuver their thinking into a different state of mind. If someone is speaking from a point of view that is dysfunctional, I may choose to covertly turn his or her thought processes towards outcomes. If someone is telling me how busy they are, I might just have them focus on the results they want and direct their attention to what is important instead of what is "busy." Sometimes they are the same and sometimes they are not.

*Key Point: You always meet them on **their** landscape, then you focus in on the reality you decide you want the other person to focus on.*

Dave Elman defined hypnosis as "bypassing the critical factor of the mind." That is an excellent if not rather ambiguous definition. I personally prefer it, but if we translate that into 21st century English, we come up with a more workable definition of hypnosis. Hypnosis is communicating with someone, or the "mind" of those in a group where the receiver of the message is using significantly less critical thought (questioning the message) to evaluate the message than they normally would.

The purpose of using Covert Hypnosis is to influence someone's (or some group's) unconscious mind(s) to change their behavior or beliefs in some fashion.

In this book, you will learn how to cause people to focus on things/events in a covert fashion. In other words, they don't know you are using covert hypnosis. It's "secret" or certainly unspoken. As soon as someone recognizes that they are not evaluating incoming messages, the covert hypnosis "has gone to work."

Covert Hypnosis is bypassing the critical factor of the human mind without the process being known to the receiver of the message.

A better way of understanding this from a social perspective is that covert hypnosis is accomplished when one person sends a message to another person and the message is received without significant critical thought or questioning on the part of the receiver.

Covert Hypnosis significantly involves state manipulation and state management.

The state of mind a person is experiencing at this moment may be productive or not. It might be depressed or not. It could be joyous or not. It could be scholarly or not. It could be sensual or not. It could be volatile or not. When using covert hypnosis, the practitioner judiciously changes the state of mind of the individual from one state to another state.

If someone has a number of useful resources in their history, you can utilize them. If they don't, you can point your subject(s) in the direction they need to go and take them as far as necessary using Covert Hypnosis. Most people do NOT have all the resources they need to make change, so you will have to help create the directions and resources for new behavior.

Imagine a six-pointed star like the Star of David. In the middle of the star, you have a large area that will metaphorically represent the "core self" of the person.

Each of the six points on the star represent "ego states" or part of the person that are not represented by other tips of the stars. One point could be "the volatile self." Another point could be the "scholarly self." Another point could be representative of the "gentle self." Another point could be representative of the "happy self." (Obviously, we could use a 20 or 30 pointed star as a frame of reference in this metaphor, but the six points make it nice and easy to understand.)

Let's imagine that a person is in the "volatile self" state. That point on the star, we'll call it point one, is pointing north. The point that is north is the state that is currently in "charge" of the entire self. If we find that dealing with the person in the state of "volatility" isn't useful at this moment, use covert hypnosis to spin the star to a more useful state. Perhaps the "scholarly self" is the third point on the star and that is the state you would like to access and maintain in your friend. Utilizing the tools of covert hypnosis, we help the volatile self disengage and spin the star so the third point faces north.

Key Point: Covert hypnosis is, in part, the intentional manipulation of another person's ego states. This can include the intensification of a state of mind, the relaxing of a state of mind, the redirection of energies of a state of mind, the re-wiring or changing of a state of mind, and so on.

The volatile self, noted above, will not easily disengage, however. Generally speaking, the more intense a state is, the more difficult it is to disengage.

Covert Hypnosis, among other things, includes shifting and maintaining specific ego states within another person or group of people.

Now, before we go any further, let's make sure we understand what covert hypnosis is and is not.

Examples of Successful Covert Hypnosis

1. A hypnotist tells a client to imagine the future clearly without formal trance induction and the client does so without saying, "I just can't see it..." IS using covert hypnosis.

2. A guy asks the girl out and she says "yes."

3. A parent telling her children to stay away from the highway without the children significantly questioning the message IS using covert hypnosis.

4. A commercial on television that you receive without significantly questioning the claims IS covert hypnosis.

5. An ad in the newspaper that you read without significantly questioning the claims IS covert hypnosis.

6. A preacher who preaches a message and you accept it without significantly questioning the messages IS using covert hypnosis.

7. A salesperson that tells you about a product without you significantly questioning the message IS using covert hypnosis.

All of these experiences meet the criteria of covert hypnosis.

Examples of Failure

1. A hypnotist who tells his client to see the future, but the client says, "I just don't know where I'm going..." is NOT covert hypnosis.

2. A parent who tells her children to do something and a fight ensues is NOT covert hypnosis.

3. A commercial on television that you receive and say, "I don't think that is even remotely true," is NOT covert hypnosis.

4. A weight loss ad in the newspaper that you read and say, "There is no way you can lose 10 pounds per week..." is NOT covert hypnosis.

5. A preacher who preaches a message and you like the preacher but you disagree with the message is NOT an example of covert hypnosis.

6. A salesperson that tells you about a product and you do not believe the salesperson is NOT an example of covert hypnosis.

You might wonder why in the case of the salesperson I didn't say that the person had to buy the product or service. Actually buying is not a required signature of covert hypnosis. A person without the money could easily have been in "state" but they simply didn't have the money to buy. It should also be noted that you cannot always measure how much in "state" a person is.

Can a person be in a state of "fear" and be in trance? A state of "anger"? A state of "depression"? A state of "frustration"? A state of "annoyance"? You bet. All these are common everyday trance states, and it can be the desire of the person utilizing covert hypnosis to ethically or unethically access these states in someone. You might be wondering how someone who is being encouraged to access a state of "fear" could possibly be in waking trance.

Hypnosis has nothing to do with "relaxation."

<u>Hypnosis is Resistance Reduction or elimination.</u>

Consider some examples.

Imagine that someone tells you that if you don't pay your taxes, you will go to jail. You may not like the person. You may not be in rapport with the person. But you probably trust them and believe them and you access the feelings of fear instantly. That is trance, and the person used covert hypnosis very effectively to get you into the state of mind that they wanted you to be in. The fear you might experience is not the reaction to the practitioner. It is to the future experience. The person is fully dissociated from reality and their resistance has dropped.

Imagine that someone asks another person what it would be like to have cancer and die a slow, agonizing, painful death because of smoking cigarettes. The person doing the imaging may not like the person, they may not trust the person, but if the person puts those pictures in their mind and follows the suggestions of the communicator, that is covert hypnosis because the listener did what the communicator asked without question.

As you can see, trust and belief are critical to hypnosis. Liking and rapport lead to trust and belief but they are not always the same experience. More often than not, liking and rapport are necessary for belief and trust.

It's not necessary for you to like someone to be "covertly hypnotized" by them.

Imagine someone puts a gun to someone else's head. That person's state shifts very quickly. Fear instantly takes over the body and a laser beam focus of attention to the exclusion of all other stimuli begins. Certainly there is nothing about "liking" the person holding the gun necessary for this trance.

That said, I believe it is very important for liking and affinity to play a role in many "forms" of Covert Hypnosis.

The Ethics of Covert Hypnosis

Obviously you will never walk up to someone, perform the ritual of an induction and have someone fall into a deep eye-closed "state of relaxation." Such is the experience of the stage and priming.

It would serve no purpose in real life and could be very inconvenient in most all cases. Everything you are learning is about utilizing the most effective tools of hypnosis, of subtle influence, of hidden persuasion.... in a very "wide awake", often intense, and wide aware state. Before we go any further, let's look at the ethics of this.

46

Is it ethical to do this or to actually "change someone's mind"? Is it ethical to influence someone without his or her awareness? Is it ethical to influence someone *with* his or her awareness?

I certainly believe that it is not only ethical, but also necessary for survival in the 21st century. I also know that the tools of covert hypnosis can be used for ill and that will never change.

Generally speaking, if you are utilizing the tools of covert hypnosis and you are doing so because of, and for, the best interests of another person, you are probably utilizing covert hypnosis ethically. If you are utilizing the tools of covert hypnosis to promote the behavior of another person to do something that is not in their best interest, that is not ethical.

This conversation wouldn't be complete without asking, "Who are you to say what is in someone else's best interest." I completely understand. Please do remember that every day, people are making hundreds of decisions for you on your behalf. These decisions are ethical and unethical.

The Congress and the President tax your money and spend it. Some of those things are for ethical purposes and others are not. You did not have a say in the matter, however. If you are a parent, you make hundreds of decisions for and on behalf of your children. You tell them what they can and cannot do. You tell other people what they will do. If you are a teacher, you are constantly making decisions for and on behalf of your students. One of the most common behaviors we take place in every day is making decisions for and on the behalf of other people.

But is it REALLY ethical?

My answer: Absolutely. Millions of communication messages are wittingly or unwittingly exchanged every single day. These messages often contain trance inductions and persuade people to take some action, or not. The difference between covert conversational hypnosis and conversation is that of intention. In everyday conversation, we tend to communicate without conscious awareness of our unconscious intentions. In covert conversational hypnosis, we tend to operate with full awareness of our intention and that of the person we are communicating with.

Imagine (note the hypnotic word induction) that you are a parent and you don't know how the unconscious mind acts and reacts.

"Don't put your fingers into the outlet, son!"

The son immediately moves to the outlet and places his fingers in the outlet. Why? The parent clearly ordered the child NOT to do that behavior. The reason is multi-fold. First, the child (in all probability) didn't know it was an outlet. It is a child's (people's) innate programming to be curious and explore that which is novel. Second, there is no unconscious or conscious representation of the word "don't." In fact, the word "don't" is what I call a "directive." This word is useful because we tend to have a polarity response to this word. In fact, in most people, the polarity response is quite strong.

The unwitting child was put into trance and told to place his fingers in the outlet. That was not the intention of the loving parent, of course. This was a trance-inducing conversation where the result was negative...and examples of these in conversational hypnosis are endless.

Covert hypnosis is not only powerful, it is very real. We accomplished getting the son to put his fingers into the outlet with hypnosis. Now that we know what we are doing, we can use covert conversational hypnosis appropriately and make sure his fingers stay occupied with more appropriate behaviors!

The Power of Suggestion Changes Perception

Covert Hypnosis, involves creating change in the mind of another without them ever becoming aware of the fact.

By example, in a clinical setting the client has come to the therapist and asked them to help make the changes necessary in their lives. As will become obvious, a person's eyes don't have to be closed to covertly generate images in a person's mind, which become new memory.

What is the foundation of covert hypnosis?

Dozens of elements are involved in suggestibility.

As we look at each of them throughout this book, you will discover what changes people's minds and you will see what is impotent. You'll see why a script is normally ineffective... but at the right time with the right words and the right conditions, your words will change minds and lives.

Suggestion Changes Perception...and can easily create false memories.

Elizabeth Loftus (one of the world's leading memory researchers) performed a fascinating experiment. She showed a film to a group of people. The film was about a traffic accident. After the film she asked the group, "How fast was the white sports car going when it passed the barn while traveling along the country road?"

Several days later when witnesses to the film were quizzed about what they'd seen, 17 percent were sure they'd spied a barn, though there weren't any buildings in the film at all. In a related experiment, subjects were shown a collision between a bicycle and an auto driven by a brunette. Then afterward were peppered with questions about the "blond" at the steering wheel. Not only did they remember the nonexistent blond vividly, but also when they were shown the video a second time they could hardly believe what they were seeing. It was nothing like they remembered it.

Loftus concluded that hints leaked to us by our fellow humans over-ride the scene we're sure we've seen with our own eyes.

In another Loftus experiment done in the 1970's, the film is different. The people view slides of a pedestrian-auto accident. They also see a slide of a red Datsun at a yellow Yield sign. The group was asked, "Did you see the other car pass the Datsun while it was stopped at the Yield sign?" The biased recall group however was asked an even more biased question: "Did you see another car pass the Datsun at the stop sign?" Later most of the biased group remembered a Stop sign instead of a Yield sign! The verbal information again leaked into the visual recall. Suggestion changes perception....and can easily create false memories.

Suggestion from an *authority figure* can often over-ride a person's visual memory to create a new memory.

Your objective is to use covert hypnosis to create images in the person's mind (see simple strategies for utilizing covert strategies in this manual) that target the behavior the client wants changed and paint pictures on the landscape of the mind that vividly show that the changes are going to be taking place.

The brain will begin to see/remember what you tell it to, if you meet the other fundamental pillars of covert hypnosis which we will discuss in detail in the coming pages of this manual. To simply read off of a script and say, "The pain has gone, how do you feel?" is impotent. Covert hypnosis is quite different. The person will begin to feel less pain. There is no power in a script. There is enormous power (or not) in the hypnotist, the client, and the alliance of the therapist and the client. Once the fundamental power structure is in place in the hypnotist, the client and the alliance of the two then change can begin to take place and covert hypnosis becomes effective.

Covert Hypnosis allows you to paint pictures on the landscape of another person's mind.

When Resistance is Likely, Distraction Creates a Receptive...and Easily Persuaded Mind

Festinger and Maccoby conducted an experiment in which they attempted to prevent members of their audience from inventing arguments to refute messages being presented to them. (AKA resistance in hypnosis.)

This was accomplished by simply distracting the audience somewhat while the communication was being presented. Two groups of students were required to listen to a tape about the evils of college fraternities. The argument was powerful and was obviously not going to be well received by the audiences.

During the presentation to one of the groups, the audience was also distracted by a highly entertaining silent film. (That group is engaged in TWO tasks simultaneously.) The other group was not disturbed by a film. They simply listened to the tape.

What were the results of the experiment? The students who were distracted by watching the film underwent substantially more opinion change against fraternities than did the students who were not distracted.

The distracted mind is easier to manipulate and create change in than the undistracted mind.

Resistance is inherent.

Expect it.

Anticipate it.

Erickson said there was no such thing as resistance. Erickson was wrong. We now know that there is resistance. There is resistance AND there is reactance.

There is resistance in the mind of every human being to that which the individual does not believe to be true. There is resistance in the mind of each person to that which creates fear within the individual.

If any ego state is not in alignment with what messages are being shared between two people, resistance will be experienced. Be aware of this now. The resistant person more often than not needs to experience pictures he creates in his mind, not pictures created by you. (See: *The Hypnotherapy Handbook, Hogan*)

Your task is simply to direct people to the right pictures!

1.   When Resistance is Unlikely, Affirm Present Beliefs.

Numerous studies have been done that reveal that people are receptive to information and attitudes that agree with their point of view. People will formulate arguments on the spot against any point of view that disagrees with their currently held belief. Therefore: Always discover current beliefs and attitudes so you can affirm them. On the other hand, do not have your client verbally state anything that you will want them to change later. Once an attitude is communicated (verbally or in writing) it will be maintained, even in the face of overwhelming evidence to the contrary.

Key Point: Resistance is unlikely when people agree with the presented point of view. In these cases, powerfully affirm the individual's point of view.

---

2.   When Ego States Battle for the State of Mind...Utilize Ambiguity.

Ambiguity allows ego states on both sides of a viewpoint to be equally accepted. By allowing different elements in the unconscious mind to be accepted, we validate the whole person and not just one part of a person's unconscious feelings, beliefs and attitudes. Erickson was a master of ambiguity.

Barton said that *ambiguity is the vehicle for expressing conflicting feelings simultaneously.* "Part" of the client wants to experience trance and another part doesn't.

You say, "Please don't go into trance until you close your eyes." Both ego states are satisfied and trance is experienced. The suggestion is a bit confusing and distracting in itself. In some cases, indirect suggestions can be helpful in facilitating trance or even creating a direction. "You may or may not find yourself wanting to be more productive in your everyday life." The obvious suggestion is to "be more productive" but because there is permission offered, "You may or may not...," there is no pressure on the "unconscious parts" that do not want to be productive. This permission for ambiguity is non-judgmental and can be useful when it is obvious there are internal battles brewing in any situation.

Key Point: Be ambiguous when building rapport with someone who has polar ego states operating in real time. This ensures that both (all) ego states will be "comfortable" and will enhance affinity with the practitioner.

Reframing: What it really means to reframe...and do it well.

Test Yourself

I want you to participate in a Reframing Game that comes from Kahneman & Tversky (1984). Simply read this scenario and write down the answers before going through the evaluation. Imagine that we are preparing for the outbreak of a dangerous disease, which is expected to kill 600 people. Two alternative programs to combat the disease have been proposed. Assume that the scientific estimates of the consequences of the programs are as follows:

- If Program A is adopted, 200 people will be saved.
- If Program B is adopted, there is a 1/3 probability that all 600 people will be saved and a 2/3 probability that no people will be saved.

What do you advise? Program A or Program B? Once you record your answer, read on.

There are two other options now.

- If Program C is adopted, 400 people will die.
- If Program D is adopted, there is a 1/3 probability that nobody will die and a 2/3 probability that all 600 people will die.

Write down your choice of program C or D then read on...

Kahneman and Tverskey found that 72% of their subjects chose the "sure thing" program A over the "risky gamble", Program B. However, they obtained almost the OPPOSITE results when the question was framed the opposite way. 78% of the same people (doctors) then chose option D which is identical to option B. (C is identical to A)

In other words, if someone chose A they logically must also choose C. If someone chose B they logically must also choose D because they are the same exact responses. However, the framing or perspective that is given seems to shift people's thinking significantly.

Covert Hypnosis Key : Reframe with this in mind - *The majority of people will do far more to avoid losing something they already have than they will to get something they don't have.*

KEY POINT: Fear of loss is a much greater motivator to most than the possibility of gain.

Need more evidence? (Say "yes", as that is the logical response!)

Fear of Loss...

The same Princeton researchers that did the above research project looked at another situation. They told one group of students to imagine they have arrived at the theater only to discover they have lost their ticket. Would you pay another $10 to buy another ticket?

A second group were asked to imagine they are going to the theater but they haven't bought a ticket yet. When they arrive at the theater, they realize they have lost a $10 bill. Would they still buy a ticket? 88% of those who lost the $10 in cash said they would buy the ticket BUT only 46% of those who LOST the ticket (which they paid $10 for) would still buy a ticket!

There is **nothing** logical or rational about the way people buy or make their decision to buy from you. Logic would tell you that people want the best product. They don't. Logic would tell you that people want the most choices possible and that they make decisions logically...Nothing could be further from the truth.

Do people really always want to experience free choice?

Even more interesting is research released from Stanford. Researchers went to a grocery store and set up tasting booths in the store. On one table they had 24 jams that the people could taste. On another there were six different kinds of jams. As you would expect, 60% of all people who stopped at the table with 24 jams tasted a jam. Only 40% of those stopping at the table with six jams tasted there.

What's shocking? Listen carefully: 30% of all people who stopped at the table with SIX jams purchased one of the jams. Only 3% of people who stopped at the table with 24 jams purchased any of them!

The ramifications are enormous...another of our famous **$10,000 KEYS** that I like to offer you every few months.

The larger number of options (in jam, religion, spousal choices, jobs) creates what we call cognitive dissonance.

Cognitive dissonance is what happens when you hold two or more beliefs or ideas and don't know which to choose. It makes us feel overwhelmed. People like to have choices...it gives them freedom.

If you give people too many choices they will simply freeze and do nothing.

This is clear in a casino...where I have been known to spend a few hours. Bettors will drive themselves crazy trying to figure out which team, horse or color to bet on. When they place their money, they become certain they are on the correct side... Later when their team loses, they can say, "I KNEW it was going to go that way, I SHOULD have listened to myself."

Similarly, women do this when they buy a dress. They see blue, they see black...they stand there helpless. Finally they buy the black and THEN they FEEL better inside...in fact...RELIEVED!

When faced with too many choices (usually two or more) most people can become paralyzed and do nothing at all. People who feel overwhelmed simply drop everything...do nothing and give birth to procrastination.

If you tell someone "you can have any of these 100 choices of paint" there is a good chance they will freak out! People are NOT used to deciding between so many options. They won't be able to decide what to do. If you say, "I can give you one of these four options," then the person finds it much easier to choose.

The truly devastating impact of the internal desire to be directed instead of being given a few options happens in brainwashing and sudden conversion experiences. Here, there is only one correct "way" or "ideology" and all others are wrong. This solves the problem of cognitive dissonance and creates what Hoffer called, The True Believer. How do YOU utilize your new found knowledge about cognitive dissonance?

The Covert Hypnosis Skeleton Key

Every 4 year old child will tell you that the most important toy in a room full of toys is the one that the other child is playing with!

Now stop and read that again. And again.

I was in high school. I asked my female friend Erin what I should do to "get back" my old girlfriend.

"A sweater on another beautiful girl always looks better."

That one nugget was probably worth $100,000 all by itself.

People want what someone ELSE has.

Grab a note card. Write that down...the one that the other child is playing with...

YOU ALWAYS want to be the toy someone else is playing with.

This is true no matter what the context is. Selling, Marketing, Managing, Leading, it doesn't matter.

YOU *want to be the toy someone else is being played with. It is here that* **YOU** *are seen as having POWER.*

Seven Crucial Distinctions for Reframing

1. People crave direction. Give them direction that wires into their unconscious drives.

2. People want to believe they are in control...and feel better when they perceive they are.

3. Help people resolve their cognitive dissonance by narrowing options and alternatives quickly and decisively.

4. Realize that your profits in business or personal life will increase with fewer choices for your friends, clients and customers. There are NOT 64 color choices for the new Lexus or Honda. There are 7 choices.

5. Remember the Pareto Principle. 80% of almost everything that happens comes from 20% of the participants or options. (80% of the money is made by 20% of the salespeople and so on.) Use the Pareto Principle to design the very FEW options you need for your clients.

6. Too many choices means that people will freeze and not know what to do. Always be prepared to direct people to the best choice for them.

7. Always think long term. People look to you for guidance and will remember the results.

I want to share a couple detailed examples of reframing in difficult therapeutic situations. I'd also like to give you an example from the world of selling, as well.

Therapy situations provide the best examples for reframing because the resistance is highest here. It's higher than in sales or dating situations....by far.

Reframing is a crucial skill in subtle influence.

Reframing is also an ethical minefield. It can be the tool that takes a person from danger and brings them to safety, or the polar opposite.

Here is what most people think of when they think of reframing.

"So can you see how having this problem has really helped you in your life?"

"Aren't you thankful now that you have had this experience so you can help others with the same problem?"

These are not reframes, they are things parents say to children that didn't faze the child and they still don't work 20 years later. A reframe **helps** the other person see the same situation or thing in a different light. A reframe does not create resistance because the person designing the frame is the person asking the questions. The person responding is actually building the reframe from the design questions offered by the practitioner.

Here is an example of a master re-frame, which is only borderline ethical in my opinion. A salesperson is selling to a customer.

Cr.: I can't afford this car. It's just too expensive.
SP: What can you afford?
Cr.: I can afford $300 per month. This is $330 per month.
SP: Can I ask you a question?
Cr.: Sure.

SP: Would you be happy driving this car?
Cr.: Of course. It's great.
SP: Is it worth $30 each month…one dollar per day to be happy?
Cr.: Yeah. It really is.

This is an old-fashioned sales closing that uses flawed logic on the part of the salesperson which creates the illusion (hypnosis) in the mind of the customer that one-dollar per day is going to make the customer happy. That, of course, isn't really what is happening. In reality it's $11 per day for this car. (330/30)

This type of communication is what is considered borderline ethical. The customer is being asked to believe that happiness is costing $1 per day. The customer is also being unconsciously directed to not consider the actual cost of the vehicle. The salesperson could have said, "Isn't it worth one more dollar per day to have a car that will really make you happy?" That would be ethical.

Quite often you'll be communicating with someone who simply wants to disagree with you because they are disagreeable by nature, or they want to protect their very fragile identity.

The argumentative person is not a bad person. They simply are frustrated. They don't have answers and they want them. When people don't have answers and everyone thinks they are crazy, they are backed into a corner.

When I was doing therapy, most of my clients were 100% resistant from the moment I first laid eyes on them. And with good reason. They had been hurt by so many.

Here is an abridged version of a conversation where I used covert hypnosis to reframe the mindset of a client when I was doing therapy professionally. I was explaining how sometimes our problems and health issues are not a result of a virus or a disease that comes into the body from without but from within. This raised the defenses within my client. Here is how I handled this woman. Watch closely what I do to defuse her frustration. Notice how I magically zap her defensiveness and then lay the foundation for healing.

Covert Reframing Magic

Ct.: But I don't think Fibromyalgia is not psychosomatic.
KH: When someone has cancer, do you believe that it's possible that their frame of mind and their environment could influence how long they will live?
Ct.: Of course.
KH: And influence the quality of their life?
Ct: Sure.
KH: Is cancer psychosomatic?
Ct.: Of course not.

56

KH: So the mind body connection is important for someone who has cancer.

Ct.: Yes. I agree.

KH: We know that some people have miraculous recoveries from cancer.

Ct.: I guess.

KH: You've heard about people who tell them that their doctor said their tumors had shrunk.

Ct.: Not very often, but yes, I've heard cases.

KH: Me too. And I wonder what it is that causes tumors to shrink. It certainly isn't the cancer. Cancer's natural track is to spread.

Ct.: That's true.

KH: So something aside from the disease is causing the cancer to remit in some cases.

Ct.: Yes.

KH: So my question is what is that?

Ct.: The mind?

KH: Yes. The mind's effect on the body. Exactly. Now think about your day-to-day life.

Ct.: I hurt.

KH: I know.

Ct.: Kevin it's hard when you hurt.

KH: I understand. Now, we know that cancer isn't psychosomatic, whatever that means.

Ct.: Right.

KH: Let's say that fibromyalgia isn't psychosomatic either.

Ct.: OK

KH: Let's just say that we don't know what causes firbromyalgia, because we don't.

Ct.: Right.

KH: Is it possible that the same mind that can shrink a deadly cancerous tumor that is programmed to kill can help reduce the pain of fibromyalgia?

Ct.: I think so.

KH: When a person experiences a miraculous healing from cancer do they think the cancer was psychosomatic?

Ct.: Of course not.

KH: When you start to feel better, how will you feel?

Ct.: I will feel great.

KH: And when you feel great, will you be thankful to have a mind that had the power to help you heal your body?

Ct.: (Smiles)

KH: Ready to go to work?

Ct.: Yes. Let's do it!

Obviously this is a therapist/client communication, but it carries over to the guy who wants the girl to go out with him, to the salesman, to the parent.

The reframing conversation is a simple process of which the content is generally not all that important to the certainty of the end result being experienced.

The girl could be hesitant about the guy.

The prospect could be hesitant about the salesman.

The husband could be hesitant about the wife.

The above session conversation is virtually identical to any other situation.

This triggers my memory of another very resistant client I had when I was a therapist.

Some "covert hypnosis techniques" have been used for millennia but only in the last 60 years have they started to be refined. During these last six decades, covert hypnosis has been used to help athletes run faster, hit more homeruns and catch more touchdown passes. Covert hypnosis has been utilized to create conformity thinking in everyone from military personnel to corporate employees to churchgoers. Covert hypnosis is a powerful skill in the therapist's office as well. And, of course, those were techniques that were known.

Now we know a lot more than we did about subtle influence, probably twice as much in 2011 as we did in 1995.

For me the turning point was Covert Conditioning which you read about earlier in this book. Here is an example of how I used Covert Conditioning. This is slightly abridged from session notes from when I was doing therapy.

Covert Conditioning Transcript

> KH: What will happen if you continue to yell at your husband?
> Client: I suppose he will leave me.
> KH: What would that be like?
> Client: It wouldn't be any fun.
> KH: What would that look like?
> Client: Well, I suppose I would be alone with the kids and there would be no one there to help out.
> KH: What else would it look like?
> Client: I think I'd be pretty depressed.
> KH: What do you feel like?
> Client: I think... I feel sad...I cry a lot...I'm really very sad.

As you can see, the client has gone into trance as she talks with me. Her eyes were wide open...in apparent every day conversation. Notice that I suggested almost nothing to the client. The client suggests to me what it will look and feel like.

My predictions of what her life will be like are not important at this time. What she visualizes as the continuation of this particular target behavior is very important. By the way, the client was seeing me for anxiety and depression. The anger she was experiencing with her husband was significant and probably relevant to her long-term improvement. Notice what happens next.

KH: I understand. (Pause) And if you stopped yelling at your husband, what would that look like?

Client: (She looks away.) I think that he would want to spend more time with me.

KH: And what does that look like?

Client: We'd have more time to talk and be with the kids...more cuddle time.

KH: And are those all things you want to see in your life?

Client: Yeah.

KH: And how do you feel?

Client: I feel good.

KH: Do you see any bad things about not yelling at your husband anymore?

Client: (Pause) No. I don't think so.

KH: Are you certain?

Client: Yes. I really have to stop screaming at him.

KH: OK. So the next time you feel like you are going to scream at your husband are you going to go inside and say to yourself, "STOP! Do something else?"

Client: Yes, I can do that.

KH: What will you do instead of screaming at your husband?

Client: I can just shut up.

KH: What else can you do instead of screaming at your husband?

Client: I could just go do something else.

KH: What else can you see yourself doing instead of screaming at your husband?

Client: (she looks away) Take a breath and tell him what I feel instead of yelling at him.

KH: Are you sure that is a good thing?

Client: Yes. (she looks back at me) I can take a breath and quietly tell him what I'm feeling and what I need him to do.

KH: Let's just pause for a minute here. See what that looks like. Pause, take a breath and quietly tell him what you need him to do.

Client: (Long pause as she looks away) OK

KH: How does that look?

Client: He listens.

KH: Do you like that?

Client: (grins) Yes. I like that.

KH: And how do you feel as you say to yourself, "STOP! Do something else?"

Client: (smile) I feel good.

Several things happen here covertly.

First we find the target behavior (screaming at her husband) and we have the client ultimately identify what they would prefer to do instead of the behavior we are targeting to extinguish. We do this before anything else.

A critical element is to have the person tell you what they want to experience instead of the target behavior. They must see this behavior not just verbalize it. They must see the consequences of this new behavior just like they did of the actual target behavior.

And of course these transcripts are simply from therapy sessions. The same conversations happen all the time with clients, relatives, salespeople and so on.

Covert Conditioning Formula

1. Identify a target behavior. This is a behavior they no longer want to experience. It could be anxiety, hair pulling, swearing, anything. It COULD be a behavior YOU don't want this person to experience.

2. Have the person see what the continuation of the behavior will ultimately mean.

3. Have the person identify a preferred behavior.

4. Have the person identify the consequences of this new behavior.

5. Be certain that the behavior is REALLY the behavior they want to experience. (Sometimes someone will tell you what they think you want to hear instead of what they want to do.)

6. You need to be certain the behavior is ecological. (That means that it is going to be good for the person and others in the environment.

7. Do not judge what you perceive to be inappropriate responses by the person.

8. Never tell the person they are wrong.

Covert Hypnosis for Performance Enhancement

While going through the session archives of clients I saw when I was doing therapy, I came across this session. An excellent example of how to generate performance enhancement and breaking through blocks.

Specific types of self-talk and imagery have been scientifically shown to improve sports performance. Other strategies fail to help individuals perform optimally.

Covert hypnosis can be used in many effective ways. What follows is an abridged and edited dialogue of a client I worked with. The dialogue takes place in the first of three meetings we had together.

Client: ...it just always seems that I blow it. I shoot five holes perfectly then I go to pieces on one hole. Then I shoot perfectly for a while. Then blow it again.
KH: What would you like to see happen?
Client: I'd like to shoot like Tiger Woods.
KH: What would have to happen for that to occur?

Whenever someone wants to have the same results as the one professional at the top of their profession, a bit of re-direction is critical. Professional athletes spend their entire lives developing a set of very specific skills which they practice for tens of thousands of hours. Therefore, the client must see that while possible to replicate such a set of skills, it is unlikely to occur if the same recipe of success is not followed. In other words, if the client is willing to quit their job, leave their family and friends, yes it is possible that if they are young enough and in the proper physical shape, that they possibly could accomplish the success of Tiger Woods. They will have bout the same chances as winning a lottery. It is never ecological for a therapist to assist the client in the decision making process of making such a move.

Client: I'd have to play a lot.
KH: And how many years did Tiger play before he achieved his results?
Client: 20 or so I guess.
KH: And are you willing to dedicate 5-7 hours every day for the next 20 years to achieve the same results?
Client: Well of course not.

(Had the client answered this question with a "yes" response, we would have had some problems!)

KH: So what would you like to see happen in your golf game?
Client: I'd like to shoot my best on all the holes on any given day, not just 15 of them.

61

KH: If you shot that well on every hole would you be a par golfer?

Client: Just about.

KH: What does that look like?

Client: (Laughs) That looks good.

KH: Tell me, what does it look like to you?

Client: Well, I see myself finishing a round happy for a change and not all pissed off because I blew it again.

KH: And what does it feel like to be happy?

Client: It feels good. It just never happens.

KH: Does Tiger Woods know that visualizing his shots before he makes them helps him be a superstar?

Client: No question.

KH: He still occasionally shoots a bad hole.

Client: Of course. Everyone does.

KH: So you would be happy about what?

Client: Shooting my best on each hole.

KH: And what if you blow the 4th hole at Valley Wood. You shoot the next six well. Do you need to blow the 11th as well?

Client: (Looks at me) Of course.

KH: What usually happens when you blow a hole?

Client: I get too excited that I'm doing well. I say to myself that "this can't last" and I'm always right. It doesn't. (laughs)

KH: (laughs) I understand. Now, when you hear yourself say, "this can't last" can you say to yourself, "STOP! It can last...and it will this time because it can last."

Client: (looking a bit confused) I suppose.

KH: OK, let's look at that. Hear that. Walk up to a familiar tee thinking that "this can't last" and then say to yourself, "STOP! It can last...and it will this time because it can last."

Client: (Pause) OK. I did it.

KH: How does that feel?

Client: Good I guess.

(Good I guess, is not a response I settle for.)

KH: Great, now in your mind, tee off and tell me what happens.

Client: (Looks away) OK, I'm on the fairway.

KH: Is that good?

Client: Yeah, absolutely.

KH: Great, now what happens next?

Client: (pause) I walk up to the ball and I hit it perfectly. Right onto the green.

KH: Excellent. Now what happens.

Client: (pause) I sink a long putt.
KH: Fantastic. How do you feel inside?
Client: I feel great. (Big smile)

The client has no idea he has been in trance for five minutes. He is totally unaware but he perfectly visualized the experience and a very positive emotional response. That sets us up perfectly for the balance of our work. There will be no resistance because he now has a wonderful goal in mind. He feels good inside! The client is ready to begin more formal trance work.

You do the same thing with the girl at the table next to you. You do the same thing with your best friend, your account clients. The process is the same. The content will be different.

The Power of the Nonconsious: Manipulating the Little Things They Don't Even Notice

Chapter Six

I want the girl to *beg you* to go out with her.

I want your clients to beg to hire you, your company, buy your ideas, products and services.

Sound ridiculous?

Excellent.

Read on...

What you want to know is what really drives the process of unconscious communication and persuasion.

The girl says "yes" because you asked with elegance.

Closing sales is a result of asking someone for an agreement.

The process is the same from context to context.

As you will see, getting the girl, closing sales, getting to "yes" will take on an entirely new meaning after implementing what you are learning in this book. It becomes...rather easy.

Instead of the ancient warrior mentality of selling where you have to beat your client over the head 6.7 times before she says "yes" you now have the science and psychology of covert hypnosis at your fingertips to make the process a pleasure instead of a contest.

In talking with people, you will get to "yes" by sliding into the mind and pushing the "yes" button.

Question: What is the difference between the top 20% of people who earn 80% of the money and the 80% of people who earn 20% of the money?

Answers:

The top 20% of people are expert communicators. They know how to ask questions and discover the needs and desires of others. Covert Hypnosis takes what was once an art and transforms it into a science. That means anyone can learn how to use Covert Hypnosis.

Those who dwell in mediocrity do so until they have powerful reasons to move in a different direction...or any direction.

People who don't live up to their potential have not set and planned for powerful goals.

Outstanding people are experts in two fields. One is the field in which they are communicating in, and the other is in communicating at the unconscious level.

Most people are influence-impotent because they do not have compelling reasons and goals to take advantage of their potential knowledge. They do not understand how other people think and they do not know how to motivate themselves so they can catch fire to act on knowledge.

Why are you going to be different? What benefits and reasons do you have to become an expert at Covert Hypnosis?

WHY?

...is the most important question in everything you do.

1. Find the BIG WHY and the girl MIGHT want to go out with you and you will get the date. Find out WHY your client needs your products and services and you will be influential, you will be successful, and you will become wealthy.

2. Find the BIG WHY and you win.

When you know what motivates a person from the INSIDE, you can influence them. When you know what motivates yourself, you can change your own behavior.

Covert Hypnosis : Become a Compliance Expert

Recent research revealed that a waitress who touches a client as she gives him the bill is more likely to get a larger tip on average, than a waitress who doesn't touch her client. That is a MAP (Mind Access Point). The waitress purposefully and ethically "pulls the string" (or pushes the client's button, if you will) and because she does so, she gets a larger tip. She knows either consciously or unconsciously that her tips are larger if she makes contact with her client.

There are thousands of MAPs installed in the minds of your clients. Knowing which strings to pull and when to pull them will determine how many sales per contact you have and the volume of sale per contact will go up as well, if it applies in your business.

Covert Hypnosis for a Waitress?

It's a fact that a server's income is mostly pocketed from tips. More than anyone, a waitress (or waiter) needs to understand the power of Covert Hypnosis.

So how would you tell your girlfriend or daughter to get more tips using Covert Hypnosis?

Here's what I taught my daughter who began waitressing a few years ago.

- Give mints or chocolate at the end of the meal
- Compliment customers on their menu choice
- Introduce yourself by name
- Touch customers
- Draw a smiley face on the back of the check (waitresses only)
- Write "Thank You" on the back of the check

Advice is one thing. What does the research actually show happens in real life?

1) Give mints or chocolate at the end of the meal

Dave Strohmetz, of Monmouth University, led a team of researchers to see whether actually giving customers the gift of chocolate would result in more tips.

First, they went to a restaurant in New York. Half of the time, when customers asked for the bill, the servers would simply bring the check over. The other half of the time, they gave a foil-wrapped piece of chocolate to each person before giving the check. At the end of the experiment, the tips were added up, and indeed, patrons receiving the chocolate did tip more; they tipped roughly 18% of the bill, on average, while patrons who didn't get the chocolate tipped 15%. That may only be $20 per night, but it's not bad!

The researchers then went back for a second shot. They wanted to find out what was causing this small but measurable effect, and in doing so, they found ways to enhance it!

This time, they compared four different methods:

- **Control Condition** – Not giving patrons a piece of candy
- **1-Piece Condition** – Giving them one piece of candy each
- **2-Piece Condition** – Giving them two pieces of candy each
- **1+1 condition** – Giving them one piece of candy each, then as the server was leaving the table, she stopped, turned back, and offered the patrons another piece of candy each *"because you are such nice people."*

Here are the results:

19% No Candy
20% 1 Piece of Candy
22% 2 Pieces of Candy
23% 1 + 1 Pieces of Candy

And here's the thing: This experiment has been done many times and in most cities the results are far more dramatic. Typically the 1 + 1 with the off handed comment *hey you guys deserve two each because you are such nice people.*

How does it work?

Very often, when people are on the receiving end of generosity, they feel the need to reciprocate.

What's the Covert Lesson For You?

Do something nice for someone BEFORE asking the Big Question.
THEN do something nice and then a second something nice BEFORE asking the Big Question.

2) A Sincere Compliment?

A study by John Seiter looked into this, again in a real-life restaurant.
The servers in the study would treat all customers exactly the same, except for one thing; after taking their order, they would either compliment the customer on their menu choice, or they wouldn't. What specifically did they say? After taking the first order, the server said *"You made a good choice!"* and after taking the second order, they said *"You did good too!"*

The study was restricted to parties of two – keep this in mind when you're applying this information – it's untested on larger groups!

As in Strohmetz's study, tip size was worked out as a percentage of the overall bill. Overall, customers who received a compliment about their menu choice tipped 19% of their bill, while customers who weren't complimented tipped only 16% of the bill! This is a simple method, taking about 2 seconds per table, and again it results in a measurable increase in the amount of tips!

Once again, an extra $20 or so for a night shift just because they complimented the people. Granted that's only $4,000 per year but still, it's $4,000 for doing absolutely nothing.

What's the Covert Lesson for You?

You guessed it. Pay a sincere compliment on a DECISION ISSUE. You will be asking a Big Question (The Date, The Sale, etc.) any minute now. Focus on complimenting a DECISION. The unconscious gesture is: "You make good decisions with me."

3) They Introduced themselves by name

In this study, a buffet was a really good way to test the effect of the introduction, because customers pretty much fend for themselves after the first introduction, so there's less chance that other factors could interfere with the results. When the server introduced herself by name, there was a far higher tipping rate when the servers introduced themselves – 23%, compared to 15% when they didn't!

An 8% increase in tips is a HOME RUN for a server. That's about $50 for a shift. That amounts to around $10,000 per year!

What's the Covert Lesson for You?

You guessed it. Forget the goofy lines. Introduce yourself by name.

4) Touch customers

In a study entitled "The Midas Touch", April Crusco and Christopher Wetzel discovered what happens when waitresses touch their customers; either on the shoulder, on the palm or not at all, when returning change. They found that the customers who were touched left the highest tips on average, *that the palm was the most profitable place,* and also <u>that the customers largely weren't aware they'd been touched.</u>

Results of Tip Size with Touching?

12% No touch
17% Touch on the Palm
14% Touch on the Shoulder

A follow up study found that when a man and a woman are dining alone, it is *more profitable to touch the female customer than the male*. The reason might be that the *servers in this study were all female*, and touching the man might have brought out some jealousy.

Covert Lesson For You?

If you are a male, test to see whether people respond better to you with a glancing touch or not. If you are female...touch away...particularly other women in front of men.

5) Draw on the back of the check?

Smart servers draw little pictures, like smiley faces, on the back of the checks. There are several reasons this might improve the tips; it might show that the server was pleased to have served the party, it might put the party in a better mood, or it might just be seen as a nice friendly gesture.

It does seem to work – but only for women. Here are the results for the waitresses:

28% Tip when No Smiley Face Drawn on Back of Check
33% Tip when Smiley Face is Drawn on Back of Check

And here are the results for the waiters...The OPPOSITE

23% Tip when No Smiley Face Drawn on Back of Check
18% Tip when Smiley Face Drawn on Back of Check

Waitresses seem to get more tips than waiters in general, and it also seems that drawing a smiley face had a *negative* effect on the waiter's tips!

Covert Lesson for You?

If you are male, behave within the stereotype norms for men. If you are a woman, offer the "cute" little gestures.

6) Write "Thank You" on the Check

When a server expresses their gratitude to the party, in the form of a little "Thank You" and signature on the back of the check, this has also proven to bring higher tips. Although it wasn't as effective as the smiley face, at least it should work for waitresses *and* waiters!

Results

16% Tip when no message
18% Tip when "Thank You" is on back of check.
18% Tip when "Thank You and Signature is on back of check.

As you can see, the signature isn't strictly necessary – a friendly "thank you" message on the back of the check is enough to improve your tips.

Covert Lesson for You?

As has been shown in dozens of studies, a handwritten post it note or a short thank you that is HAND WRITTEN increases response, sales, and as you just saw, tip size.

Knowing when and where to touch someone can dramatically increase your income.

KEY POINT: It's not the sentences we say, it's the nuance. It's all about the tiny elements. The little factors. The hidden nonconscious touch or word that changes minds and generates thousands of dollars per year in extra...free...income.

Want to read more to find out the details?

References:
Strohmetz D. B., Rind B., Fisher R. & Lynn M. (2002). Sweetening the till: The use of candy to increase restaurant tipping. Journal of Applied Social Psychology, 32(2), 300-309.
  Seiter, J. S. (2009). Ingratiation and Gratuity: The Effect of Complimenting Customers on Tipping Behavior in Restaurants. Paper presented at the annual meeting of the International Communication Association, Sheraton New York, New York City, NY Online PDF
  Garrity, K., & Degelman, D. (1990). Effect of server introduction on restaurant tipping. Journal of Applied Social Psychology, 20,168-172.

Crusco, A. H., & Wetzel, C. G. (1984). The Midas touch: The effects of interpersonal touch on restaurant tipping. Personality and Social Psychology Bulletin, 10,512-517.

Stephen, R., & Zweigenhaft, R. L. (1986). The effect of tipping of a waitress touching male and female customers. Journal of Social Psychology, 126,141-142.

Hornik, J. (1992). Tactile stimulation and consumer response. Journal of Consumer Research, 19,449-458.

Hubbard, A. S. E., Tsuji, A., Williams, C., & Seatriz, V. (2003). Effects of touch on gratuities received in same-gender and cross-gender dyads. Journal of Applied Social Psychology, 33(11), 2427-2438.

Rind, B., Bordia, P. (1996), "Effect on restaurant tipping of male and female servers drawing a happy smiling face on the backs of customers checks", Journal of Applied Social Psychology, 26(3), 218-25.

Rind, R., & Bordia, P. (1995). Effect of server's "thank you" and personalization on restaurant tipping. Journal of Applied Social Psychology, 25,745-751.

Rind, B., & Strohmetz, D. (1999). Effect on restaurant tipping of a helpful message written on the back of customers' checks. Journal of Applied Social Psychology, 29,139-144.

Covert Hypnosis Using Story

Chapter Seven

Each story you write and tell has a purpose: *to influence*. In training Covert Hypnosis, I enjoy telling stories that relate to selling, therapy and first encounters. But really they are all the same conversation. If you can do one, you can do the other. You are simply changing content, not process.

Simply telling a story is not going to influence anyone.

Read this story and then go back to the beginning of the story and read the notes in **italics that explain specifically what covert tools are being utilized.**

Don't read anything in [brackets] until you have read the story in it totality.

The Birth of An Influencer

Autumn 1972
Selling: My Only Hope

I started selling when I was 10 years old. I had to. I was the oldest of five children and we had no money. My stepfather was going to die in less than 18 months and Mom's time was divided between her job and taking care of Dad who was confined to a hospital bed in our home. It was a heck of a way to live... We lived in a "lower-middle class" suburb of Chicago. If I wanted to have money for anything (and I did) I would have to sell something.

I sold my services in the wintertime as the kid on the street who would shovel your driveway. $1 per hour... The Chicago winds would blow out of the North and off the lake with a bitter coldness that I'll never forget. Sometimes I'd take the $3 I would earn and give it to Mom. Sometimes I'd keep the money and buy

Pepsi and Reese's Peanut Butter Cups. In the summer, I would sell my services cutting people's lawns or pulling weeds. (I hated pulling weeds.)

[I'm sharing with you some powerful self-revelations here. My family was poor enough and I'm sharing with you that one of my values is family and the importance of helping to take care of a sick Dad, an overworked Mom and four other kids. I'm telling you I'm a good child, with a good heart, without saying, "I'm a good kid with a good heart." These are important elements in the lessons I want to teach the listener/reader of this story.]

Realizing that there was no hope for me in the lawn and garden services, I knew at age 10 I would have to do something where I could utilize my time in a far more efficient manner. I saw an ad in a Sunday newspaper for Cheerful House Greeting Cards. I read that I could earn from fifty cents to two dollars for each box of cards sold. I immediately sent the company my $10 for a sample kit. ($10 was a lot of money in those days.) In return Cheerful House sent me five boxes of Christmas cards. Some quick math calculations revealed that if I just sold the five boxes I'd make one dollar per box sold! The sales literature said that there would only be four "selling seasons" per year, so whatever money was going to be earned would have to last a LONG time.

[One of the key lessons of success is the lesson of saving. If a 10-year-old kid can save, so can any adult listening to me share this story in a seminar!]

I got home from school the next day and as soon as my paper route was done I was ready to go make some real money! I knocked on my neighbor's door. It was Mrs. Gossard. I showed her my cards and she bought a box. My first dollar was earned! Then I went to Mrs. Singer. (She couldn't buy a box.) Mrs. Hendricks bought two boxes; Mrs. Serdar bought a box. Mrs. Makela bought a box. Lots of other people didn't. I was gone until 8:00 and had knocked on 30 doors and sold about 18 boxes of cards. I looked at my watch as the sun was setting. I knew I had to go home and help put the kids to bed. I had checks totaling about $60, of which my math whiz brain figured, $20 was mine...

Mom was so excited when she saw the order sheet. I told her that I'd give her all the money I earned. She said, "No. You earned it, you are going to keep it." Wow! The next day I left the neighborhood to start selling in a neighborhood I never went to. I was out from the time my paper route was done until sunset. I sold only four boxes of cards. Some of the people's houses were...scary looking and being a skinny little kid...I decided that I wouldn't go back there again! Nevertheless, I made about $4. I showed Mom when I got home and she told me that it was mine to keep.

[The story is REAL because all the names are named. That's the first key here. I don't

want to say, "I knocked on everyone's door in the neighborhood and made a bunch of sales." That doesn't covertly take you out of the 21st century and bring you back to 1972. By naming the names of everyone on our block, you get a flavor of what it was like...right down to the sunset. This is covert hypnosis using a kind of age regression and visualization. It's very elegant and very powerful at getting you out of the 21st century. When you listen to this on CD or in person, you are immediately swept from your world into the world of the young salesman.]

The problem was that I knocked on about 50 doors to earn that $4. I couldn't believe that more people didn't buy my Christmas cards. They obviously weren't as smart as the people in my neighborhood. The next day was Saturday and I remember getting up, delivering the Saturday Morning Waukegan New-Sun (They had to be delivered by 7 A.M.!) cutting the lawn, and then at noon off I went on my bicycle. I went into neighborhoods I had never been to and knocked on over 100 doors that day. I didn't stop to eat lunch...or dinner. I sold 6 boxes of cards. I got home to find that there was no Hamburger Helper left. (I was eternally grateful.) I told Mom that I didn't have a very good day. I made $6 but I was driving across highways and I was kind of scared of the neighborhoods I was going into. She suggested I stick with the neighborhoods where people knew me and that I wouldn't be crossing the highways anymore. (She would later tell me she was scared to death that her son was going into some of the neighborhoods!)

[The Hamburger Helper is important to the story. It clearly indicates this was a common foodstuff that I was sick of...a foodstuff of poor people. You also learn that I am delivering newspapers and doing odd jobs. You are learning the lesson of persistence, which is necessary for success!]

We totaled the order sheet. I had sold 28 boxes of cards. My total earnings would be about $30. I would get paid after I delivered all of the cards to my clients. I couldn't wait!

I learned a lot that week.

I learned that people were more likely to buy from me if they knew me. I realized that if people had the money, I could talk them into buying an extra box for someone else as a gift.

[Another teaching lesson here. People buy from people they know and like. How do you incorporate that into direct mail for example? Permission marketing. How do you incorporate that into sales? Developing relationships. How do you incorporate that into therapy? Building rapport with your clients and listening to their stories!]

I learned that selling cards was a lot better than cutting the lawn, pulling weeds, shoveling the snow or delivering the newspaper.

I learned I could only work four weeks per year selling cards. Selling cards was going to make me $100 per year next year but I'd need to think of something else to sell if I was going to make more money.

More importantly, after delivering the cards to the people a few weeks earlier, I realized how much fun it was to see people smile and say "Thanks, Kevin." "They're beautiful." "You got those to me faster than I expected."

[The great thing about selling is that people are happy with what you are selling them. This is a critical message with two purposes. One: Sell a product that makes people's lives better. Two: For all the rejection one receives in selling, realize that those who do business with you will be happy (or you are selling the wrong product/service!]

Most importantly, I made $30 for about 20 hours of work that was not physically killing my scrawny 10-year-old body!

I sold greeting cards for the next four years as a source of income. I sold flower seeds and vegetable seeds. (I also continued to sell my body shoveling snow, pulling weeds, cutting lawns, and doing anything I could.) The most fun was selling cards, though. The women were (for the most part) fun to talk with, the work was all sitting down in their living room and some of them even gave me cookies and milk those few days per year when I was selling. I was actually having fun working at something.

[Covert message: selling is FUN!!]

The ad from Cheerful House Greeting Cards changed my life. Not because it made me rich. It didn't. It gave me hope that I could escape living in poverty. The Boy Scouts wouldn't need to bring me clothes and turkey dinners on Thanksgiving anymore. (The Boy Scouts delivered clothing and food to our home on Thanksgiving on a couple of occasions. I remember appreciating the clothes and food…and hating being needy.) I knew whatever I was going to do when I was older, it would be selling.

I was right.

I discovered as a 10 year old that the ability to think quickly and talk with people could give me a chance to escape being poor and maybe…just maybe…be rich. Selling was hard work in some ways, but it was fun. It certainly beat "physical work"!

Selling would give me security, freedom, independence and the ability to be productive…to be valuable to other people. It was something I could do well.

[Here is the main message: Selling/being in business for yourself gives you freedom and I could have just told you that but I weave the idea into the story and it MEANS something!]

Fast forward to1998.

[No pause. You are still "in trance." I still have your attention in the past and I'm now moving you forward in time, but NOT to the present! You are going to see how the 10 year old still learns and becomes more successful as time goes on.]

Autumn 1998

I've been earning a six-figure income for a few years. I've owned my own business, consulted or sold for other people since 1987. The idea of receiving an hourly wage and punching a time clock is almost a phobia. Business is good. I have several books in print including one, *The Psychology of Persuasion*, that is doing pretty darned well in the bookstores...But...

[Six figure income. That's a good thing. Doesn't mean I'm rich, just fairly successful. More importantly, I have some accomplishments, but all is not perfect! There are still lessons to learn and experiences to have!]

I've stalled. I've stagnated. I've been earning $1,000- $2,000 per speech I give. Nothing wrong with that but I've been there and did that. What is going on? No one is offering me more than that. I am baffled. People compare my speaking style to Anthony Robbins and my physical and offstage presence to Kelsey Grammer, David Letterman and Drew Carey. Now, what more could a guy want? That's enough talent to feed off of for FOUR lifetimes.

[Stagnating at $1-2,000 per speech is a problem that could be sought after by a lot of people. This is the first point. The second is that I'm favorably compared to some well-known personalities and this is all shared in the context of 1998, in an eyes-open trance.]

Enter Dottie Walters, the author of "Speak and Grow Rich" (Dottie owned the world's most prestigious speakers bureau and published Sharing Ideas magazine for national speakers.)
I see her "Speak and Grow Rich" course listed next to mine in the Open U catalog. I have no time to take a full day off and learn what I already know regardless of whom it is with. But for years I have wanted to meet Dottie. She would now be about 70 or maybe older...and it was her book, *Speak and Grow Rich* that helped me focus my world into teaching and speaking in public for a significant portion of my current living.
I decided to take the Saturday off and go see Dottie. If nothing else, I should thank her for being inspirational in my life!
I experienced her class with about 20 other students. I enjoyed watching the woman speak for 5 hours. She was able to keep the group enthralled with stories she had no doubt told for decades. Her approach was simple and somewhat

"grandmotherly." She was kind and direct. I was in love. (Not to mention watching her do back of the room sales was inspiring!)

[Setting up the second part of the story is very important here. I'm meeting an elderly and kind woman who has been in my profession longer than I have been alive. I'm doing well in life, have all the "book knowledge" but still need more. This is a powerful covert message I want my listener to know. It's just not the facts that people want...they need INSPIRATION and a NUDGE to take action.]

I didn't get what I came for, though. I hadn't really learned anything "new." But I was in love. I approached her after everyone had left the class and her grandson had finished packing the few books and videos that hadn't been snatched up by the audience.

"Dottie, I'm Kevin Hogan. I want you to know you have been an inspiration in my career."

"Thank you Kevin." She looked up into my eyes. She was tired. I've been here before. The last person wants to keep you forever. You (I) have been on stage for six hours and you want to find the bed in the hotel and fall flat on your face and have them wake you in 15 hours for breakfast...

[I'm covertly reminding you that I know that Dottie doesn't really want to talk with me and that I'm taking up her valuable time...and hoping that you will do the same for me after my presentation!]

"Dottie, I want you to have this." (I hand her my book, *The Psychology of Persuasion*.)

"Thank you dear."

O.K. Kevin, her brain is fading. Either ask or get the hell out of here. She has a date with a hotel pillow and you are being as charming as a bottle of mental Drano.

[Now, here is a wee bit of humor inserted into the story. I want to create the picture I'm hemming and hawing because it is such a natural and normal thing to do when you meet someone you idolize!]

"Dottie, I have one question for you. I have been doing about $1500 per speech for the last couple of years. It doesn't change. They don't offer more than $2,000. What do you suggest? You tell me, I'll do it. Anything. What is going to take me to the next ($5,000+) level?"

"Have you asked, Kevin?"

"Pardon me?"

"Have you asked for $5,000?"

"Well, not really. I mean...no...you know, I haven't."

She put her hand on my arm and patted me like I was a little child.

"Well honey, just ask." (She looked at my book and smiled.) "Just ask."

"Thanks Dottie, I will."

As I walked out of the door on that brisk Minneapolis afternoon I wondered just how stupid I must have looked. Successful author towers over sweet woman asking the dumbest question on the face of the earth. Thank God no one would ever know about this moment.

[Covert messages all over the place here! First the answer to what I think is a difficult question turns out to be super easy. Just ask. Second, I paint the picture of the fact that I'm embarrassed as a successful author needing advice. Just like you the salesperson listening to me present this material live in our seminar today.]

Fast Forward: One Month.

[Still in trance! I'm simply moving you forward in time just a little bit!]

Early Winter 1998

I have a sore throat and a terrible cold. My nose is stuffier than it ever has been in its life. I feel terrible. CNBC is on in the background. The market is not doing well and I'm not making money today.

(…ring)

[Losing money in the market means making money in the market on other days…enough to where it's important enough that I have CNBC on in the background right?!]

"Who could that be?" I talk to CNBC when no one else is around.

"Kevin Hogan, can I help you?" (It didn't sound like that…maybe they bought it on the other end.)

"Is this Dr. Hogan?"

"Yes it is." (Dr. Hogan has actually left the building for dead. This is his associate who has not yet succumbed to the flu…)

[Did you catch the DOCTOR part?! ☺]

"Oh…you sound terrible…this is Richard Marks (Not his real name) with the Sales Association (Not their real name either)."

"How can I help you?"

"Well we were at your website and are looking for a speaker for our winter meeting in Minneapolis. What are you charging nowadays."

Here it is, Kevin. You spent the last month finishing your book, *Talk Your Way to the Top.* It's over. The book is at Pelican. What are you going to tell this guy? Your voice sounds like hell. You've just yelled at CNBC. You…just ask, honey. Just ask.…

[Oh yes, and the fact that I have books in print and that I talk to televisions like every other football fan and market watcher in the world!]

"$5,000 is my fee but I'd sure like to know more about your group and what you are looking for."

Richard tells me about his group, tells me they want me to talk about "body language" and asks if I will settle on $4,000, which is what his budget is approved for. What's the difference between 4K and 5K anyway? You're working for ONE HOUR Kevin? You moron. It's an hour drive and you are working for an hour.…Just ask honey…just ask.

"No, my fee is $5,000 and I think I can give you exactly what you are looking for. An hour of massive entertainment combined with an hour of data all happening simultaneously."

"I'll have to check for approval on $5,000. I'll call you back. Thanks Kevin, we'll talk soon."

I thought to myself, "You stupid moron." (CNBC was running a commercial with Ringo Starr in it…I could use a little help from my friends…Ringo…)

"What the heck are you thinking? Guaranteed $4,000. Been paid that once for a full day, never for an hour and you say, $5,000. Idiot. Idiot. Idiot." Sue Herrara talks with Ron Insana about how the market is taking a hit today and I'm feeling like a bigger idiot by the micro-second. The phone doesn't ring for the rest of the day.

[Not only am I telling Richard this, I'm telling your audience this! I'm telling you that I stick to my guns and don't sell myself cheap…though I'm going to beat myself up for sticking to my guns!]

Fast Forward: Next day.

(Ring)
"Kevin Hogan."
"That really you?"
"Who's this?"
"Richard Marks."
"Hi Richard, good to hear your voice." (I'll take the $4,000. Just offer it again, now, and I'm yours.)
"Kevin we got the $5,000 approved and would like you to….blah blah blah blah…(Get out of here. DOTTIE, I LOVE YOU… Just ask honey….I never doubted you Dottie, I swear to…just ask…and I wrote *THE PSYCHOLOGY OF*

PERSUASION. I mean, how long does it take to realize that you are unable to follow your own advice...just ask honey...DOTTIE, YOU ARE THE GREATEST...)

[I can get excited, just like YOU would if you were offered $5,000 for a one hour speech. Your sales depend on your attitude and although I was nervous, you can see that I get a rush when good stuff happens. No arrogance.]

"How does that sound Kevin?"
"Yes, absolutely, let's run through the details again. My head is foggy from this flu."
Deal closed. Check received in 6 business days. That was the last time I doubted that still small sweet voice in my head. Dottie is with me always...

[A little humor to close the story puts a smile on everyone's face. This is a covert hypnosis masterpiece and it is 100% true!]

Have you ever suffered from low self-esteem? We all do. I tell you this story because every time I think of it I remember that I'm worth an enormous amount to people, to society, to myself. I also think of my childhood because it reminds me that no matter how tough things get, they aren't going to be that bad ever again.

When you persuade or take control of any situation, **you** determine your outcomes.

Whether you are 10 years old or 70 years old, you are going to determine your own fate in selling. You are a free agent and can choose to sell almost any product or service you want. Once you have the product or service picked out that you want to sell remember this fact:

In general communication, people want to know what is perceived as a Unique Positive about you. In sales and marketing, people don't buy your products, they buy you.

You must represent a great product or service. What you sell is critical to your self-image and your self-esteem. It needs to be the best, and if it isn't, dump it and go get on the team that is the best. Every product has problems. Every service has its weaknesses. My question is, did you pick the best of the group? If not, go sign up with the best. Because, once you do, the rest of the story is about YOU!

Selling is an inside job. It all takes place inside of people's minds. Selling is a simple science that encompasses beliefs, values, attitudes, lifestyles, emotions, feelings and psychological shifts. Selling is the most wonderful profession on earth because it gives you what you want:

- ✓ Freedom
- ✓ Security
- ✓ Productivity
- ✓ Independence
- ✓ Sense of Accomplishment

No longer are you a slave to anyone. You are your own boss and you are the master of your life. You'll never work 40 hours again. You'll work 50 or 60 because they are for YOU and the people you love. Selling is the solution to the destructive "dollars per hour" mentality that exists everywhere. You'll never get paid an hourly wage again. You'll be "unemployed" every day for the rest of your life and you will never feel more in charge of your own life!

Covert Hypnosis Lesson 1. Through the stories in this module I was able to teach you about my dedication to my family when I was a child. You learned that I cared about my family. You learned that I wanted to take care of them.

Covert Hypnosis Lesson 2. Through the stories in this module, you learned my exact process of finally asking to be paid what I am worth. You saw my struggle with my own self esteem and discovered that you are a lot like me. If I can do it, you can do it. That message was critical to get through from my conscious mind to your unconscious mind.

Covert Hypnosis Lesson 3. You now know that I have been successful in the field of influence, and are therefore more likely to accept what I tell you as factual and therefore, you are more likely to act upon those messages.

Covert Hypnosis Lesson 4. I have disclosed personal weaknesses to you so you know that I am not a superman...nor do I think I am. If you want people to like you and respect you, you must let them know that you are not arrogant. You are just like they are.

Covert Hypnosis Lesson 5. You develop your own story(ies) in the same way! Put REAL thought into the process and practice telling your stories so when it is time to tell it to someone who matters, it resonates and moves quickly.

Stories and Metaphors

People want to hear the following to be influenced by your stories:

1. **Information-** Our instincts drive us to learn and be curious. It is a survival instinct. We need to make sense of everything and fit it together into a religion, a system, a box. Stories help you give people information in a simplistic (best kind for most people) fashion.

2. **Faith-** They want to believe in you. Stories about how you helped another person in a similar situation are very convincing. In fact, people believe a good story more than they do meaningful statistics. The fact is that a story is more memorable and convincing than a lot of data. The problem is that stories are completely unreliable and do not represent reality in any way...but this isn't a course in reality, it's a course in covert hypnosis. People want to BELIEVE.

3. **Meaning-** People want a sense of meaning in life. We need our myths and related rituals. We want to believe God created the earth, that Jesus went to heaven, that Mohammed ascended, that Buddha is back as the Dalai Lama and that we all will live again. We want to believe our company is the best. We want to believe our school is the best and that "I have the best doctor in the state." *We are driven to need to believe and create a sense out of our life experience.* We need to believe there is an ultimate reason, plan and purpose for this life we are living.

4. **Viral-** When people hear your story, they will tell it, if it is powerful and you will have created an idea virus.

Six types of stories that subtly influence.

(see <u>The Story Factor</u> by Annette Simmons)

1)   "Who Am I"

Funny is a good way to start...it covertly lowers defenses. A slightly self-deprecating story goes a long way at setting another person or group at ease.
The personal flaw/self disclosure story is a good story to build rapport.

2) "Why Am I Here"

You can't fake being authentic so you might as well be authentic and "be yourself" while you put all of your best feet forward!

Are you here for a selfish purpose or are you simply ambitious. You aren't selfless, no one is, so don't try and fake it.

Successfully answering the call of the first two brings trust/rapport.

3) The Vision

Are you laying bricks, building a wall or building a cathedral?
Vision gives our struggle meaning.

4) Teaching

I want you to be successful utilizing Covert Hypnosis. Here's why. I remember when my son was two. He was crawling toward a light socket....

The next reason I'm teaching you this is because of a guy named Osama bin Laden and all those he spread his virus to and all those who create rigid rules for after life success to the point of destroying people in this life...

5) Values in Action

In 1995 someone did me a big favor. In my entire life no one had done me a really big favor. I received a call....

...and now I am loyal to him forever...

...and that's how I am with my students who participate in mutually reciprocal relationships.

6) I Know What You are Thinking

Create the proposal or idea. Fight it. Show why it is a good idea, in spite of that argument which fought it. This is how the brain will interpret the situation in the future.

Shaping the world, shape a few...

Stories have shaped the world in a very covert manner. What we believe is truth in our specific culture is simply similar to what other cultures have created.

Most every culture has:

- A creation myth
- A flood myth
- A savior myth
- A resurrection to life myth
- An ascension myth
- A life after death myth
- A certainty of truth myth

Covert Hypnosis Exercise: (choose one)

a. You want someone to quit smoking. Tell a story that gets that message across.
b. You want to sell something (maybe your service as a therapist). Tell a story that gets the message through loud and clear that the person should buy or hire you.
c. You want someone to go out with you or spend an evening with you. Tell a story that gets that message across.

Remember: A story is just a story. A story that a listener/reader can identify with is powerful. A story that has subtle messages woven into a powerful story is one that will change minds!

17 Keys to Using Covert Hypnosis in Story

The intention of communication is to influence.
Most communication does not succeed in achieving the intended result.
Covert Hypnosis (Intentional Subtle Influence) is sometimes best used in a story...and in fact, makes the story far more likely to succeed in achieving the intended result...influencing others to your way of thinking.

Captivate or Die

...the room was packed with people. We were all sitting down to eat at a table. 22 of us. One big long table. We were on our lunch break from training. I was sitting next to Ron Stubbs who was engaged in a conversation with our friend, Katherin. I was sitting opposite a gal...whose face is a blur and name escapes me because the face is a blur. But the moment was memorable for me.

...the waitress had been gone for almost 20 minutes before lunch was actually served. The woman across from me had been talking for almost the entire 20 minutes. My head was nodding because I wanted to be affable. I was already tired but she never recognized that I didn't hear a word she said after maybe the first five or six minutes.

I do remember she told me all about her trip to Sedona. The energy vortex and all that. Any time I hear "energy vortex" or anything like that there is a part of me ready for engagement. But on this day, I was tired and soon the stories she was telling me drifted from the energy vortex to a trip she had just taken with her boyfriend and then...I don't remember...anything.

I was sipping a tall diet Coke with lemon (I never liked lemon in my diet Coke and should have pulled it but I didn't...) and nodding. I heard Ron and Katherin talking about the training and the modules they were going to be training. And I heard the hum of 10 other voices in the room chatting away, most lively though I wasn't in tune with any of them.

Ron whispers in my ear, "Hey buddy, (he knows I hate being called "buddy") you in trance or what?"

I know he said this because he told me later that he did.

Apparently I blinked my eyes.

The woman across from me said, "Don't you think?"

It dawned on me she had told me a story about something for what seemed like forever (I found out later she had been talking for some 20 minutes straight) and I simply drifted into the ether. Fortunately only Ron noticed.

He laughs in my ear. I immediately get uncomfortable. I like Ron. One of my best friends in the world, but get outta my ear, man.

"I can see that." It is an automatic response I've learned over the years that gets you out of trouble when you don't understand, can't hear or have spaced out from boredom.

Ron put his left arm around my back grabbing my left shoulder. His Right hand grabbed my right shoulder. He looked at the gal.

"I need him for 2 minutes and you can have him back."

Katherin looked at me with a big grin. I saw that she knew I was lost in space.

"I just saved your a-s, you owe me."

And he did. He actually saved the entire class because the woman's stories had shut me down and sent me past Neptune.

He talked a little about what he wanted to go over that day and then, mercifully, lunch arrived...

Captivate Your Listener

Stories can captivate to the point where you are there with the person and experiencing everything as if you are there with them.

They can also totally shut down the listener. It takes very little time to drive someone past boredom and drop them off at exhaustion junction.

When you are telling a story, it almost always should have a purpose.

1. What intention do you have? What do you want the other person to think or feel after telling this story? What is your purpose?

You say to yourself..."I am telling this story to Kevin because I want him to_____" and you make sure your story moves Kevin in that direction.

If people thought in advance WHY they were telling a story, they would tell far FEWER stories.

Stories can kill rapport or captivate to a plane far above rapport to a place of connection that is almost electric.

My intention of telling you a story must be clear to me, or I don't tell it.

Note: Just because you intend to tell a story for a specific result doesn't mean you will get that specific result. It often will be filtered through people's beliefs, biases and values and the story could be "offensive" or "felt" in a negative way. That will happen particularly when you tell a story to more than one person.

Know two things: It's not the intention of every story you or I tell to be to deliver a "calm message." Many messages MUST ignite emotions to influence people.

The other notion is that if you get similar feedback from multiple people, you might want to reconsider the value or usefulness of a specific story.

With this caveat: The best communicators are often those who generate the most emotion, positive and negative in others. When you think about Bill Clinton or Ronald Reagan, you have two very different people and sets of beliefs, but you also have two successful communicators that were generally respected by the majority of people...even those who disagreed with them. Emotion influences.

Key Point: Capture, hold and focus the audience's attention until they go into a natural waking trance. Share information in a simplistic fashion that appeals to the audience's innate curiosity and need to learn.

2. Give certain powerful SINGULAR self-revelations that reveal and teach the audience your values, beliefs, the goodness of your heart, and the emotional and experiential reasons for it.

That said, put all the emphasis on SINGULAR. If you tell a story that is a biography or a travelogue of your ENTIRE life-trip, you space the other person out and they lose interest ...completely.

If you want someone to know that you value loyalty or that you believe in God or that you are a Red Sox fan or whatever, you want to STICK TO THE SINGULAR. PICK one covert message and stick with THAT message.

3. Avoid communicating too much - and too much information in any one story.

A good story maxes out at about 4 minutes in conversation with one person. You get one of those about every half hour. With small groups, you have to make your stories tighter and more concise. With large groups of say 50 or more, you can tell a longer story if it is emotion or action packed. Perhaps 6-7 minutes.

You want to self reveal because you must have the person you are communicating with be able to empathize with you....to know who you are "inside." But self reveal in a non-threatening fashion.

Always put words of self flattery back into the mouths of the people who originally said the words. So if you want to tell how smart you are, you will make sure the story you tell is one where someone ELSE tells you how smart you are.

This is the beauty of "covert." It's why a testimonial means so much more to the average person than a scientific study.

And, a testimonial that is SINGULAR in it's message is ALWAYS more effective than a testimonial that says you are smart, good looking, and a good gardener...

... Quick Summary and then your next 7 Keys...

(This is profound...please take notes...you'll never see this kind of info again in your life....)

A good story must:

a. Have a clear purpose, or intent, a particular influence you wish to achieve by telling it.

b. You have to be clear in your own mind, "I am telling this story in order to get my listeners to ...!" People babble and babble and say nothing, have no clue what their intention is and worst, while babbling they have no idea that the other person can't hear them any more because their mind is just west of Neptune. YOU always have a clear intention AND pay VERY CLOSE attention to feedback, verbal and nonverbal, from your listener.

c. **Capture, hold and focus the audience's attention until they go into a natural waking state of captivation.**

I used to call this "trance." That was an error on my part. **A State of Captivation** is accurate. When a person is completely wrapped up in what you are saying and there is nothing else happening in the world, you have a **State of Captivation**.

You have created a tunnel between you and your listener, and you are meeting in the tunnel. You will meet them at their end and take them by the hand and bring them to your side.

What grabs attention?

- Something they passionately agree with you about (Prolife/prochoice, handgun/ban handgun, etc.)
- Something controversial that creates a significantly attention-getting emotion inside of them. (Anything that causes emotion that is NOT SO GREAT to take attention away from your story...nor too dull so that they pay no attention.)
- Peripheral things that have nothing to do with the actual later content of the story. (Camera focuses on the cheerleaders between plays to hold attention in commercial breaks.)
- Setting, environment. where the story is told... (the restaurant you are at)...or if you are good...where the story takes place in the mind of the person you are talking to.

There's more, but the key is this. You want to wake up your listener. Get them OUT of their walking-through-life trance and then bring them into your world. You WANT to stimulate an emotion but not to a degree that they become compelled to argue with you or debate you about something. You stir emotion...you don't boil it. Stir and you captivate. Boil and you eliminate.

"There's a fine line between courage and recklessness...a fine line between chaos and creation." **Paul McCartney**, Fine Line, *Chaos and Creation in the Backyard*

McCartney 2005. That's the deal.. Your story is told because they are fascinated and they don't want to walk away. They are not repelled. They are magnetized with interest. There can be tension. It must be relieved at times during the story.

Any of the 16 desires that we deal with in Covert Hypnosis do the trick IN THE RIGHT PROPORTION.

A scary story works as long as the person feels no compulsion to run. It makes their heart beat faster but not to the point of a panic attack.

You tell some detail but make sure you keep unnecessary detail OUT. Detail can become VERY boring, very quickly...in seconds you can lose captivation and even simple attention.

Rapid digression can recapture a drifting mind if you then put the mind back into the story at a quick pace.

Lots of things captivate...but it's important that each sentence ends with certainty that your listener is fascinated.

Now, on to more Keys.....

4. Share information in a simplistic fashion that appeals to the listener's innate curiosity and need to learn and acquire knowledge.

Never try to be too smart...or stupid... for your listener. Bring everything to their level of comprehension and Do NOT make a mistake by going too high or too low. If I'm not in the military don't tell me you are going to the PX (the store) to get some food. Meet the listener on THEIR landscape.

People want to know things. They want to know secrets. They want to understand the way things work IF it's easy to understand. Otherwise you can forget it and move on. Keep your story simple and emotion filled if the subject of your story is not about technical things.

5. Give certain powerful self-revelations that reveal and teach the listener (or audience) your values, the goodness of your heart, and the emotional and experiential reasons for it.

People want to know you and trust you. Believe in you. Tell a story in your absolute most humble voice that reveals who you really are to the listener. Arrogance is explosive...and never good. It breaks rapport and causes decaptivation and attention deficit.

6. Create vivid visualizations by giving descriptors that appeal to both the senses and the emotions.

Trigger as many safe or relatively safe places in the brain as you can. Communicate what you see, hear, feel, smell. Cause the other person to almost hallucinate those sensations as well. That's captivation. Emotion and Sensory.... Therein is the holy grail....

7. Regress and/or progress the audience through time, deliberately avoiding the present as you do so.

Get them out of today back to whenever. The present is where they feel uncomfortable. Once in the future or past you can take them somewhere that you have discovered to be helpful in meeting the needs of captivation.

Get them in the moment. Never talk about your biography. Tell a story..story...and never tell another without demand until they have told one, as well.

8. Be REAL, be true, and be your own experience.

The story won't be the same every time because it won't be scripted. BUT THE HEART, THE SOUL will be awesome. No matter the situation, beware of telling a story without thinking about WHY you are telling each part. You need to have INTENTION. PURPOSE. And it must align in some way with your listener. Parallel, not perpendicular.

9. It must somehow provide historically verifiable convincers of that reality, e.g. Names, dates, places, appeals to the audience's collective experience/memory, etc.

People want to have what they consider evidence that something is true. Names, dates and places don't PROVE something is true but they at minimum create an illusion in the listener's mind that the story is true.

And truth matters. When people hear person, place, thing, date...they can be there with you and when they are THERE you ARE telling the truth, BECAUSE THEY CAN SEE, HEAR and FEEL IT, too.

The story can be fiction or fact, but if the listener hears name, date, place, time...it is not fiction...it becomes part of their memory...it becomes part of their understanding of truth and who you are. And when people "know" who you are they LIKE YOU MORE INSTANTLY.

10. When you are telling a story that involves other people, have the characters come alive by speaking directly in the first person, rather than indirectly in the third.

"He said, ...'I'm doing the best I can, man.'"
(Scotty, Star Trek)
vs.
"He said that he was doing the best he could!"
As you make that character real, it gives LIFE to your story. I can't tell you how many people tell me they remember the story about the little girl in the wheelchair I met in Chicago during my first book tour. There are others that people tell me they remember...but they all remember Barnes and Noble, Chicago. July 1996.

11. Your story must contain important embedded intentions, lessons, or keys, to achieving your, or their purpose. (That's a mouthful.)

Example: I'm telling a story to a woman that Al really wants to take on a date. I'd like her to attend *Influence: Boot Camp* in February. Two separate intentions that can both be met to create a triple win.

."..and by the way, Al wasn't the only one who went to *Influence: Boot Camp* last year that got a book deal utilizing information he learned."

Now she knows that Al went to *Boot Camp*, and that he got a book deal and that the information he got at *Boot Camp* was stuff he could actually *use*. Multiple purposes can be sandwiched into a story about Al with ease. One sentence, then I can return to telling a story about Al and how amazing he was when he presented at *Boot Camp*.

12. You must place yourself in a context and situation that makes you relatable to the audience.

This is accomplished by either direct or visualized common experience. They must be able to go inside and go, "Yeah, that was just like when I ...." Or, if they have no similar reference, it must at least appeal to the sense of curiosity, "Yeah, I've always wondered/imagined what it would be like to ..." .....Yes. I'm just like the listener.

"Who'd have ever thought it... there I am... Kevin Hogan, a kid from Chicago, wondering if my tie looks good.... wondering if it's obvious that my heart is pounding away, seated across the table from one of the most important people in Poland."

It's easy to relate to someone being nervous and we all like to be with someone important so it makes the story that I'm about tell completely relatable....something you can connect with easily and instantly.

13. Sometimes you want to....Have meaning!

Your story can contain points of information that could just have been told directly, but are instead woven in as part of the tale. AND the lesson is usually learned BY ME (the storyteller) from someone else in the story. That way I'm NOT preaching. I'm learning and relating what I learn....as it happens...in the past.

"I never realized how important it was to X."

And that is my message for the listener or audience. I want them to X, but I'm not telling them to X. I'm simply telling them that I previously had never REALIZED how important it was to X.

14. Very "graciously" tell your listener or audience how great and REAL you are! Really! But YOU don't tell your listener, the people in your story do.

."..and Kevin we got a letter from the management of that Barnes and Noble...they said it was the best experience they ever had with an author."

You can't tell your listener how wonderful you are, but the people in your story can...

15. The charismatic cover charm and irresistible attraction is achieved by:

- Putting words of praise on the lips of other people in the story, (as they happened!)
- Offsetting what could be boasting with self-deprecating humor or humility.
- Revealing your vulnerabilities, inadequacies, weaknesses and plain ordinary "human-ness."

Every great story I tell has lots of self deprecation...lots of vulnerability. Plenty of personal exposure and human weaknesses. That's what my audience wants and that's what they connect with. All the self deprecation. It's the trademark of great story.

16. Give the listener opportunity to believe, have faith, and create their own trance-identified solutions in YOUR story.

You want her to think, "Well, if she did that, then I can/could ..." or put another way... .....If you can get them to say x vs. tell them x, they will much more readily acquiesce and with more power and attitude.

17. Provide clear inspiration, a "nudge", to a specific action! Be viral!

Be simple, powerful and memorable enough that they will repeat it, both mentally and verbally, and fully re-experience it when they do!

All the classic stories in the repertoire can be told to someone else that they meet on the street. and it's always followed, "oh my gosh...he's such a great guy, or, such a great speaker...you know what he said?..."

Notice the power of being "in the moment."

Compare and contrast these examples CAREFULLY

He looked at me like I was nuts. "Kevin, you idiot. What are you doing? Have you lost your mind?"
vs.
He looked at me like I was nuts and called me an idiot.

She locked eyes with mine and said, "Kevin Hogan, I love you."
vs.
She locked eyes with mine and told me she loved me.

He looked at me, shocked. "Kevin, you did that? It's amazing! You are incredible. How did you do it?!"
vs.
He looked at me shocked. He told me I was amazing and wanted to know how I did it.

It's this simple...or this hard.
Now, here is the next big disaster or disaster averted!

KEY BONUS POINT: You are telling a story. Not a biography. One story.

Stories are almost always events. One day, or one hour or two similar related events...one causing the other.

If you tell TWO stories before your listener has told one, you are at the cliff's edge. It's time to be quiet.

Remember in covert hypnosis, the key is subtle. The single most common problems in Story are bragging, boasting and boring.

THOSE BOASTFUL WORDS must come from someone else's mouth or they don't get said!

Quick Summary of the 17 Keys to Using Covert Hypnosis in Story

1. What intention do you have? What do you want the other person to think or feel after telling his story? What is your purpose?
2. Give certain powerful SINGULAR self-revelations that reveal and teach the audience your values, beliefs, the goodness of your heart, and the emotional and experiential reasons for it.
3. Capture, hold and focus the audience's attention until they go into a natural waking state of captivation.
4. Share information in a simplistic fashion that appeals to the listener's innate curiosity and need to learn and acquire knowledge.
5. Give certain powerful self-revelations that reveal and teach the listener (or audience) your values, the goodness of your heart, and the emotional and experiential reasons for it.

6. Create vivid visualizations by giving descriptors that appeal to both the senses and the emotions.

7. Regress and/or progress the audience through time, deliberately avoiding the present as you do so.

8. Be REAL, be true, and be your own experience.

9. It must somehow provide historically verifiable convincers of that reality, e.g. Names, dates, places, appeals to the audience's collective experience/memory, etc.

10. When you are telling a story that involves other people, have the characters come alive by speaking directly in the first person, rather than indirectly in the third.

11. Your story must contain important embedded intentions, lessons, or keys, to achieving your, or their purpose. (That's a mouthful.)

12. You must place yourself in a context and situation that makes you relatable to the audience.

13. Sometimes you want to....Have meaning! Your story can contain points of information that could just have been told directly, but are instead woven in as part of the tale. AND the lesson is usually learned BY ME (the storyteller) from someone else in the story. That way I'm NOT preaching. I'm learning and relating what I learn....as it happens...in the past.

14. Very "graciously" tell your listener or audience how great and REAL you are! Really! But YOU don't tell your listener, the people in your story do.

15. The charismatic cover charm and irresistible attraction is achieved by:

16. Putting words of praise on the lips of other people in the story, (as they happened!) Offsetting what could be boasting with self-deprecating humor or humility. Revealing your vulnerabilities, inadequacies, weaknesses and plain ordinary "human-ness."

17. Give the listener opportunity to believe, have faith, and create their own trance-identified solutions in YOUR story.

18. Provide clear inspiration, a "nudge", to a specific action! Be viral!

COMPARE:

Option 1: "Kevin: I'm such a great speaker and writer and renaissance man."(sucks)
vs.
Option 2: Someone else saying,..."Kevin you are just an amazing speaker, a brilliant writer, how did you become this renaissance man?" I shrink away not knowing what the renaissance really is. I think that's a good thing but I don't know...

Notice how in Option 2, you covertly tell the world all this neat stuff because your fan said it to you. No one can argue or react negatively to the fan. But, they can think you really suck if you say it yourself - about yourself.

These powerful keys can be used one on one or in presentations and in many other ways as you will discover when you put these keys into practice.

Hypnotic Language Patterns

People who study hypnosis learn that there are many ways to get a person into a specific frame of mind and then get them to think about anything the hypnotist desires. Without digressing too much, our goal in hypnosis is to get people to imagine something or a specific outcome. Imagining something is often the first step to getting it, or avoiding it.

In the case of selling, we want people to put their attention on our products and services. Then we want them to tell us how they will go about buying our products and services. People will not give you these secret codes to their thinking just because you ask, however.

You need to use the scientifically proven techniques in a very artful manner. There are specific words and phrases that yield amazing results in gaining compliance.

Below are some of the phrases that have been shown to get a person to come to a conclusion that is all but predetermined.

You will notice that the hypnotic language patterns are in bold face and we assume that whatever follows the pattern will be acted upon. In other words, in the first example, the hypnotic command is to *"buy this car, that's your decision."* It follows the hypnotic sentence fragment, **"I wouldn't tell you to..."**

All of the commands are written in small type below and the hypnotic language is in bold. A command is the specific action we want the person to take. Most of these patterns are not necessarily what would be considered "good English" or "grammatically correct."

I'm going to use a selling example for the language patterns. You can easily change the context to dating, relationships, parenting, presenting, anything you want. These patterns which have tested out well, are all "content free."

Exercise:

BEFORE you learn how to use the 16 core drives and desires, write two or three examples for each of these patterns for you, or your own product/service/desire.

I wouldn't tell you to buy this car, that's your decision.
I wouldn't tell you to invest more money in stocks, you need to figure that out on your own.

(I wouldn't tell you, but notice that the command is still coming!)

How do you go about deciding to buy a new car?
How do you go about deciding how much you are going to invest?

When you ask how they go about deciding, you learn specifically how they decide and then they give you the specific instructions on how to sell them!

You might want to... now, join the club for only one year then renew.
You might want to... now, buy this beautiful car.

(You don't **have** to, you just might!)

What is it that helps you know whether you should buy an X or a Y?
What is it that helps you know whether you want to upgrade **now** or wait awhile?

(Again, you are really asking for their specific decision strategy.)

You don't have to decide **now.**
You don't have to invest in several funds; one or two is just fine.

("I will if I want to!")

Why is it that some people just don't see the value of owning a quality car?
Why is it that some people just see greatness and others it eludes them?

(Not you Mr. Client, but some people…)

I don't know if signing up **now** is what you want to do.
I don't know if deciding **now** is absolutely necessary so you don't lose out.

(Actually I do know but I'm being very gentle.)

Would you like to see a bigger house?
Would you like to see this in blue?
Would you like to see our client service people call you regularly?

(You are asking for specific features and benefits that they might want…or not.)

Some people are investing a great deal of money right **now.**
Some people are snapping up houses like they are going out of style.
(Some people…is your client.)

If you could have a perfect car, what would it be like?
If you could have the perfect speaker for your function what would he be like?

"If you could have…" = "imagine"
It goes straight to the unconscious mind and goes to work like a mind virus.

If you could choose any mutual fund what qualities would you want it to have?
If you could choose a better insurance company what would be most important to you?

(He can choose and his brain will tell him so, now!)

Have you ever seen a truly amazing sales trainer?
Have you ever seen a speaker that motivates the day AFTER they leave?

(Again, this is the same as "imagine." It's a no-pressure question that darts through the brain at high speeds causing a "yes, I want it" response.)

Would you be surprised if I told you that most people aren't as astute as you are?
Would you be surprised if I told you that this car gets 30 mpg?

("Would you be surprised if I told you," implies you have the shocking truth.)

Imagine what would happen if your portfolio averaged 12% per year!
Imagine what would happen if you lived in a house that you could really be proud of!

(Once again, we have "imagine" lighting up the brain like a Christmas tree.)

Are you interested in making more money short-term or long-term?
Are you interested in making the online experience for your clients easy and fun?

(He knows he should be interested and now he has to say yes or pick which is best for him.)

If I could show you a way to make more money **would you** hire our firm?
If I could show you a way to literally look 10 years younger would you do it?

(This is a perfect, pre-closing question. You wouldn't ask it unless you COULD show him, so now you get the "yes" response and then you close after you show him.)

What would it be like if you had an extra $25,000 per year in income?
What would it be like if you had a body that people would be magnetized to?

(Imagine that....)

You may not know that this is going to be fun.
You may not know that we are going to be working together for a long time!

(He'll know right after you say, "You may not know...")

Can I show you seven ways to increase your personal sales?
Can I show you how to work out in such a way that you will be stronger and look better?

(Getting permission to sell your client is kind and effective.)

I'm wondering if deciding today will make you feel comfortable inside.
I'm wondering if investing today is going to make you the most money long term.

(I'm wondering while you imagine.)

Don't you think that it's time for a new President to lead our country?
Don't you think that a mutual fund that has a proven track record is better than...?

(It's hard to say no to anything that follows, "don't you think that.")

Don't you feel that you are happier when you have someone do your taxes for you?
Don't you feel that you are better off with a new car than an old one?

(Same as previous comment.)

Your Thoughts and Comments:

After you have learned the 16 Core Drivers THEN return to the language patterns and do them again for a context in which YOU will use them!

The Ultimate Covert Hypnosis

Chapter Eight

WIN/WIN Relationships
Create Near-Term Wealth and Long-Term Happiness

There is a special energy that is exciting about communicating with the intent of influencing others. Occasionally the experience is seen as a chess game where there are two opponents who must "buy" and "sell" from each other and only one will ultimately win and one will ultimately lose. Far more often, *the persuasion setting is one where both sides MUST win.*

In some situations, you will never see the other person again. Selling your house, a timeshare, or a car is typically a one-time interaction between the salesperson and the client. The pressure experienced by both salesperson and client is far greater in each of these settings because it is a "one shot deal." The necessity of a win/win scenario is still critical to the long-term success of the client's finances and the salesperson's reputation.

The "feel" of these kinds of transactions is very different from long-term relationship selling, though. Insurance people, have a slightly different kind of pressure on them. People who sell to a client every week or month (pharmaceuticals for example) have an even different type of pressure. One thing is certain: Engaging in Win/Win deals will make you sleep at night and be proud of the work you are in.

My personal insurance agent is Denis Dunker of Cannon Falls, Minnesota. In all but two years of my adult life he has served as my casualty insurance agent.

He has never had to close a sale with me. He has always utilized MAPs effectively and ethically in working with me. On many occasions in the past I have "demanded" that my coverage be improved. That is one of the tell tale signs of someone who is a master at walking on someone else's mind map! When the client demands the salesperson sell them more and more, the salesperson has become a master.

Every couple of years Denis makes it a point to drive the 45 minutes that are necessary to get to my home in the Twin Cities. He drives past several other State Farm Insurance agencies on the way up here for a visit or a luncheon date. In theory, I should have had my business with one of those agents he drives past, but Denis has built a long-term relationship, a friendship and has always shown great respect and interest in my work. Those are all important to me and they are all related to many of the 16 basic desires you will learn about in the next two chapters.

> **All *people need respect and desire friendship.***

Denis probably didn't know that being a friend and respecting someone's work is part of my instinctual drive...he simply likes people and works hard to do what is in his client's best interests. Today Denis is a wealthy man and has a substantial client base that will take care of him and his family for the rest of his life. He never has asked me buy an insurance product I didn't want. In fact, he has never "closed" a sale with me. He has always allowed me to "close myself." He utilized my personality, which includes analyzing data, being in charge, being a decision maker, and has acted as my advisor instead of what other less astute individuals may have done...and lost my business. Here is Denis's key to success:

> **Build rapport...ask questions!**

Denis has taken care of me for over 20 years and hopefully will do the same for the next 20 years. He is an unconscious master of selling and I don't think he is fully aware of it. On his next island vacation trip, I'm sure he'll not be too concerned...as he sits on the beach with his wife sipping from the tall glasses...That's what happens when you care about people...they demand you sell to them...because they know you care...just like Zig Ziglar said.

When I think of Win/Win on a different level I think of the great expense and the great fun involved in a trip to Disneyland.

When was the last time you went to Disneyworld or Disneyland? Remember how much fun everyone had? The rides were great. The shows were great. Meeting the cartoon and fantasy characters was a thrill for the children. The day or weekend at Disney may have been the focal point of the vacation. You look at your pictures from Disney and think of how thrilled the kids were to get there.

In between the parking lot and the park was a ticket booth where you paid over $100 for your day of fun. You may have been shocked at how much the price had gone up since the last time you had been there. Was it worth it? Looking back, was it worth it? You bet. You paid a lot of money to allow your family to have a great deal of fun. It was definitely worth it. It was a win-win deal. Disney's tradition is to continually generate enormous revenues from the masses of the world populace in exchange for an experience of great fun and enjoyment.

Win-Win thinking is not a platitude with a wink attached to it.

Win-Win is at the core of every long term successful relationship in the free world. Win-Win Thinking is the foundation for every technique utilized in this book.

Two Levels of Awareness

Decisions to comply or not are made and lost on two levels of awareness and communication. One level is called the conscious level of awareness and the other is the unconscious level of awareness. After you read this book, there will no longer be anything mysterious about the unconscious level of awareness. The unconscious level of awareness is that which you are not consciously aware of but are still responding to in your mind and body. Communication is ongoing at both levels of awareness all of the time during the persuasion process and no one is ever *fully* aware of what is happening at both levels of awareness.

Here is what is even more fascinating. ***Before two people see each other in the persuasion setting, many "sales" are made and broken.*** Even before a client and a person ever meet or know they will meet, sales are made and broken. You will shortly learn how to prepare for what used to be largely unknown in the persuasion process: the beliefs and attitudes of yourself and those of your counterpart.

Four Features on the Covert Hypnosis Map

*The skills of Covert Hypnosis continue with an understanding of the beliefs, values, attitudes and lifestyles of both the person who will influence and the person who will comply. **This is important for dating, relationships, management or sales and marketing.***

What do these four words mean and why are they important to your success?

Beliefs are what people know to be true, with or without enough evidence to have made a rational determination that the belief itself is actually true.

104

Beliefs are what someone else knows to be true. This doesn't mean that the client is right or wrong. It's their belief. It's foolish to argue about beliefs. It's foolish to debate beliefs. People's lives are supported by their beliefs and people are normally slow to change them.

Values are what people hold in esteem or significance in their life. Some people consider love, happiness, peace of mind, money, security, freedom, justice and companionship among the highest values in life. There are hundreds of values. Values arise from the core desires and drives that unconsciously motivate us. Values are normally more difficult to change than beliefs. Therefore, don't try. Better: *Utilize* the values of another person. Acknowledge them and appreciate them.

Attitudes are people's states of mind or feeling as they pertain to specific issues. Unlike values, which are over-riding themes in a person's life, attitudes are specific. They relate to specific things in life.

Lifestyles are how people live considering the means, values, beliefs and attitudes they currently have. Lifestyles are all about how we behaviorally respond to our beliefs, attitudes, and lifestyles.

Beliefs, values, and attitudes are unconscious "filters" of our experience. We see everything in life through the glasses of our beliefs, values and attitudes. Once we open our eyes to our own beliefs, attitudes and values, it makes it easier to understand other people's values, attitudes and beliefs. In the course of an average day, we don't discuss our attitudes, values and beliefs but we do perceive and experience life based upon these filters.

Once you know a person's beliefs, values, attitudes and lifestyles you can ask them for anything in an appropriate fashion and they will in all but the rarest instances say, "Yes!"

Understanding your own beliefs, values, attitudes and lifestyle comes first in the persuasion process. Long before your counterpart meets you, you spend time with your belief systems, values, your attitudes about life and your work, and live within a certain lifestyle that often make or break a communication before you meet the woman who will say "Yes!" to you today. Take a few moments to learn about yourself first and understanding others will be easy.

Values: Opening The Doors of the Mind

Take twenty minutes and write down the answer to each of these questions.

A) What are the 10 most important things to you in life?

_____

_____

_____

_____

_____

_____

_____

_____

_____

_____

B) Rank the above ten values in order by placing the numbers one through ten by the value.

C) Write down the 10 values in the spaces provided below and to the immediate right, write down specifically how you know when you have that value. (If you wrote love, for example, then write down, exactly how you know when you have love next to the word love.) Take your time, as this isn't as easy as you might think.

My Top Ten Values and Evidence of Them

1)_____

_____

2)_____

_____

3)_____

_____

4)_____

_____

5)_____

_____

6)_____

_____

7)_____

_____

8)_____

_____

9)_____

_____

10)_____

_____

Understanding your values is the beginning of mastering covert hypnosis. Your values are what you move toward. These are the states of mind and "things" that you want most in life.

One element that separates great people from those who are mediocre is the ability to discover what is important to others in business, relationships and life. As you learn what is important to others, you work hard to meet their values and needs and find that what you hold in highest esteem, while wonderful for you, is not what you are selling. You must sell your products and services to meet the values, beliefs, attitudes and lifestyles of others around you.

Magical Questions...
    ...that Open the Doors to the Mind

There are three key magical questions that allow you to uncover another person's values instantly.

They are very simple to learn and once you can utilize them in any context, your personal power as a communicator is enhanced dramatically.

The reason you want to know another person's values is that once you know what is most important to another person in the persuasion process you are virtually guaranteed to gain compliance.

Generally speaking, you want three pieces of information. I am using selling situations in most cases in this book. You can obviously adjust this for the therapy, dating, and relationship setting.

1) What is most important to you in X?

(X as in "buying" or "considering the purchase of your products or services.")

"What's most important to you in deciding how much life insurance to buy?"

"What is most important to you in deciding what computer system to use?"

"What is most important to you in buying a new home?"

"What is most important to you in deciding what to invest in for your retirement?"

Your counterpart or client will respond with whatever is important. He may respond with one word like "quality" or "service" or he may respond with a 20-minute monologue that you will recap into one or two sentences.

Regardless of how your person responds, his response and your summary of his response now become "Y."

2) How do you know when you have Y?

(P) Person: I want a car that is a good value.
(M.S.) Master salesperson "How do you know when you have a good value in an automobile?"

(P) I want enough life insurance to protect my family when I die.
(M.S.) "How do you know when you have enough life insurance to protect your family?"

(P) I want a house that is big enough for my whole family to live comfortably in.
(M.S.) "How do you know when a home is big enough so your family is comfortable?"

[Once the client responds to your inquiry, they do so by stating something that is often ambiguous. For example, they may say, "We like quality." Therefore, the master salesperson wants to know, "How do you know when you have a quality X (house, automobile, mutual fund, insurance company)?" This is called, "evidence" in this book.]

3) If I could give you Y, would you Z?

If you can meet their highest value, quality, or desire using the example above, will they work with you, or hire you, or buy your product? It is very difficult to say, "no" at this point because of the framing of questions one and two. Consider the following examples.

"If you can be certain that this is an A+ rated insurance company will you feel comfortable?"

"If you can be certain that this is the best value in automobiles will you feel comfortable owning it?"

"If you feel sure that this is a quality home, will you feel comfortable living here?"

The Fourth Magical Question

On occasion, the client will say no to a "stage three question." If that ever occurs you have one more magical incantation that will turn the key.

4) What else is most important to you in buying/owning an X?

At this point you merely cycle back through the value elicitation process noted above. There are times when the client does not know what is most important to him in the purchase of your product. Question four eliminates the concern and continues the magic cycle to a positive solution!

You now know the magic formula for eliciting values. This is one of the single most important factors on the journey of success that you will learn in this book.

Two charts appear below. The first chart is an assessment of what men and women value the most in life as far as their "ends values" are concerned. Ends values are states of mind like happiness, freedom and love. This chart was compiled from a study where a number of values were shown to participants. The participants then created a hierarchy of those values. This first chart will help you have a basic understanding of what you will discover in the marketplace when you begin eliciting values from your clients.

The value you can gain from this important ranking is two-fold. First, you see the values that shape America. Second, you can observe the difference between men and women and their hierarchies.

The second chart reveals the personality traits that Americans value most. If you can mirror the American values, you will appeal to the greatest number of people.

Ends Values and Composite Rank Orders for American Men and Women

(adapted from *The Nature of Human Values* by Rokeach)

Terminal Values	Men (665)	Women (744)
Comfortable Life	4	13
Exciting Life	18	18
Sense of Accomplishment	7	10
World at Peace	1	1
World of Beauty	15	15
Equality	9	8
Family Security	2	2
Freedom	3	3
Happiness	5	5
Inner Harmony	13	12
Mature Love	14	14
National Security	14	14
Pleasure	17	16
Salvation	12	4
Self Respect	6	6
Social Recognition	16	17
True Friendship	11	9
Wisdom	8	7

Instrumental Values and Composite Rank Orders for
American Men and Women

Instrumental Value	*Men*	*Women*
Ambitious	2	4
Broadminded	4	5
Capable	8	12
Cheerful	12	10
Clean	9	8
Courageous	5	6
Forgiving	6	2
Helpful	7	7
Honest	1	1
Imaginative	18	18
Independent	11	14
Intellectual	15	16
Logical	16	17
Loving	14	9
Obedient	17	15
Polite	13	13
Responsible	3	3
Self-controlled	10	11

Changing Values in America

American values are not remaining static, however. Each year we re-shape our society and the individuals within the society re-shape themselves. It is a slow process but there are definite changes that have been evidenced. Notice how many values and attitudes have been re-shaped in just the last two decades.

Changing Values in America
(adapted from: The Futurist)

Old	New
Self-denial ethic	Self Fulfillment ethic
Higher standard of living	Better quality of life
Traditional sex roles	Blurring of sex roles
Accepted definition of success	Individualized definition of success
Faith in industry/institutions	Self Reliance
Traditional family life	Alternative families
Live to work	Work to live
Hero Worship	Love of ideas
Expansionism	Pluralism
Patriotism	Less patriotism
Unparalleled growth	Growing sense of limits
Industrial growth	Technology/Info Age
Receptivity to technology	Technology Orientation

The United States and Canada are changing countries. Values and beliefs are shifting with time and growth. You become an expert in Mind Access by having the foundational knowledge necessary for sales success as detailed in this book. You become a sales success by applying the strategies and techniques you learn in this book in your everyday life.

The Linear Covert Delta Model

There are hundreds of ways to present information to clients, groups, loved ones, lovers, and buyers. The LCD model of covert hypnosis is really just one of my top ten favorite models of persuasion.

When we are making our presentations and proposals to others in the persuasion process we should note the following key elements are occurring whether it is a one on one lunch date or a public speaker before a group of 1,000. This model has been proven effective and I recommend you utilize it in your business.

Specific strategies for each of the elements below are detailed elsewhere in the book. For now, we want you to have a useful framework for persuasion. Some of this will be very familiar to you. A few of the points will be new distinctions that you had forgot about or perhaps they are brand new to you!

1) Establish and Maintain Rapport

Rapport can be defined as being "in synch" with another person. Generally people are more likely to be in rapport with someone else if they like that person. How do you know if you are in rapport with someone?

Answer this question:

Does the person respond to you in a positive manner?

If so, you are in some degree of rapport. Remember what Ziglar said, "They don't care what you know until they know that you really care." Therefore, you will want to begin to develop a sense of empathy and sincere curiosity about others. Rapport occurs on different levels of communication. You can be technically skilled at acting and appear to be in rapport, but if you don't sincerely care about your client and the people you are working with, what is the point? There are several methods of developing rapport.

2) Use Content to Build Rapport

Discover what their interests are and if you are already not in tune with the interest, learn about it. *People love to talk about what they love and what they know about!* When I lead sales training seminars, one of my favorite stories about building rapport is the "learning about fishing" story.

Living in Minnesota, many of my clients are avid fisherman. How would I connect with my clients knowing absolutely nothing about fishing? I grew up a Chicago Cubs fan, a child prodigy in mathematics, and even though I lived very close to Lake Michigan, unlike most kids, I never enjoyed fishing. In Minnesota, a big deal is made every year when it is time for the "fishing opener." To my mind, "opener" means opening day at Wrigley Field. To the mind of many of my clients the only Wrigley related thing they know about is the chewing gum. It seems I am doomed at meeting many of my clients at more than a superficial level...until one day...

...I decided to learn about fishing by asking all of my clients that love fishing to tell me their favorite fishing stories. I began asking questions that to them must have seemed absolutely ridiculous. Over the last few years, I have built an array of knowledge and stories about fishing. I can direct you to all of the best lakes for fishing and I can tell you what to fish for at these lakes...and I've never been fishing in the state, not once.

You can build a great deal of rapport and long term friendships by showing

114

and experiencing sincere interest in what is important to other people. Sharing the experiences of your client's hobbies, lifestyle, and interests is called "using content to build rapport."

3) Use Processes to Build Rapport

There is more to building rapport than swapping fishing stories. Becoming in synch with another person or a group can take a great deal of skill, in addition to the sincere interest that is necessary in building relationships. Many people will not feel comfortable discussing their families, hobbies and lifestyles with you, a perfectly nice, perfect stranger. How does the ice get broken when stories are very uncomfortable for the client? Many of your contacts were taught as children to not talk to strangers. Many of your contacts were taught to keep private matters, private. How do you help these people become comfortable with you?

4) Pacing

When in doubt, an effective way to begin building rapport with anyone is by pacing. Pacing is essentially synonymous with the term "matching" or "mirroring." In other words, be like your client, because he likes people who are like him. There are a number of techniques that can be used to effectively pace your client, to begin building rapport. Rapport is one of the pillars to success in sales and in life.

5) Use Your Voice

Imagine that the person you are communicating with is in an upset mood. He has a sharp edge to his voice and you get to make your presentation. Many people attempt to get him out of his mood with enthusiasm or a cheery story. In fact, the rule of thumb is, *"when in doubt, pace your client."* If your client has an edge in his voice, let your voice have an edge. If he sounds angry, let yourself be angry, however briefly about something that occurred today as well. This vocal pacing will help put you in synch with your client. Eventually you will lead your client out of the negative frame of mind, if you choose to. (And keep in mind that there are many times when a negative frame of mind is necessary to making a sale.)

There is more that you can do with your voice than match the tone of your client. We all speak with a measurable average number of words per minutes. Many people drawn to the sales profession happen to speak quickly. Part of this experience is due to the nature of the business where we are obligated to be quick and to the point.

Unfortunately, if your client speaks slowly and you are speaking quickly to meet a time constraint, you probably will lose the sale. People tend to speak at a rate that is consistent with how they process their thoughts and internal representations. if people tend to think in pictures (movies), they tend to speak very quickly. People who tend to speak very slowly process information through their feelings and emotions. In between are what we call the radio announcers. These people are those who speak with a more rich and resonant voice. They normally think in words.

Building rapport is fundamental to covert hypnosis. One specific strategy is to speak in the same rate and pitch of voice as your client.

---

6) Why Pace Breathing?

Admittedly, one of the more difficult pacing techniques is that of pacing your client's breathing. Breathing is one of the most unconscious of all body functions and pacing of breathing is one of the great rhythm generators of all time. Two people in the heat of sexual passion often are breathing at the exact same pace. Two people sitting side by side in deep meditation often experience the same exhale and inhale points.

When leading a group in hypnosis, hypnotherapists find that having the group breathe together actually creates a unique bonding rapport in the room.

It is this Mind Access Point that you will now enter.

As you watch your client breathe, begin to breathe in when she does. When she exhales, begin to exhale when she does. It is best to practice this pacing technique when you are not in verbal communication with people. For example, if you are waiting in line somewhere, and someone is talking to someone else, begin to pace their breathing. You can practice this at home by pacing someone who is unaware that you are doing it. Our research shows that by pacing another person's breathing, *the liking between the two people rises!*

7) Physiology and Posture

Unlike pacing someone's breathing, pacing someone's posture and physiology is much easier. If you sit erect and stiff and your client is seated in a comfortable, slightly bent over manner, you are not likely to develop the rapport you hope for.

Pacing physiology too closely can be a mistake. If every move your client makes is mirrored immediately back at him, he will begin to feel uncomfortable. The most effective manner of pacing physiology is to match the posture and general body position of the other person. When we discuss "leading," below, you will learn how to appropriately test your pacing skills with your client and be certain you have established rapport.

8) Leading

Developing a sincere interest in relationships and friendships with others is the first step in the persuasion process. Pacing your client is the second step. Leading comes third. A lead is successful when the person follows you. If you are sitting across from your counterpart and you both have similar physiology and you are both enjoying each other's company you have an opportunity to now begin leading, which is the beginning of the active process in persuasion.

Will your counterpart now follow you into your presentation? You have been following him for minutes and minutes. You've matched her vocal pacing and her physiology. You have shared mutual interests. Now it is time to take a non-verbal break from pacing and start leading. If your counterpart follows your lead you have successfully built rapport at the unconscious level and you can begin your persuasion momentarily. There are a few key methods of determining if you are in rapport with your client and we will move on to them now.

9) Lead with the Tone, Rate or Pitch of Your Voice

If you have been successfully matching your counterpart, you have an opportunity to lead by altering one of your vocal qualities. You may, for example, increase your speaking rate a little bit and induce a more enthusiastic attitude in the tone of your voice to help you bridge the conversation to your product or what you are pitching. The context of your discussion will help determine when and if this is appropriate.

When you notice that your counterpart follows your lead with a more enthusiastic voice, an increased rate of speech, a higher or lower tone of voice, you can feel assured you have successfully developed rapport.

10) Leading with Physiology, Posture, Movement

A person that is in rapport with you will often mirror the simplest movements you make identically.

Imagine that both you and your counterpart have been sitting with a hand to your chin for several minutes. Now, imagine that you believe you are ready to "test" to be certain you are in rapport. If you are sitting at a restaurant, you can take your hand to pick up a glass of water and watch to see what your counterpart does. If she follows you by also picking up her glass of water, or, even picking up a pen or a napkin, you have successfully led your client to the next stage of the persuasion process.

If your counterpart does not follow your lead, you need to begin the process of building rapport again.

---

11) Induce Reciprocity

Building rapport begins within you. The entire process of building rapport is built upon the foundation of concern, caring, compassion, interest and a desire for the well-being of your counterpart.

Pacing and leading is a process that creates comfort for you and your counterpart to know that you are moving along at a pace that is appropriate for them. The entire process of building rapport, pacing, and leading could be as little as one minute and as much as an hour or more. After rapport has been established you can enter into the body of your presentation. There are many ways to begin the persuasive presentation, but, my favorite is to give my client something. I regularly give a book that I wrote, called *The Gift: A Discovery of Love, Happiness and Fulfillment,* to my clients. You may not have a book to give, so here are some ideas to consider when deciding how you will induce reciprocity.

What you will give to your client to induce reciprocity will be in part based upon the average profit per sale and the significance of your gift. You should know that gifts tend to be reciprocated with sales in direct correlation to the dollar value of the gift that is given.

Specialty items, like pens, date books and calendars are perceived as advertising items and do not induce reciprocity. You must think of something appropriate that you can give to your client that will be appreciated. Inducing reciprocity is not just a sales technique, it is a way of life. There is almost a metaphysical energy that seems to emanate from the giving of gifts. Expect nothing in return when you induce reciprocity. The simple act of giving helps you develop a caring and compassionate personality. *That* is what people are buying when they buy from you....*YOU!*

People don't really buy into ideas, products or services....
they buy YOU!

---

12) Share Part of You, With Them

Show your confidence in your counterpart by helping them with one of their potential clients (or problems). In other words, offer to help them in any way you can. Can you make a phone call for them as a referral? Can you help them bring more business to their store by taking 50 of her business cards? What can you do to freely help them with their business that is above and beyond the scope of your sales call. *OFFER TO HELP*.

I've done this for years in selling and marketing and you can't believe how many times my kindness has been returned a thousand times over, over the years. Would you be willing to write them a testimonial on your letterhead for your client to show *HIS* clients? That is the kind of treatment you would like from your clients, so why not offer it out first!

13) The Common Enemy

Nothing binds two people, groups, or nations like a common enemy. Find their enemy and align yourself with their viewpoint. Do they hate the IRS? Do the same people try to hurt your mutual businesses? Jibe with them. Once someone shares with you who his enemies are, you have built a relationship for life. Drugs? Gangs? Taxes? Unemployment Compensation Insurance? Lawsuits? Government? Criminals? What are the common threats to business and society that you both dislike and you both know hurts your business.

You won't find a common enemy in every persuasive interview, but if you are thinking of the theme, the opportunity to put both of you on the same side of the table will occur during 50% of your interviews. Once you have a common enemy you have rapport and a lifetime relationship.

14) Tell a Short Story About Someone Like Them

If you can build a reservoir of stories *(short stories)* about people who have become your clients, you can utilize this covert persuasion tool. Tell today's client about another client who recently bought from you. This client should be someone they remind you of.

You can build an entrancing sales presentation around such stories and they make great lead ins to the core of your presentation.

15) Respect

Sincerely show respect for the person via a compliment. Always be looking for things to like about other people. Compliment them.

A little respect goes a long way and you cannot underestimate the value of a sincere compliment of respect in the environment of influence.

16) Knock Their Socks Off

The shortest amount of time we spend with any counterpart is normally that of the actual communication itself.

When you do actually begin the process, the very first thing you do is this: *Blow them away with an astonishing claim, an amazing fact, something that few would know. Show them something amazing that no one else has shown them.*

Make the biggest claim that you can substantiate. The client will always remember and consider this introduction. Start strong, finish strong. Your claim for your product or your service should be colossal and it must be true. Knock their socks off.

17) Always Give More Than You Promised

Napoleon Hill always made sure his audiences knew the principle of going the extra mile. Follow the example of those who sell who become millionaires. If you promise something make sure that your client gets exactly what you promise and then some. Remember that phrase: ...*and then some!*

18) The Power of Understatement

After making your big fat claim you can quickly work your way into your persuasive presentation. This is the time to make sure you don't over-inflate your product or service. You made your big fat claim, now support it with the power of understatement. In other words, if your mutual fund portfolio has a track record of 12% return per year over the last 10 years, then understate that by saying, "Now, if you average 10% per year..." For 10 years you have earned a 12% return, but you are being conservative for your client and he knows it and *appreciates it.*

19) Be Precise: Then Beat Your Precision

If you know that this automobile is going to get your client 19 miles per gallon, tell him that. Then tell him a secret. ."..but, if you use Mobil One oil, you can literally add an extra 3 miles per gallon of gas and that translates to an extra $100 of gasoline savings per year." Be precise, then be better than being precise.

20) Get It Done Faster, Easier, Better

You live in an age where your client wants everything to be better, cheaper, faster, quicker, smarter, easier, and more luxurious. So promise what you can, and then deliver...and then some. If they tell you that your competitor will get them X, then if you can really do it, you tell your client that you are going to get them X+2. Never be beaten because of the lack of going the extra mile.

What can you do for your client that no other agent will do for them? What can you do for him or her that no one else in the business does? Answer these questions then do it.

21) Be On the Edge of Your Seat

Pay attention with bated breath to every word your client has to say. It should be clear that what your client has to say is the most important thing in either of your worlds at that moment...and it is. If these were the last words you would hear while you were alive you would want to know what your client has to say.

Live your sales presentation as if the significance of each word will change your very life. Relationships are cemented when you do this. With the attitude of respect, going the extra mile and intense excitement about your client and his life, you won't need to use a multiplicity of closing tactics on your counterpart. He will demand that you sell him your product...*now*.

22) Asking for Compliance

As you begin to experience this kind of a relationship in the communication setting, the idea of gaining compliance is literally just that of consummating the relationship. Your client knows you care, they know you have their best interests at heart. You know their values and what is important to them in life and in the process of this sale. They know that you are going to help them solve their problems and they know that you will be there for them when you need them. It's the same as a friendship. Specifically how you want to do your paperwork is up to you. Simply ask a question or make a statement.

Your client is your friend. You are now involved in a relationship that will be long in duration and loyal in nature. Aside from leading the client to take action now, you don't have to "close" in the traditional sense of the word.

"OK John, we can wrap this up and do lunch again next week on me. I'm thinking a half million life insurance, level term 20 years. By then you are likely to be self-insured. Agreed?"

"Janet. Can I make a suggestion? You have $80,000 ready for retirement. You still have 30 years until you are going to need the money. I know you are averse to risk and I know that bonds and money market funds aren't going to do it for your retirement. Are you ready to divide the money evenly between Small Cap Growth and Large Cap Growth funds?"

"Bill. In my mind you need to be careful not to overextend yourself on your payments. I think you should finance for four years. If you go six years, most of the extra money is interest and that's a waste of money. In addition to that it will be forever before you own equity in the car. On the other hand, if you find yourself in a bind you can always refinance later on. Most banks will look at this as a new or virtually new car for the first year. Take it home now and pay it off faster and then you own it. OK?"

"Christina, as I look at this your company will be able to save thousands of dollars with our new system F90. You could spend a lot more on other systems I sell but this is the one that will optimize your return on investment. But, it's up to you. What do you want to do?"

Now, I know what you are thinking.

"They can say no!"

"These aren't alternative choice closes!"

Nonsense.

People don't buy because they don't need a product, they don't trust you, you haven't shown benefit to having the product, they don't like you, they don't have the money and perhaps a few other stray reasons.

The 21st Century Model of Covert Hypnosis is one that is based upon the foundation of trust and liking. It demands Win/Win or No Deal scenarios. If the client can't benefit from your product you wouldn't ask them to buy it and if they don't have the money they can finance it or simply not buy it. If financing is a reasonable and ethical option, and it normally is, then you can make the product affordable for the client in payments. Your client is your friend. No longer are they enemies that have to be outwitted.

The client is your friend. They are someone to be cared about and nurtured. When they see that in you, you won't need to worry about hundreds of closing lines and techniques. It turns out in real life, that closing is actually the easiest part of selling.

Building rapport, identifying the driving needs (those that they see and do not see) and wants of your client and understanding how and why your counterpart "buys" is really where the time in the persuasion process needs to be focused. That's what the next several chapters will cover in detail.

The Covert Model for Changing Minds
Chapter Nine

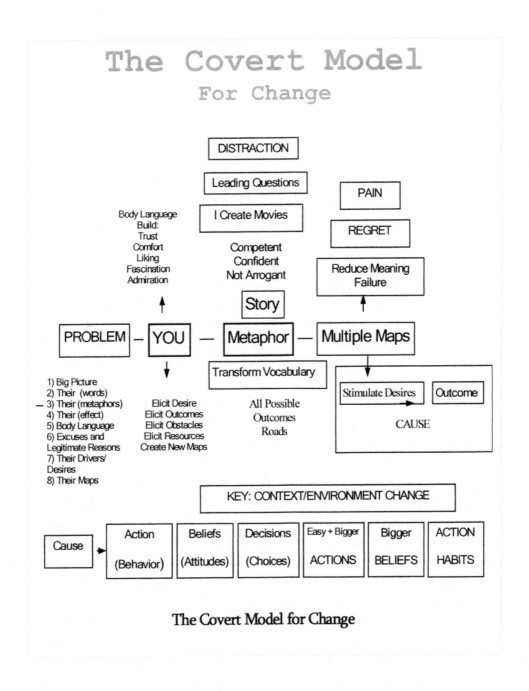

The Covert Model for Change

Remember, Covert Hypnosis is the utilization of techniques and strategies to change the perception and behavior of others in a completely unconscious way.

The Model for Change

This is the model for getting others to change behaviors, do things a different way, begin success thinking and find success. There are many other models out there, but this one has been found to be most successful.

Overview of the Model (See Map Above)

Cause

There is a cause for most behavior. Feelings, thoughts, ideas, imagination, fears, desires all be causes of behavior. As children, a cause could be the mother, father, or other family members.

The cause leads to an action or behavior. For instance, your mother may ask you to go to the store to buy a specific item. She may request that you go to the Seven-Eleven store instead of the grocery store. In order for you to change the behavior of which store to choose, you consider the input (or the cause) of your mother making the specific request. Your brain is accustomed to going to one particular store to get the items. But this time the request is different. If you were to go to the store you are accustomed to, the brain would already have neural pathways laid down with the route to the store on it. You could just about turn off the brain and go to the store "unconsciously", because the brain knows this pathway so well.

By the time you are an adult, billions of neural highways in the brain are neutralized, because of non-use. The actions you perform over and over lay down very clear neural pathways that you become so accustomed to, that they become "unconscious" actions.

When in Poland, I heard people speaking, and saying terms such as "wprost." My brain was not used to hearing the subtle "fff" sound before the "p" sound. It took many many times of hearing that "fff" sound for my brain to lay down a new neural pathway and allow me to hear the word in this more subtle way.

So, similarly, when I go a new way to the store, or choose a different store, it takes a few times of going a new direction in order to lay down a new neural pathway for this action to become "unconscious."

What is another way of looking at this? When you were a child, you probably attended church in some fashion. You went to church, you went to synagogue, you went to the mosque. Every Friday, Saturday or Sunday, you attended some form of spiritual service. Whatever action you do shapes your attitudes and beliefs. This is where new clusters of behaviors and future attitudes start to form.

As we go to the same service over and over, it is beginning to shape who we are and who we will become.

When we defend our beliefs to others (especially in a public way), it reinforces our behavior and actions. As people develop their defenses to their beliefs, what's happening is that these beliefs are being reinforced, strengthened, in a much more powerful way. What happens next is that people will begin to make choices based upon their very strong beliefs and attitudes. We inject emotion into attitude, belief, memory and learning. Adrenaline and stress hormones released as we defend our beliefs add to the emotions connected to our attitudes.

When presented with a choice or a decision on your own, you will start to make the choices of the behaviors you did as a child of 5 or 6, because you defended them publicly. As you go through life you will tend to make decisions based upon these past proclaimed beliefs and attitudes you have defended, despite or in spite of great evidence to the contrary, leading to greater actions.

Why do terrorists perform terroristic acts? They are very dedicated, and have proclaimed their beliefs in public many times and in many ways. Is there a question that they will perform acts that they believe uphold their beliefs? No, there is no doubt that these people will engage in terrorist acts which they believe uphold their beliefs. Why? Because that's what they are programmed to do. Their actions created their beliefs, their beliefs created these decisions, which lead to huge actions.

Actions → Beliefs → Decisions → Bigger Actions → Bigger Beliefs → ACTION

Are there the same principles in the Christian community? Yes. For example, Tim McVey, who, after the events at Waco, TX when the federal government went berserk over the Branch Davidians years ago, decided to take matters into his own hands.

A soldier in the Gulf war, McVey came home and watched an incredible thing unfolding before his eyes. He saw members of his own government, his own group, taking action against civilians within his own country, who did not have the means or training to defend themselves properly against a military unit. He had a belief that those actions were wrong and inappropriate, according to his upbringing and according to his own training. He either acted alone, or in collaboration to bomb a building in Oklahoma housing some of those same FBI/ATF agents, in retaliation for their actions.

This is true of people in every belief structure all throughout the world, throughout evolution. And there are these thin bands of people who will utilize violence in order to kill that which they believe is wrong. Including people.

These big actions become bigger beliefs. They become HUGE beliefs. They are fundamentalists in whatever it is that they believe, whether it is what church to attend, what sporting event to watch, what product they should buy…

Loyalty

Loyalty can be a factor in our attitudes and beliefs. I have a friend who owns several McDonald's franchises. I feel a certain loyalty toward him, and when the opportunity arises, I will go to McDonald's over Burger King or any of the other options out there, simply due to my loyalty to him. Not that the food tastes better! My actions reinforce these beliefs and as I perform this action, loyalty will become an even greater and greater belief.

When someone displays non-loyalty to me, I will recognize and respond accordingly. Vengeance is one of the 16 Core Desires that you'll find in human behavior. And in men, in salespeople, in people who are of persuasion, the dynamic of vengeance, that drive and desire is very large. So expect that. And just like in a military person, that vengeful piece will be found, but also on the flip side of the coin, the loyal piece will also be found. You will often find vengeance and loyalty as the same part of the package in a person. That belief will cause other actions and habits.

I will always do the loyal thing; I will support my country, my friends, my family. It is a very strong belief system.

Cause (mom, dad, peers, genetics, temperament) leads to actions, behaviors. This causes new beliefs, new attitudes, and new clusters of neurons in the brain. This leads to bigger actions, bigger beliefs, validating new beliefs.

Kids in the schoolyard have cigarettes. They offer it to you. You smoke it. It's awful. You might get sick, throw up, etc. But you smoke it. You believe you are cool when you smoke. You continue to smoke. You reinforce the action and continue to believe you are cool. Given the opportunity, you no longer need someone to ask you to perform the action (smoke the cigarette, drink the alcohol, take the methamphetamine, etc.). You decide and choose to do it yourself. And then you go on to bigger things, instead of just having a glass of wine, you might begin to drink hard liquor, which causes you to believe that it's okay, and nobody should be telling you what to do anyway. This causes you to have long-term actions and habits. Unfortunately, lots of these things are deadly.

8 Keys to Understanding the Problem

The above type of programming is the beginning of the model (even though it's on the bottom), because it is your original programming. It leads to reinforcement, bigger beliefs, bigger actions, and habits.

It is difficult to change just thinking about what needs to be changed. Action is the only way to make a change.

If you're 30 pounds overweight and need to lose weight, just thinking, "Man, I'm fat and I need to lose weight", will not help. The only thing that helps is the action you take to lose the weight.

Our goal is to get our target (client, wife, husband, whoever) to change something (a belief, a habit, a behavior). First of all, a person will present to you a problem. The problem could be anything from needing insurance to having a horrible relationship, to being overweight. There is some behavior or set of circumstances in life that could be better. Use this model to assist them in making an ethical change.

If a person says, "I'm feeling kind of down about X."

I say, "What's up?"

They answer, "I'm depressed because...I broke up with my girlfriend."

"What's going on with that?" This is an ambiguous and non-loaded question that will assist you in finding out what specific emotions are going on with the person, and what specific behaviors they may be doing that are causing this person to be unhappy.

I listen and say, "What else?" I am not ready to direct this person's behavior at this point. I don't want to covertly, or otherwise, plug something in yet. Except for the fact that they can trust me.

1 - The Big Picture

They will explain the big picture to me. Pay attention to the words they use to describe their situation. Determine if they use terms like, "I am really annoyed", as opposed to, "I am so depressed I could just die", or, "I feel like I'm already in the grave", "I feel like sticking a gun to my head and pulling the trigger", or, "I feel like there's this big cloud hanging over my head and it follows me wherever I go."

The absolute single most important factor about why people do anything is the context that they are in. If you want to know what you are going to remember about any event, it is based upon the context of the situation you are in.

2 - Words/Vocabulary

The first thing I listen to is the person's vocabulary. If this is not how this person normally talks, I will note that.

3 - Metaphors

I listen to their metaphors very carefully. "I feel like I've been given a mountain, and I just can't climb it." If I can get inside of their metaphor, I can change their thinking and begin to give them the tools they need to make positive changes.

If I don't know what the metaphor is, and if I begin to speak before I have this information, I don't have the ability to give them the tools they need for their own specific metaphor.

You can change any metaphor by giving them the tools it takes to change their metaphor. You MUST listen first. Don't waste yours or their time. Discover their metaphors and stories. Before you start communicating.

4 - Cause and Effect

I am listening for cause and effect. Does the cause make sense and lead logically and rationally to the effect? People commonly mis-attribute cause and effect. They may believe that because they wore orange two days in a row, then met the person they are dating; maybe orange is their lucky color. Does this really make sense?

5 - Body Language

Look at the person's body language. How are they communicating? Slouched? Long face? Sad?

You need to understand their body language. Body language is 2/3 of the message. Does their body language match their verbal communication?

6 - Excuses & Legitimate Reasons

"I can't do that because…"

They may have convinced themselves of a belief for whatever reason ("I'm too old", "I'm not smart enough") Legitimate reasons are different. ("I'm deaf")

Remember, deafness may be a legitimate reason not to do certain things, but it also may be an excuse not to do other things.

7 - Core Drivers and Desires

What are their core drives and desires? Covert Hypnosis: An Advanced Course Volumes 2 & 3 (http://www.store.kevinhogan.com) taught you all about the 16 core desires of human behavior. What makes them tick?

8 - Maps

What are their maps? A map is how a person looks at their problem and if they have a destination, and if they have a road going to the destination, and if they have alternate roads to get there. Is it a good map? What do you see are the drawbacks on this person's map? How can you accelerate the person's map? Improve on it?

You Begin to Take Control

The information is presented to you. Now, at different levels in the mind and body, specific things will begin to happen. There are elements you will use to assist you in helping your client.

Body Language

You will use body language and para-language to begin to build trust, comfort, liking, fascination and admiration. Body language is anything I utilize my body for. Movement, how I look, how I look at the person, how I look *to* the person.

Para-Language

Para-language is the use of stressors and tone of voice and pitch and frequency to communicate ideas and words through the qualities of your voice.

To get an idea of the power of para-language, see the difference in the apparent intention of the sentence as we stress each word:

"THAT is a really good idea."

"That IS a really good idea."

"That is A REALLY good idea."

"That is a really GOOD idea."

"That is a really good IDEA."

Take a voice and articulation class if you feel you are not able to utilize this concept.

Build Trust

In order to build trust, maintain an open posture, use affirming communication. To build comfort, stay open, give a head nod now and then, and smile when it's appropriate.

We need to approve of the other person, and show admiration. Be fascinated by what they have to say, admire them while communicating with them. If they sense this, they will open up, and you will be allowed in to make the changes they need.

Elicit Core Desires

Elicit (ask questions about) core desires. If they tell you the absolute most important thing in their life is their family, you know that the person likes to nest and they have their connections. Ask what else is important. This is elicitation.

Elicit Outcomes

What do they want? If they break up with their significant other, ask what they want. Do you want them back? Do you want someone else?

What is the outcome, so that we can develop the map to the desired outcome? Find alternatives. If you can't get your number one outcome, what is the number two outcome?

People won't know what to do. Assist them in finding the alternatives that would be acceptable.

Elicit Obstacles

For every single outcome, there are a number of obstacles. ASK the person what the obstacles will be for each and every outcome. Predict every obstacle.

Elicit Resources

Find out what resources the person has to defeat obstacles. Chart the obstacles, and elicit the resources. "Have you ever had that happen before? How did you deal with that before? How did that turn out?"

Create New Maps

Affirm their input in the outcome and the new map.

...Now comes the hard part.

Intervening

There are a number of ways to intervene. You are going to talk for perhaps 10 minutes. Stay within the person's attention span. You have computed in your mind what the map is. It's your job to get the other person to see the map.

Use transformational vocabulary

When they say they have a dark cloud over their head, following them around, you are going to remind them that all the water that could fall out of that cloud, eventually will, and it will dissipate ultimately, into sunshine.

Utilize their metaphors

When they say they are devastated, you say, "you are pretty annoyed?" Bring them up a level from devastated to annoyed. Match and alter. If they say, "I feel so hurt", you say, "you know you look pretty hurt." Do not disrespect them. Bring the level of the metaphor up one or two levels.

Use Story

Preferably the person will tell us a story. Ask them, "How do you think that we could make this all work out?" If they say, "I don't know!" Then, you tell them a story. You can tell them, "You know, you are going to go on down to the used car place and you are going to get yourself a used car. Used cars are seen in a different light than they were years ago and it can certainly save you tons of money, AND solve the problem you are having with your current car." Create the story for them if they cannot come up with the story themselves.

Create movies

The movies you create will have the person confident, competent, but not arrogant. Create stories they can see in their mind with alternatives, where they can believe they overcame them, etc.

Ask leading and probing questions

"How are you going to find the next girl of your dreams..." "How are you going to find your next job..."

Distraction

Distraction is a critical intervention. Maybe the person needs to be distracted from their problem so that they can get past their problem. A lot of times, the brain will get out of its stuck state, and find the solutions it needs.

Multiple Maps

All these interventions lead into making multiple maps. We need multiple maps for all the possible obstacles and the roads around and through all the obstacles. Deal with the past, the short run, the homerun hitter. Take care of them in advance. Get it down on the map. This will prevent inertia for your friend/client/loved one.

If you don't get to the destination with one map, rip it up and make a new map.

You have as many maps as you have days in the life.

Anticipated Regret

Lastly, **utilize the power of Anticipated Regret** by creating (pointing out) the pain they will feel if the person does not grab the map book and go. "What will happen if you don't..." Have them experience the regret first, and know what it will be like to regret not having the degree, the job they want, the person to love.

The person has desires that will be stimulated when coming out of a session like this. They will start to see their outcomes. They see these desires being fulfilled, the outcomes become clear. This person becomes AT CAUSE for themselves. They don't experience the effect of their mother, their father, their brother, their peers. They believe they can take massive amounts of action, they know the obstacles, their resources, and their outcomes.

The person is taking action. They know they will run into obstacles. But that's okay. They are prepared for rejection, they are able to take it, and they will survive. The person who gets past no, is the person who gets the girl, gets the job, gets the money.

These actions create new beliefs, which create new choices and new decisions for you.

If you are AT CAUSE, you are getting and choosing what you want!

If you don't have a map, it is impossible to get anywhere. The goal is to create maps to stimulate desires, elicit outcomes and lead to BIG actions and habits.

The Core of Covert Hypnosis
The 16 Human Desires

Chapter Ten

A boss, seeking desperately to motivate his low-morale employees, decided he would give everyone in his company a generous raise. He expected the extra money to make his employees happy and increase their productivity. Instead, employees were resentful. "He's just throwing money at us" was a common response. "He doesn't care about what's really important to us." It wasn't that he didn't care, but rather that he had no clue what motivated his employees—what drove them.

According to the latest academic research, there are sixteen core desires found in human nature. These are the desires that motivate us to move in one direction or another in our lives. The desires all take place at the unconscious level, though on occasion we may actually become aware of our desires, our instinctual drives.

People, on average, have a very high desire for competition. That's one of the 16 basic desires and without that desire you probably couldn't be successful in selling. Lots of people have a very low desire for competition. These are people who should not be in sales! The basic desires include the desire to have power, the desire for tranquility, the desire for having a family and the desire to belong. There are numerous others that round out the 16. In the next section we will catalog them all and have you learn how to enter into the MAPs that trigger the desires.

Each of these desires can be objectively measured, which is nice for you and me because then we know that someone didn't just dream these 16 up one night and write a book.

The 16 core desires have been thoroughly researched at Ohio State and I'm convinced that:

Understanding the 16 desires that humans experience makes motivating others and getting them to want to "buy" us not only easy, but also virtually instantaneous.

Where did these 16 desires come from? They came from our evolutionary drive to reproduce, locate and eat food and from the fight-or-flight response. All 16 desires stem from these basic drives. The remaining desires all come into play because they assist the core desires or attempt to "control" or squelch them in some fashion. The interplay between genetic predisposition and environmental factors is obvious in the 16 desires and it is something you will not only become proficient at identifying but also something you will learn to utilize.

Your client/counterpart is nothing more or less than a human being. (We know you have often wondered it this were really true, but rest assured...) Your client is alive and here today (in part) because she is a carrier for her genes and more specifically for her DNA. DNA is something that replicates over millennia and you and your counterpart are both alive today because your genes "found a way to replicate."

Before we go any further, I know you probably believe in God and that God made you in his image. You are probably right. If you are right and he did, then the DNA that has replicated is probably going to have some staying power! Let's do a mini-lesson in evolution to see just who and what you are so you can see what MAPs will trigger strong responses in your client.

You don't have to believe that your ancestors are apes to utilize this information! In fact, understanding the theory of evolution allows you to understand just how unique you are and how many things had to go right for you to be here. Nothing you are about to read will even ask you to set aside your belief in God or your religion. What you are about to read is what happens after God puts your great-great-great-great-great grandparents on earth and they begin to have children and reproduce. Enjoy!!

In every cell of your client's body there is DNA. On this DNA there are genes for which we now finally have a complete roll call. We don't know what they all "do", but we "know" them all. (The census has been taken, their "jobs" will be discovered later.)

Because the material in this chapter is so vital to the science of persuasion, I want you to get a free mini-lesson about evolution and genetics from the inventor (author) of *Microsoft Word* and author of *Virus of the Mind*, my friend Richard Brodie. Richard has one of the brightest minds on earth. I've had the privilege of his friendship and have been his travel companion on many

134

occasions where we discuss the significance of what he will now share with you. Richard's ability to explain the complexities of evolution and genetics in an easy to understand fashion is something that always leaves me awestruck.

"... the theory of evolution by natural selection explained the facts well enough that it held on for a long time. But Darwin had never heard of DNA.

"The selfish-gene theory shifted the evolutionary spotlight from the fittest individuals onto the fittest DNA. After all, it is the DNA that carries the information passed from one generation to the next. The individuals of a species don't, strictly speaking, replicate copies of themselves. Parents don't clone themselves to produce children who are exact copies. Instead they cause copies of pieces of DNA to be reproduced in a new individual. The pieces of DNA that are best at causing themselves to get replicated become most numerous, and it is they that participate in the survival of the fittest, not whole individuals.

"Those pieces of DNA that play this game, causing themselves to be replicated by whatever means, are called genes. The fact that evolution seems to revolve around their well being rather than ours makes them selfish genes.

"Paradoxically, one way that scientists confirm the selfish-gene theory is by noticing unselfish behavior in animals. Female worker bees have evolved to labor all their lives to support their mother, the queen, and have no children themselves, because by a genetic quirk their mother's offspring share more DNA with them then their own offspring would. It serves their selfish genes better to behave that way than to go off on their own." (Virus of the Mind: The New Science of the Meme, Richard Brodie, 1996)

Four "drives" are critical to the survival of genes. (Yours, your clients, your children, your friends, all of your "relatives" who live in every nation on earth.) Each of these drives or programs is running all the time but they are running at the unconscious level in your mind. You probably don't ever think about these drives in the course of the day. They are simply part of you and every living creature on earth...understanding and appealing to these drives is what will double your persuasion abilities...or triple them...or more.

1. The first is food. *We all need to have food to keep the body alive that allows the genes to live in your body.* You are hosting your genes and your genes "want" your body to eat. They don't much "care" what you eat but they "want" you to eat until you reproduce and copy them into other little clients. (Genes don't think, by the way, they simply have instructions for influencing your physical appearance and behavior.)

2. *The second experience necessary to the survival of genes is the ability to flee in the face of danger.* If it makes more sense to the survival of your genes to run from danger than fight, you will instinctively do so. Now, remember that YOUR genes are not only in your body. Many of them are also in the bodies of YOUR children!

135

3. **The third experience necessary to the survival of genes is the ability to fight in the face of danger.** If it makes more sense to the survival of your genes to fight than flee, you will instinctively do so. Now, once again, remember that your genes are not only in your body. They are also in the bodies of YOUR children! In addition, also remember that some of the same genes are in the bodies of other humans as well. As Richard points out in *Virus of the Mind*, if your family is together and you all come into danger at the same time, it may be in your genes' best interest for you to intervene between the threat of danger and your children. Sacrificing your life for your children is selfish on the part of your genes. It's all part of how genes get replicated…

4. **The final experience necessary to the survival of genes is that of reproduction. You must reproduce or your genes will not be copied.** The desire to have sex is the key "moving toward" program that is running your life. Your genes are "telling you" to make as many babies as you possibly can. Your genes don't care if you just got laid off from work. Your genes aren't interested in your financial situation or changing diapers…they simply "want you" to reproduce. To your genes, there is no distinction between reproduction and having sex. Therefore, anything that you can do that appeals to the desire to have sex is going to appeal to the unconscious minds of the majority of people on earth. We will have a lot to say about this later!

Each human being is driven instinctively by these four needs. In fact, these four needs form the foundation of what are known as the 16 basic desires. Before we arrive at the core desires of human experience, let's take a careful look at the four programs that are running our life:

1) The desire to eat.
2) The desire to flee from danger.
3) The desire to fight when in danger.
4) The desire to have sex/reproduce.

Remember this key point:

> **You don't fulfill these desires to keep you alive, you fulfill these desires to allow your genes to survive.**

Question: If you only knew these four astonishing facts about your genes (and we might as well say your "self"), how would you persuade?

Answer: You persuade so that what you are selling them appears to meet the needs and desires of each of these four key drives. In general, any persuasion message that meets your instinctual needs is likelier to be acted upon than messages directed at other desires.

This may seem obvious (or not!) but how do we apply this immediately into our careers as people?

Look at some specific examples:

Life Insurance: If your client buys life insurance, his genes are protected. His children will survive until they are old enough to reproduce. His children will be able to eat and his children will be able to have the resources to ward off danger. Now you don't say that when you are selling life insurance, you frame your presentation in such a manner that these points become clear.

Real Estate: If your client buys a home from you, she has a place to cook her food. She has a place that is safe from the dangers of the world for her and her children (her genes). She also has a place where it is safe to reproduce and nest.

Clothing: If your client buys clothing from you, she has (hopefully) improved her appearance so that she looks more attractive, thus increasing her chances for reproducing her genes. Buying new clothes will (hopefully) also help her stay more attractive so she is more likely to be viewed in a positive light by others for mating, continued mating or so she can earn more money to protect her genes.

Almost every person, product or service has a connection with at least one of your instinctual drives and **by highlighting these drives** you make you or your products and services far easier to "buy" and make you or your products far more attractive to a buyer.

If you sell clothes at Macy's, you probably won't find your sales going up if you say, "Oh, and if you buy this skirt, you will ultimately have lots of sex and marry a guy who has lots of money to take care of your biological need to reproduce." Framing your communication so that it is artistically grounded in science is going to be the key. The woman you are selling clothes to already knows at the unconscious level that clothes that enhance her appearance will improve her "face value." Your job as the sales person is to reinforce the fact that, "you look absolutely stunning in that dress."

Emerging from the core desires and needs to have sex, avoid or ward off danger and eat, come 13 other desires. Dr. Steven Reiss of Ohio State is the first individual I know of to successfully catalog each of the 16 basic desires. Others (William James, for example) have recorded most of the human desires, but Reiss, in my opinion is the first to scientifically categorize and distill them all. The balance of this chapter will discuss the 16 basic desires and how they relate to persuading.

For further reading about the 16 basic desires, I recommend, *Who Am I? The 16 Basic Desires that Motivate our Actions and Define our Personalities* by Stephen Reiss. Reiss's new book, *The Normal Personality* is also required reading for anyone who really wants to understand the 16 Core Desires in greater depth!

The 16 Core Desires

In detailing the power of the 16 Core Desires, I've chosen to use examples from Selling instead of therapy, dating, first encounters or management. The reason, of course, is simple. Selling is Pure Persuasion and if you understand a sales tool it's very easy to get the same results when you see "her" over "there."

You should also know that I have trained this material internationally. I used to use questions (you'll see hundreds in just a moment) that were appropriate to a laid back, comfortable, relaxed form of communication.

It didn't work. There were too many idioms.

So the questions you read are INTENTIONALLY stilted on occasion, and you certainly wouldn't say the exact words that you read here. Your only action is to understand the concept. Get the concept for each of the 16, and you will have the world at your fingertips.

Perhaps the responses we show under stress are those that are most telling about our motivations. We will do a great deal to avoid pain but what specifically will we do? As noted earlier we are going to be protecting our genes' survival and those responses may indeed be "calculated" but what response protects the genes the best? Over time, however, people may miscalculate and develop tendencies to respond to a majority of fearful situations in a flight *or* fight mode.

When you become afraid, do you tend to respond to fear by fighting or fleeing? Most people don't really know themselves very well, so let me give you a few examples to consider.

1. You see a police officer on the highway while you are speeding. Do you challenge him to come and get you (fight) or slow down (flight)?
2. The IRS sends you a notice that you are going to be audited. Do you go in and fight like hell or do you start making up receipts and reconstructing records (flight)?
3. A tall stranger approaches you (you are alone) on the street late at night. Are you prepared to run or fight?

4. Your boss yells at you about something. Do you scream back at him? Do you quietly apologize?

As you can see, there are many situations that can represent danger to an individual. Now that you have thought of a few of them, you can look at the continuum of behaviors below and how people see themselves and others along the continuum. Which side of the spectrum do you tend to be on? Notice that timid people, (people who consider themselves wise enough to flee from danger see themselves as cautious, prudent and careful.) They see other people who may consider themselves to be brave, as foolhardy and reckless. Where do you see yourself?

With this thumbnail sketch of evolution we now turn to the first three (four) core instincts and desires.

Desire for Tranquility and The Flight Fight Response

Many people move toward tranquility as a basic human desire. When this is thwarted, people respond with the flight-fight response. Show people danger and they go into preparation mode. They prepare to fight or flee. In order to do so they may need your product or service!

> **What is the danger if your client doesn't buy your product or service from you, now?**

You sell new automobiles.
- ✓ What is the danger if your client doesn't have a new car?
- ✓ What is the danger if they have one of the other type of cars?
- ✓ What is the danger if they own one of those SUV's that tip over?
- ✓ What is the danger of not having the best for your family?
- ✓ What is the danger of waiting for a different day to buy from you?

You sell skin care products.
- ✓ What is the danger to your client's skin if they don't buy your lotions?
- ✓ What is the danger to their appearance if they don't buy from you?
- ✓ What is the danger of using the competitor's products?
- ✓ What is the danger of waiting for another day to buy?
- ✓ What is the danger to your "face value" if you don't protect your skin?

You sell yourself as a personal coach.
- ✓ What is the danger to your client if he doesn't hire you?
- ✓ What is the danger to your client if he doesn't utilize you regularly?
- ✓ What is the danger to your client if he uses a less qualified coach?
- ✓ What is the danger to your client if they wait to hire you?

I will answer one question for each of the above examples for you then you respond to the rest.

1. If your client doesn't buy a new car from you, they put their family at risk. They are running the most important things (their loved ones) on earth in a ten or twenty year old vehicle. The brakes could fail, the car could stall at an intersection, and the tires might not give you the 10 extra feet you need to prevent a serious accident. Question: Is it worth it? I didn't think so.

2. If your client doesn't buy skin care products from you, they put themselves at risk on many levels. First, the fact that they are considering skin care shows they care about themselves. Do you know how many people don't care about themselves? Do you know what this does to people's self esteem? Do you know how this affects every day life for the person? Their level of happiness or depression? On another level, the skin is the largest organ in the human body. It needs to be cared for. Skin care products will keep it looking better for a lot longer and that makes your clients not only feel better about themselves but let's other people see them in their best light. Other people will respond better to your client who will look more attractive because of your products. That isn't fair, that's just the way life works.

3. You are a personal coach. If your client doesn't hire you, then you have possibly created harm for them. You charge $200 per hour but let me ask you this. If your client could have saved or earned $10,000 in exchange for that time isn't it worth it? If you could have coached them to save their marriage are you willing to put a dollar figure on that? If you could have shown them five ways to draw more interesting people in their lives do you really believe that isn't worth $500? A person's daily life is all they have. Are you going to let your shyness about your personal income stand in the way of another human's rich experiences?

As you can see, a big part of your job as a persuader is to highlight the risks inherent of not buying your services from you, now. That's the big picture of danger. Now let's fine-tune utilizing your clients' instinctive responses to dangers so they become buyers.

You will notice that throughout the rest of the book you will find many continuums of behavioral experience. On one side will be one desire, say, "timid." On the other side will be the other end of the continuum, in this case it's "brave." Now at some times in your life, you are brave and others you are timid. However, research clearly shows that you will respond typically from one point on the continuum.

I want you to find where you are on these continuums. Then look at how you perceive yourself to be by reading the "Believe themselves to be" section. Next look on the other side and see how the other think of themselves. Finally, go back to the next set of descriptions under your side. It says, "Others believe to be." This means that other people perceive you in this fashion! (What is THIS information worth to you?!?!?!) On the other side you will be shocked at how accurate the phrases are that describe how you feel about others. That's how these charts work. (For more details about each of the desires, see Reiss's *Who Am I?*)

Desire for Tranquility

Timid ←--→ Brave

Believe themselves to be:

Shy	*Fearless*
Cautious	*Courageous*
Wary	*Bold*
Prudent	*Daring*
Careful	*Confident*
Mindful	*Valiant*

Believe others to be:

Imprudent	*Fainthearted*
Reckless	*Cowardly*
Foolhardy	*Neurotic*
Unaware	*Worrier*
Daredevil	*Overprotective*

Imagine a tax accountant is attempting to sell their services to a fairly timid person when it comes to their own personal safety. When it comes to the rest of their genes (their children) they are quite the opposite as might be predicted from our previous discussion. Perhaps part of the conversation might go like this.

"Mr. Johnson, when you give me your tax information I want you to be as careful and prudent as you can. I don't want you to get into any trouble. But your kids deserve to live as well or better than they are and not have all of this extra money going to the government, which is going to blow it on pork projects. Let me shoulder the responsibility for going to war with the IRS. I'll be up there on the front lines fighting for every dollar you deserve."

Wow! Mr. Johnson gets to be prudent and the tax accountant is going to be courageous on Mr. Johnson's behalf. She's going to fight the war for Mr. Johnson. He can live with that! She will shoulder the responsibility and fight for Mr. Johnson. She has closed the sale!

This is just one example of being aware of people's response to dangerous situations and then utilizing that information into a communication for the purpose of making the sale.

The following exercise can help you double your income. But there is a danger. If you don't do it, you will probably stay in the same income bracket you are in for eons. Do the risks of skipping this exercise outweigh racing through this text, which you bought to change your life?

Exercise:

Write down all of the possible dangers your client could face by not buying your services/products from you, now. Write down the possible dangers to your client if she waits, even one day. Write down all of the dangers in light of the evolutionary needs we have discussed. Do this now. (If you don't, you will fail to see the value of this information and are unlikely to utilize this material. That means no increased sales. Please do this exercise!)

The Drive to Eat

People have an instant response when presented with food. If they like the food that is presented (in thought, on television, on radio or set on a plate in front of you) a MAP is about to be entered. If you show people food (that they like) and you associate it to your product or service you are on the right track.

Do you sell groceries, fast food, own a gourmet restaurant, or have anything to do with the multi-billion dollar food (or dieting for that matter) industry? If so, you have an obvious MAP you can enter into. The need for food consumption is one of the core desires. Utilize that fact!

Are you in that multi-billion-dollar multi-level marketing business that sells herbs and vitamins? Nutritional supplements you call them right? It's a terrifying thought to consider that *all* the food you are currently eating isn't giving you enough or the right nutrition isn't it? *It could threaten your very survival!*

It's funny, though. Every time someone approaches me to buy their supplements they tell me how much better I will feel, how healthy I will feel. Those are fine reasons to use such a product, but wouldn't it be more effective to simply tell me, "Kevin you're 40 years old. If you want to make it to 90 on your current diet, well, you are hallucinating. Supplement Q810ZX is going to keep you out of the nursing home and on the beach frolicking...if you know what I mean..."

Now, I don't know about you...but there's something there that appeals to me. There is food, there is danger, there is frolicking. (What is frolicking anyway? I don't know but my genes seem to be responding to the notion...)

You can tell people you sell herbs and vitamins or you can tell them that they will still be frolicking when they are 90. Are we on the same page?

BUT! Maybe you don't sell Reese's or own a McDonalds. What can we do for you? How could your product or service possibly relate to food consumption? (Food consumption is an obvious survival need for both your client and his genes, but so what?!)

Question: If you sell Mary Kay cosmetics what does that have to do with food?

Answer: Maybe nothing…maybe everything.

If you sell Mary Kay and you know that cosmetics help a woman appear more attractive to men, then that brings certain benefits to the woman. She appears more attractive and therefore, she attracts a wider range of men. She has more choices as to whom she can be with. Her genes have a better chance of being replicated and her genes have a better chance of being passed on in further generations if she can locate men that will help her provide a safe environment to raise children in. It sounds so simplistic. It sounds very old fashioned.

Here's the reality: It's the DNA, the genes, millions of years old and it isn't interested in the feminist ideology or much of anything except getting the genes replicated. Finally, the fact that the genes are more likely to get copied…they will be cared for… means that food consumption will not be a problem.

Appealing to the evolutionary need of food consumption is absolutely critical in the persuasion process. (Have you ever wondered why successful people close a lot of deals at lunch? Even they don't know…and now you do.)

- ✓ After all, we all have to eat.
- ✓ It puts the food on the table, you know.
- ✓ You don't work – you don't eat.
- ✓ An apple a day keeps the doctor away.

(By the way, do you see how "danger" is threaded into the last two common phrases. Welcome to the world of scientific selling.)

What subtle implication of easy access to food can you link to your product or service? What implication of limited access to food can you link to your product or service if your client doesn't buy from you?

You sell automobiles.
- ✓ Who will be the first person your client takes to their favorite restaurant in their new car?
- ✓ How will having this new vehicle make their access to their basic needs easier?
- ✓ How will having this new vehicle make your client more aware of his or her own physical body?
- ✓ How will having a new vehicle help your client feel going shopping?

Desire to Eat

Hearty Eaters ←--→ Light Eaters

Believe themselves to be:
Connoisseur   *Physically Fit*
Happy   *Slender*
Sensual   *Healthy*
Gourmand   *Sensible*

Believe other half to be:
Self Denying   *Lack willpower*
Unhealthy   *Unhealthy*

The desire to eat, to be nourished, is something we always consider as important in the science of persuasion. I find it useful to close deals over lunch and dinner and so do others. Research shows that people are more likely to say, "Yes" when dining than when doing business in an office setting. Certain foods have certain effects on brain chemistry of course, and this is part of the reason. We also have many traditions about sharing food and "breaking bread" as way of bonding and celebrating.

Many people in the United States do try to control the instinctual need to locate and eat food. It is extremely difficult for most people who are overweight, for example to actually lose weight and keep it off. Whether food is abundant or not, people look for and consume as much as they can. It's prepared into the nature of who you are. 90% of all people who diet gain their weight back in less than two years.

So how will we utilize the evolutionary urge to find and eat food in the persuasion process?

First, it's very important to place the implications of having no food or too much food in the client's mind. Second, on a cautionary note, you should know that people who are extremely overweight or underweight have serious problems and this becomes an area that people should steer clear. Entering minds through MAPs is necessary to increase sales, but we don't need to encourage anorexia, bulimia or obesity!

The Icing on the Cake

It's obvious from the chart that people who are light eaters perceive themselves to be sensible, slender and healthy. So, when they go out to eat with us, doesn't it make sense to have something that will be healthy for us both?

Wouldn't it also make sense to eat something along the same lines that our client does to show our wisdom as far as being healthy goes?

It's also obvious from the distinctions in the chart that people who are heavy eaters consider themselves to be happy and sensual in nature. I'm sure that we will be able to model this behavior for one lunch ourselves and not raise a fuss about the amount of food they consume. Hearty eaters love to talk about food and I'm certain that you will find ways to weave their favorite restaurants and meals into conversation.

Sex, Romance and Sensuality

Here is the key to your persuasive success. Here is the key to most people's buying pattern. The drive to reproduce (the behavior for which is romance, flirting, and the act of sex) is virtually unparalleled in humans. We could write a book about how this single drive is what life is all about.

Because this drive has been suppressed for over 3,000 years by many world cultures and religions, there are many tricky nuances about specifically how to utilize this drive in the process of persuading. The genetic urge for reproduction runs squarely up against many society's moral values that make it wrong to want to reproduce. Therefore, when using the Sex MAP you have to be very careful indeed.

Men and women both want to be perceived as attractive. Men are hardwired to spread their seed everywhere and do so as often as they can. Women are hardwired to find a secure location for their offspring and fill it with as many babies as possible with one mate who will provide for that brood. That's at the unconscious level, of course.

These very specific instinctual needs then meet society. For the most part today, the evolutionary urges are regulated by laws. You're generally permitted one wife if you are a man and there is a limit to the number of children that is considered "reasonable." To be sure there are some religions that encourage the birth of many children. These organizations even make rules that make it almost impossible to not have kids. However, almost all of these organizations see the folly of having multiple wives and set ground rules so it can't happen.

All of this is very interesting and it makes you want to talk about it all day, but what does sex have to do with persuading?

Just about everything.

There are several reasons people enter into the selling profession and most of them relate to three of the four core instinctual drives...and one of the other 13 basic desires plays a very strong wild card in the mix.

People as a group tend to be fighters. They are aggressive and face challenges daily that they overcome, get around, move beyond and they love to win. Every day for a salesperson has an element of danger in it. People wake up unemployed every morning. If they sell, they live another day, if they don't, they...must return to working for someone else. (You may work for a big company as a salesperson and think that you work for the big company. You don't. They work for you. You are paying the salaries of the rest of the employees with all of the net profits from your salaries after you are paid. Only when you become a liability do you actually work for the company. This happens when your net profits do not pay for your salary and commissions.) There is something incredibly attractive about people who are in control of their own destiny to people of the opposite sex.

Women in particular are attracted to providers; and what are salespeople? They provide for everyone.

People work to eat first. This doesn't mean they are overweight or even hearty eaters. Not in the least. But people work to eat. People who have jobs that pay the same amount every week don't work to eat. They work for their total sustenance. They have no control over their lives in any meaningful sense of the word. No one eats until the salesperson eats. No one. If no sales are made, no other employee gets their paycheck. Once again the salesperson is the provider. They work to eat first and nothing is more attractive (**to women in particular**) than someone who can provide food for the group. Most people don't know this but now you do!

People have intense sex drives. (At least driven people do.) Selling is one of the few professions that require proactive action on the part of the individual. Look at these professions: Carpenter, attorney, medical doctor, chiropractor, psychologist, social worker, teacher, priest, etc. Almost every profession or job that is not a sales position requires people to come to them. In selling it's the opposite. You have to go to other people. Persuasive people therefore must have an enormous set of strengths to overcome everything from rejection to the fears of interpersonal communication with every type of human being. Persuasive people are generally speaking, fearless in the communication setting. They are the ultimate adaptors. They have the ability to communicate with every type of person and therefore they are the most interesting people to communicate with. They have adventures to tell that are unparalleled by other professions. Persuasive people are ultimately attractive to others.

The drive to reproduce keeps the persuasive person successful. The persuasive person is someone who channels his intense evolutionary desires into profits. The sex drive, coupled with the desire to eat and the flight/fight response come together to create a lean, mean fighting machine known as a persuasive person.

Now that you know that you are driven by your instincts in such a fashion, let's look at our clients/counterparts.

Your client/counterpart has the urge to reproduce, too. You aren't the only person that "feels this way."

> People will "buy" you, or, your products and services if, at the unconscious level, they know this will improve their ability to reproduce.

Please remember that genes don't think. They just replicate and have their orders to replicate. Those orders are causing drives in your client.

Question: How does your product appeal to your clients' instinctual drive to reproduce?

Answer: Almost all products and services will help this desire or can be linked to this desire if you think about it in the right fashion.

You sell mutual funds and stocks.
- ✓ Who is buying your product? (Men) Who is attracted to men with resources?
- ✓ How might your client benefit sexually from having more money?
- ✓ How might your client be perceived more attractive if they are successful?
- ✓ How does owning stocks and mutual funds NOW, make your client more attractive in contrast to waiting?

You sell real estate.
- ✓ How might your client benefit sexually from buying property or homes?
- ✓ How might your client be perceived as more attractive if they own a beautiful and elegantly decorated home?
- ✓ How does owning real estate NOW, make your client more attractive in contrast to waiting to buy later?

You sell automobiles.
- ✓ How might your client be perceived as more attractive if they own a new car?
- ✓ How does buying a new car now make your client more attractive in contrast to waiting?

"So you know Charlie, if you buy a home, own Cisco and IBM and get a new Lexus you're going to have some amazing sex this week."

While that might be true, we aren't going to quite frame things this way in the persuasion process.

"Can you imagine how you will look flying down the highway in that new Lexus? Man, I'm telling you, you will be unbelievable." (His unconscious mind fills in all the blanks.)

"Isn't owning your own place what it's all about? (For a man, the unconscious mind fills in the blanks.)

"When you two own this home you will be able to finally settle down." (For women, "settle down" = "make babies" at the unconscious level.)

"Won't your wife feel more secure if you go ahead and invest in stocks that will ensure your long term security?" (The woman is nodding her head. It's biologically wired in!)

Appealing to the needs of reproduction, sex and desire for sensual experience is a powerful motivator. Every man's magazine (Maxim, FHM, Details, Arena, Loaded, Playboy, Penthouse) is sold with a cover that features a beautiful woman on the cover. Every woman's magazine (Cosmopolitan, Mademoiselle, Ladies Home Journal, People, Entertainment Weekly) is sold with a cover that features a beautiful woman on the cover. Attraction and desire sell. Period.

Appealing to the nesting instinct sells, too. Better Homes and Gardens, Country Living, American Home all are sold to women who want to nest and "settle down." They want to stay put and make their surroundings safe, secure and attractive. These desires are hard wired into the woman's genes and they are exhibited in her behavior. What are you doing to sell to these unconscious urges and needs?

Have you ever gone into the Romance section at Barnes and Noble? There are thousands of books there with the same cover, same theme and same story. Women devour this material like men devour pornography. Women want to be romanced and they can't get enough of it. How are you linking your product or service to these needs?

Here is the continuum of the urge to reproduce in human beings.

Find where you are on the continuum then see if how you perceive others matches the chart. It should.

Then see how people on the other side of the spectrum perceive you.

This will help you sell more efficiently both people who are like you and people who are very different.

Sexual Desire

Pleasure Seeker ←--→ **Ascetics**

Believe they are:

Flirtatious	*Conservative*
Romantic	*Virtuous*
Sensitive	*Saintly*
Carnal	*Spiritual*
Lustful	*Cerebral*
High Sex Drive	*Self Controlled*

Believe other half to be:

Puritanical	*Wild*
Prudish	*Hedonistic*
Hung up	*Lacking in Control*
Impotent	*Superficial*

There are also large numbers of people who have successfully suppressed their sex drive. These people are sold by tapping into the MAPs of self-control and virtuosity. As you listen to what people say when they talk to you, discovering their most powerful drives will be simple. As with all skills, it just takes practice!

In the next section we will look at the balance of the drives that all emerge from the three core drives that we have discussed. By now, I think you are starting to see how your instincts drive your behavior and you are now probably starting to see an emerging picture of others around you that may have been foggy, until now.

The Second Tier Desires

Each drive in this chapter emerges from the core drives we've already studied. However, they are definitely distinct from them and are important in developing a complete picture of yourself and more importantly, your client/counterpart. After reading this chapter, your client/counterpart/loved one will essentially be an open book.

People tend to be very competitive. They have to be to survive. They certainly have a strong tendency to cooperate with others but they are definitely competitive with others in their profession.

However, let there be no question that some people are juiced by being part of a team. Competing as part of a team energizes other people. Still others love to compete one on one. Who are you? (Remember you may fall in the middle of the continuum!) You may also find that you are on one end of the spectrum at home and another at work.

Desire to Compete or Seek Vengeance

Competitive ←---→ **Cooperative**

Believe themselves to be:
Go Getter
Winner   *Conflict-avoidant*
Competitive   *Kind*
Aggressive   *Forgiving*
Will get even if necessary   *Turn other cheek*

Believe others to be:
Failure   *Bent out of shape*
Loser   *Aggressive*
Non-assertive   *Competitive*
Passive   Angry
Always wants to win   Always need to win.

Vengeful behavior probably began as a way to punish aggressors who stole possessions from the individual or the group. Those who would take revenge upon others may have been the protectors of the community. Perhaps 10,000 years ago they were higher on the totem pole in the society and had to protect the group from outsiders. These vengeful people became leaders because of their drive for "justice" and need to be "the best." Vengeance, of course, has its downside in behavior. Men still kill out of jealousy in our civilized society. The need to get even can be very intense, especially in men.

Individuals that have a difficult time controlling their anger, those who compete, and those who seek revenge fall on the competitive side of the spectrum. People who tend to avoid competitive situations definitely fall on the other side. These critical distinctions help us sell our client/counterpart. Imagine that your counterpart falls on the competitive side of the spectrum. Here is how we want to enter his MAPs.

You sell securities. (Stocks and mutual funds)
✓ What matters most is what you end up with at the end.
✓ "Don't you deserve more because you've worked harder?"
✓ "Aren't you as good as the rest of them?"
✓ "Don't you deserve as much as anyone else?"

You sell real estate.
✓ "Would you like to own the nicest house in the neighborhood?"
✓ "Is it important that you get the best price possible?"
✓ I know you. You just want the best.
✓ What it all comes down to is are you getting the best deal.

You sell advertising.
✓ "Whose image do you want to pop into people's heads first?"
✓ Don't YOU want to be known as the go-to guy?"
✓ "Do you want a bigger ad than (your competitor?)"
✓ "What do you think the best long term strategy is to knock them out?"

Drive to Nest

Research continues to show that better educated and higher IQ people are having fewer and fewer babies. (How's that for an evolving mess?!) What is going on here? I'm not certain, but understanding a person's drive to have a family is very important indeed. Obviously this drive emerges from the instinct to reproduce, but it is not the same thing. Wanting to have lots of sex is not to be confused with wanting to have lots of children. Your genes don't know the difference but your 21st century brain sure does.

I often look around the office of my clients to see if they have several pictures of the wife and kids or if they have the one obligatory picture of the family...probably several years old. That helps me understand this most important desire.

Stephen Reiss notes that if raising children is essential to your happiness, then you fall on one side of the spectrum. If having kids is mostly difficult you fall on the other side of the spectrum. There seems to be no difference between men and women on average with the desire to raise children, so be careful of stereotyping!

When I listen to people talk about their children, I want to know how much affection for those kids is resonating in the person. (I am not interested in how people view other people's children in most cases.) If they say, "my kids are great," I haven't heard anything to MAP into. If they say, "My kids are my reason for living. They make me thank God every day." That I can MAP into and here's how I do that:

> You sell cars.
> ✓ "Won't your kids love having this new car?"
> ✓ "Doesn't it make you a proud Dad to be able to bring this home?"
> ✓ "What have your kids been asking you to get?"
> ✓ "How important are your kids in your decision to buy a safe car like this?"

> You sell securities. (Stocks and other Financial Investments)
> ✓ "Do you factor in your kid's future when you make your investments?"
> ✓ "What's it feel like to be a responsible parent in an age where no one cares?"
> ✓ "What weight do you assign to your kids when making these decisions?"
> ✓ "Are you looking for enough to put the kids through college?"

As you consider the continuum below, where do you fall on it?

Are you responsible and domestic? Do you just relish every moment with your children? Are they the center of your universe? You're on one side of the spectrum.

Do you sense kids are more work than they are worth? Do you feel that children conflict with your desire for freedom? Are kids going to just tie you down for 20 years? You are on the other side of center.

The Nesting Instinct

Family ←--→ Non-Family

Believe themselves to be:
Cocooner   *Out and about*
Domestic   *Independent*
Responsible   *Free*

Believe other half to be:
Selfish   *Burdened*
Irresponsible   *Tied Down*
Immature   *Imprisoned*
Unaccountable   *Obligated*

Exercise: The desire to nest and raise children is common and dominates the decision making process of most parents. How does your product or service MAP into both groups? Answer now before going on!

The Desire to Connect with Others

It is an interesting fact that people who have many friends and rich relationships tend to be healthier, live longer and heal faster when they are sick. There is an inborn drive to connect with other people that serves an important purpose in ensuring the replication of those little genes. In ancient times it was very important to gather together in groups so you could survive everything from attacks by enemies to animals. The same instinct can be seen in the modern world. People tend to live in cities. The cities are expanding to where there was once just farmland. People may not like everything about being in close proximity to others but for the most part it is how we feel comfortable.

To be sure, there is a significant percentage of the population that feels the need to live in rural areas or lead very private lives, tucked away from others. This is not the norm, however, and it is not the drive that has perpetuated the safety that is found within a group.

Social connections for the individual can be very important. Each week many people take time out of their everyday lives to congregate at their local church. They renew friendships and make new ones with like-minded individuals. The same experience is true of people who go to Rotary, Lions, Kiwanis and other fraternal organizations. Similarly, most people tend to find more security in working for a BIG company in contrast to a small company. The drive to connect with others is powerful and there is a price that may have to be paid for those who don't connect with others. Everything from the safety the large group

154

provides to the healthier life one experiences with lots of connections makes it clear this instinct pays dividends.

Not everyone prefers the group, though. They've fought the desire to be one of "the group." They've "gotten over" the need for acceptance. They might just want to be left alone and appreciate the solitude of peace and quiet. The stress and hustle and bustle...just aren't worth the effort for these people.

Wouldn't it be useful to MAP into the specific thinking that is driving your client?

Where do you fall on the continuum of connectivity? Do you feel happiest when you are in a group? Do you feel like there are groups to which you "belong"? Do you like to have fun with others? Do you consider yourself a very friendly person? If so, you are on the side of the instinctual drive to connect with others.

On the other hand, do you tend to be serious and studious? Do you find time alone preferable to time with others? Do you find the group repulsive? Do you find yourself lonely or alone (in either a positive or negative sense)? If so you are on the other side of the fence.

Now as you think about your clients think about where some of them fall on the spectrum.

Desire to Connect with Others

Sociable ←--→ Private

Believe themselves to be:
Warm	*Intimate*
Approachable	*Secret*
Friendly	*Serious*
Fun	*Unhappy*
Lively	*Lonely*

Believe other half to be:
Cold	*Out There*
Reclusive	*Loud*
Aloof	*Lack Depth*
Private	*Superficial*
Serious	*Shallow*
Shy	*Boisterous*

You sell cars.
- ✓ "Won't it be fun to go out in your new car?"
- ✓ "Traveling becomes fun again with this car doesn't it?"
- ✓ "Won't it be nice to drive up to the office in this one?"

You sell real estate.
- ✓ "Won't it be nice to throw a party in your beautiful new home?"
- ✓ "Isn't it going to be fun entertaining here?"
- ✓ "Isn't it nice to have a neighborhood with so many nice people?"

You are a travel agent.
- ✓ "Won't it be fun to take spring break in Orlando with all the people?"
- ✓ "Won't it be great to take a cruise and meet people just like you?"
- ✓ "Can you imagine Las Vegas at Halloween and all the people you will see?"

Exercise: Write key questions and sentences that will help you enter your client/counterpart's Mind Access Points. Include sentence and questions for people on both ends of the spectrum, not just the side of the instinctual drive!

Seeking Power

Power is the ability to influence the behavior of others.

Poland's leading magazine is called *wProst*. It's as influential in Poland as *Time* in the United States. *WProst* did an extensive interview with me in 2000. They printed the interview and a nice photo to boot. The caption read something like, Kevin Hogan, "The Guru of Business Psychology." *WProst* lent power to my work for the people of Poland who didn't know me from your brother in law. On my next trip to Poland, I received the royal treatment. Everyone from the people in the hotel to the people who came to the Sales Conference I spoke at in 2001 wanted autographs and pictures. Why? Because *wProst* said I was the Guru of Business Psychology.

Particularly interesting about this specific experience is that the millions of people who read this magazine believe what they read. The magazine, like magazines in all countries, shapes opinions about who or what is important. It creates perceptions in people's minds that may or not be accurate. In my case, the stamp of approval was important to my message being well received. I used that instant rapport in many ways that were useful for the audiences I spoke to.

Power is a two way street. People have to be willing to give someone power and someone has to desire the power for that power to be utilized on a long-term basis. Power is a fascinating subject, but let's see how to tap the drive for power with your client.

The word alone creates images in your mind. The drive to reach the top of some pecking order (to become a big fish in a small pond) is common among men. They seek power in different ways. Some strive to political power. Do you know how many multi-millionaires there are in the House of Representatives?! Why would a man who is a multi-millionaire spend millions of dollars of his own money to get a job that pays $110,000 per year?

Power.

Other men seek power in different ways and on different levels. The evangelist who is enlightened seeks the followers to listen to his message. The author wants people to read his book and the judge wants to be the representative of justice. The police officer wants the power to control behavior and the mayor wants the reigns of the city. They want to have the biggest burger joint, the biggest airline, the prettiest wife, the most fans, the most clients, the most money and on and on. They all want power and to some degree or more they get some power.

Unfortunately, the drive for power can get ugly. The striving and acquisition of power can cause wars and literally cost millions of people their lives. Power is a potent drive that can help individuals to ascend to do great good or ill. This deep desire of human nature is chiefly a drive of male behavior in contrast to female behavior. (Understand that both men and women want power, the point is to what degree the genders want power.) There is no question that great power is sought and acquired by far more men than women.

Whether your client is male or female isn't that important. Everyone (almost everyone) wants to influence human behavior. We all want our children to obey. We want the neighbors to change some of their behaviors. We want the idiot at the stoplight in front of us to turn left so we can get going. We all want to influence the behaviors of other people. This is the striving for power.

How do YOU help the other person acquire power?
How does your product or service help your client/counterpart acquire power?

If your client can see how you can help them become more influential, and power IS influence, then you can virtually ensure a sale.

Look at the continuum below and see where you fall on the continuum for the desire to have power. If you find yourself to be ambitious, influential, working 60 hours per week and have a dominant personality, you fall on one side of the spectrum.

If you aren't particularly ambitious, tend to be people-oriented and a good support person, you probably fall on the other end of the spectrum.

Find yourself on the continuum first then consider where your clients/counterparts tend to fall on the spectrum.

Seeking Power

Leader ←-----------------------------------→ **Follower**

Believe themselves to be:

Enterprising	*Simple*
Aspiring	*Humble*
Motivated	*Undemanding*
Ambitious	*Not ambitious*
Influential	*People oriented*
Hard working	*Submissive*
Dominant	

See the other half as:

Allergic to work	*Lofty*
Unmotivated	*Demanding*
Lazy	*Domineering*
Weak	*Not caring*
Unsuccessful	*Controlling*
	Workaholic

How do you use the drive of power to persuade?

You sell cars.
- ✓ "Doesn't driving a Mercedes give others the impression of you that you want them to have?"
- ✓ "Doesn't owning a new car make a statement about what you can have?"

You sell real estate.
- ✓ "Some people say it's a good investment to have the least expensive house in a neighborhood. Doesn't it say something to have the nicest house in the neighborhood?"
- ✓ "When people see this house, how will they respond to you?"

You sell securities.
- ✓ "Money is power and power is freedom. Isn't that what you want?"
- ✓ "Doesn't having money mean that you can do anything you want?"

Exercise: Write key questions and sentences that will help you enter your client/counterpart's Mind Access Points. Include sentence and questions for people on both ends of the spectrum, not just one side of the instinctual drive.

Seeking Status

Everyone wants to be important to someone else. Some people want to be important to larger groups. Status and power often dovetail, but not always. The desire to be perceived as important is a driving force in human nature.

In the last ten years, newsgroups on the Internet have become an interesting battleground for status. People who never have been well known publicly can obtain social status (good and bad) in various small groups by posting regularly to these various groups. Everyone looks the same in text so people with time on their hands can be seen as players in whatever field of interest they feel they have a right to make public comments about.

"15 minutes" is a well-known phrase in America that refers to everyone's average amount of fame they will experience at some point in their life. Many people want more than 15 minutes. Some people are motivated by their drives and desires to be seen as having "more" or become well known in certain ways. Some people will buy a mansion. Someone else might drive a ridiculously priced car or an enormous diamond. All of these are "status symbols."

The people that produce status products realize this and can command a premium for these types of products.

Some of your clients may only need to be important to their family. Some may feel the need to be important to the large group. Knowing where the MAPs are is vital.

Do you find yourself buying the best or the most expensive things in certain areas? Do you buy things to impress other people? If so, then you fall on one side of the spectrum.

On the other hand, you may find yourself unimpressed by royalty, status, prestige and the accoutrements thereof. If you don't care what others think, then you fall on the other side of the spectrum.

First determine where you lie on the continuum then think of many of your clients and decide if they are driven by status.

Desire for Status

Social Climber ←---------------------------------------→ **Egalitarian**

See themselves as:
Moving up	*Equal to everyone else*
Prestigious	*Libertarian*
Important	*Fair minded*
Worthy of recognition	*Democratic*
Prominent	*Down to earth*

See others as:
Unknown	*Stuffed shirt*
Insignificant	*Highbrow*
Unimportant	*Snob*
Low class	*Arrogant*
Poor Taste	*Show off*

How do you use status to sell your product or service?

You sell securities.
- ✓ "Imagine how people will look at you when you are retired compared to the rest of the people who don't care about their futures."
- ✓ "When you are wealthy from all of these investments, please remember the little people who helped you get there."

You sell cars.
- ✓ "Just imagine how you are going to look driving this new car!"
- ✓ "People will think you have really made it when they see you driving this!"

You sell real estate.
- ✓ "There is no doubt that this house is a statement. You have arrived."
- ✓ "This house says that "you have worked hard and you deserve the best."

Exercise: Look at your product/service now and decide what phrases, sentences and questions you could ask someone on either end of the elitist/egalitarian spectrum.

Seeking Independence

The group offers protection and social contact. Those are two elements absolutely necessary for the perpetuation of your genes! Once secure in those two factors, the individual comes to an age where it is time to set out on their own.

In ancient days, this was necessary to find food. The group had formed. Lots of people congregating together in one place is not going to be positively correlated to having animals stop by to sacrifice themselves for the community dinner.

The desire to strike out of the collective is very important, indeed. Today we find that people often need to make a change after having relied on the group for so long.

In ancient days there was much more work to be done than in our 21st century society. Capturing food and preparing it was a hard day's work…if not a week or month. The need for self-reliance is not only an instinctual need, it is a key drive for success and achievement in life.

People who are "independent" feel they are self-reliant. They say things like, "If you want it done right, you have to do it yourself." "I just want to be free." And indeed, like a bird put in a cage, the individual struggles to become free. The birdcage becomes a prison though, and over time the individual becomes reliant upon others.

The need for self-reliance is conditioned out of the person and they learn a new set of behaviors. These we will call "interdependent." Interdependence serves many functions.

Interdependent people are easier to love because they are home more often! They appear to have more invested in the personal and social aspects of relationships and they are more connected with others in their home and their community. Interdependent people see themselves as loving people who are much more devoted to their spouses and families than independent people.

As you look at the continuum for independence/interdependence, where do you seem to belong? Are you more freedom seeking and autonomous or do you tend to act far more devoted to those around you than the average person?

Desire for Independence

Independent←---→ **Interdependent**

Believe themselves to be:
Self-Sufficient
Reliable
Self Reliant   *Loving*
Autonomous   *Trusting*
Free   *Devoted*
Resistant to the herd spirit

Believe the other half to be:
Immature   *Inflexible*
Weak   *Prideful*
Dependent   *Strong Willed*
Needy   *Bullheaded*

How will we link into the MAP of your client who has a strong drive for independence?

   You sell securities. (Stocks, bonds)
   ✓ "Won't it be nice when you can rely solely on yourself when you are older?"
   ✓ "Have you ever known anyone who was wealthy who wasn't their own investor?"
   ✓ "Do you find that having money build up makes you more independent thinking?"
   ✓ "Would you say that investing for your future will give you financial freedom?"
   ✓ "Isn't it nice to not be a slave to anyone?"

You sell Mary Kay distributorships. (or any face/face direct sales!)
   ✓ "Isn't nice to be able to do something on your own?"
   ✓ "Doesn't it feel good to be your own boss?"
   ✓ "What's it like being on your own?"
   ✓ "How good does it feel to know that you aren't a slave to someone else?"

You sell real estate.
   ✓ "Isn't nice to not be a slave to rent any more?"
   ✓ "What's it like to have you or own home finally?"
   ✓ "Isn't it nice to live well and build your independence at the same time?"

✓ "How is buying this home going to help you achieve financial independence?"

Exercise: Look at your product/service now and decide what phrases, sentences and questions you could ask someone on either end of the independence/interdependence spectrum.

Desire of Curiosity

Sherlock Holmes. He searched and found the clues that pointed him to the truth. In his cases there was always a villain who left a trail of clues, albeit minute and often almost impossible to notice. Holmes was the great detective. He told fascinating stories of his travels, he was aware of every move someone would make and he was brilliant. Holmes would have made a terrible detective had he not been curious.

Richard Brodie, who you met earlier in the book, introduced me to a friend of his on a recent trip we all made to Las Vegas. Jeffrey Gitomer had just arrived in town. I was familiar with his book, *The Sales Bible*, and his masterpiece about client service called, *Client Service is Worthless, Client Loyalty is Priceless.* I had never heard Jeffrey speak but I knew from his writing style he was going to be a no nonsense kind of guy.

We met at a little restaurant just off the strip. Jeffrey and I were both exhausted from flying into town. We exchanged pleasantries and immediately he began.

"I see you wrote this book, *The Psychology of Persuasion.*"

"I did, have you read it yet?"

"No."

"I thought your 'Worthless/Loyalty' book was great."

"Good job kid." (He called me kid. For future reference: As of the publication of this book I will be 45. Had I been much younger than this, the reference to kid would have been particularly annoying. However, the fact that Jeffrey is at least 10 years my senior, I forgave him…in less than one week…)

"How's 'Loyalty' doing?"

"It's fine. Define selling for me in two words."

I drank my wine….or most of it, at that request. Define selling in two words. Geez' Jeffrey, summarize War and Peace in two words…this is what I get for being last at the table. Richard has obviously prodded you into getting inside of my head and pushing buttons instantly…OK, here we go.

"Build Rapport."

"No. Guess again."

Guess again!? Build rapport is a heckuva answer for this off the cuff, "Who Wants to Be A Millionaire" at Batista's restaurant. I look at Richard. He is restraining a smile. His girlfriend, Heather has not restrained her smile. She is clearly thrilled that I am getting tutored...

"I can't guess heads or tails on a two sided coin. You tell me, in two words Jeffrey, summarize selling."

"Ask questions."

Well duh. You have to ask questions or you're just a videotape that is constantly replayed over and over...and...why didn't I say that? It's a better answer than "build rapport." This is the kind of guy I could really be annoyed with, if I wasn't ready to learn so much...

"Good answer."

"I know."

Ask questions. Why? Because we don't know their answers. We can only imagine we know their answers until we ask. Then we know their answers. That's what persuasion IS all about. (By the way, lest you think the distinction had been *previously lost on me, there is an entire section in The Psychology of Persuasion* highlighting the significance of asking questions!)

Aristotle was a philosopher some two millennia ago. He wrote about curiosity and I think there is a lot to be learned from his writing. There are four things that humans are intensely curious about.

---

1) We want to know what things are made out of.
2) We are curious about the forms and shapes that things take.
3) We are curious about the beginnings and causes of things and events.
4) We are curious about the purposes or goals of people, things, and events.

We were curious about these things thousands of years ago and we still are. Begin to tap into people's curiosity!

Genuine curiosity about all that goes on around us is a survival and success mechanism. Curiosity helps individuals become capable of solving problems and that once again helps keep our genes flowing! People who are very curious consider themselves to be intelligent, thoughtful and aware. On the other side of the spectrum are people who are not interested in intellectual pursuits. They tend to lives simpler and more practical lives. They consider themselves "street smart" having learned from experience. Interestingly, people on both ends of the spectrum consider people on the opposite ends to be boring and this brings up a critical point:

The only way to avoid being boring is to ask questions!

Your only hope to not bore someone to tears is to be certain you know where they are on the Curiosity continuum! Simply communicating our wealth of knowledge and interests to another person is one of the riskiest communication behaviors there is. If you have someone on the other end of the spectrum as your listener, they won't listen for long.

Look at the continuum below. Where do you find yourself? If you are often seeking intellectual pursuits, trying to find out why you are here, are in search for the truth and general want to know "more," then you fall on the intellectual side of the spectrum.

On the other hand, if you find yourself to be more of the "street smart," and practical, down to earth type, you fall on the other side of the spectrum. Now, that you have "found your self," think about some of your clients and counterparts. Where do they fall on the continuum?

Desire for Curiosity

Intellectual←--→ Non- Intellectual

Believe themselves to be:

Intellectual	Non-Intellectual
Engaging	*Sensible*
Fascinating	*Sane*
Smart	*Practical*
Interesting	*Down to earth*
Aware	*Street Smart*

Believe the other half to be:

Intellectual	Non-Intellectual
Boring	*Boring*
Ignorant	*Nerd*
Superficial	*Arrogant*
Dull	

How do we frame our questions and statements to MAP into another person's desire of curiosity?

You sell real estate.
- ✓ "Are you looking for a home that is close to a church?"
- ✓ "How many rooms will you need Internet access in?"
- ✓ "Will you use one of the bedrooms as an office or library?"

You sell securities.
- ✓ "Would you like a complementary 90 day subscription to Investors Business Daily?"
- ✓ "Would you like a list of the best investment websites?"
- ✓ "Are you interested in technical analysis of these stocks?"

You sell cars.
- ✓ "Would you like to look at what Consumers Reports has to say about this car?"
- ✓ "Would you like to see what Edmunds.com shows the value of your trade in is?"
- ✓ "Are you interested in seeing how this car compares to our competitors?"

Exercise: Consider your product or service. How can you MAP into the thinking of your clients and counterparts with the desire of curiosity? Write down several questions, statements and themes.

Desire for Acceptance

"You better go back to driving a truck, son." That's what the manager of the Grand Ole Opry told Elvis in 1955. The manager had determined that Elvis Presley simply didn't have what it would take to be a star.

A person who lacked in self confidence never could have gone on to fight his way to the top. The non-assertive individual desiring acceptance of group norms would have immediately packed his guitar and decided to go back to driving that electrician's truck. Thankfully the need for acceptance by the group is over-ridden in cases like that of Presley's.

I spent an enormous amount of time researching and writing the book. The first draft was written in 1991. I submitted the manuscript to a publisher that in less than two years would go bankrupt and my manuscript was returned. That was 1993. Beginning in late 1993, I began submitting the manuscript to publishers all over the United States.

Week after week I would receive rejection letters. Many of them said that I had no chance of being published without an agent. But I was determined that the book was an excellent piece of work that would help people sell and persuade others to their way of thinking. I was **certain** that if people read this book they would love it and more importantly, that the book would help change their lives.

As of 1995 I had received over 240 rejection letters for *The Psychology of Persuasion*. Then I wrote one letter with a personal touch...

For years I had admired Zig Ziglar. He was always one of my favorite authors and speakers. I knew Pelican Publishing in Louisiana published him. I wrote Pelican and told them that I was going to be the next Zig Ziglar.

I had already begun a somewhat successful speaking career, had self published two books by this time and was ready for a hard cover. Trust me, I told them, I'll make it happen.

240 rejections…then they said "yes."

Since that time I have been in a Win/Win relationship with Pelican and we're still receiving great reviews and inquiries to speak about *The Psychology of Persuasion*.

Had I followed my "common sense", I never would have sent out any manuscripts after the first 50 and certainly none after 100. I was absolutely certain, though, that I was going to be a popular author.

Today of course, you see *The Psychology of Persuasion* in bookstores from Los Angeles to Warsaw and London to New Delhi. It's been published in China and Brazil. Defying the voice that said "give up" that was programmed in by the group was something I never questioned.

I was certain that *The Psychology of Persuasion* was a great book. I've never regretted not listening to all the other people who told me I was wasting my time…and getting a real job that "paid benefits." I'm a salesman…paid benefits…geesh…

The desire for acceptance though, is what keeps people in large groups and the desire for acceptance has its benefit.

People who desire acceptance tend to "go with the flow" better than people who are defiant in the storm.

People who "go with the flow" tend to experience less stress and make fewer waves. There are a lot of benefits there. More calm, more relaxed.

Virtually everyone would prefer that they be accepted and liked by the group. That said, not everyone **needs** to be accepted and herein lies this desire.

Those people who need to be liked tend to very non-assertive by nature. They are literally needy.

As you look at the continuum below do you find yourself being more a "go with the flow" kind of person or do you see yourself as being more assertive? Which side of the continuum do you fall on?

Desire for Acceptance

Go with the Group ←---→**Assertive**

Believe themselves to be:
Insecure   *Assertive*
Lacking in Self Confidence   *Confident*
Not Assertive   *Self Assured*
Go with the flow   *Persistent*

Believe others to be:
Conceited   *Needy*
Too Confident   *Immature*
Slick   *Overly Sensitive*

How do you sell the person who needs acceptance?

Imagine you sell cars.
✓ "This is the most popular car out there."
✓ "This car will make you look and feel great."
✓ "Don't feel pressured to buy this car. Just drive it and see if it feels right."
✓ "This car is safe and reliable. You will feel comfortable owning it."

You sell securities.
✓ "I work for people who don't feel comfortable investing on their own."
✓ "I've been doing this for 15 years, why don't you let me take the pressure off you and show you what will make your future more secure."
✓ "This is a simple growth mutual fund. Nothing aggressive. Just consistent and steady. "
✓ "Most people who want a solid future will have a balanced portfolio. Does that sound like you?"

You sell real estate.
✓ "This is a pretty conservative home that you will feel safe in."
✓ "This is a pretty conservative neighborhood. I think you will be comfortable here."
✓ "Would you like to handle getting a loan on your own or do you want me to take all the stress out of it and do it for you?"

Exercise: Consider your product or service. Decide now how you will communicate with people on both sides of the acceptance spectrum. Write down sentences, questions and themes that will appeal to people on both sides of the continuum.

Desire to Have Honor

We aren't really "just" animals anymore.

Consciousness is something that is experienced by just about every living person. The need to be decent to people is something that is respectable. This need certainly has its root in the evolving race we are in.

If people didn't cooperate with others, there would be no economic expansion, no long-term relationships and eventually the groups that collect into urban areas would all turn on each other and self-destruct. That doesn't happen though, because many people have honed the desire to be honorable into a key personal value.

Obviously, the counterpart has its place, too. There is a certain amount of checking and double-checking that takes place in honorable people.

Sometimes there are so many reassurances that need to be made that things don't ever get done. Sometimes expedience is more useful than principle.

In ancient days, disloyalty was severely punished. In times of war, loyalty is severely punished.

You can be certain that loyalty and honor are rooted deeply in our behavior. Always remember that many have grown to make the trade-offs that disloyalty offers.

A sense of individuality and freedom come with expedience. Breaking away from the group to strike out on your own becomes important to many.

As you look at the continuum below, where do you find yourself? Are you more focused on principles, loyalty, morals and duty or are you more of an opportunist, practical minded and expedient?

The Desire of Principled Loyalty

Principled ←---→ Expedient

Believe themselves to be:

Devoted	*Resourceful*
Dedicated	*Quick Thinking*
Patriotic	*Problem Solving*
Moral	*Practical*
Have Character	*Opportune*
Dutiful	*Like everyone else*
Loyal	*Pragmatic*

Believe others to be:

Disloyal	*Self-Righteous*
Self Serving	*Holier than thou*
Lacking Character	*Sanctimonious*
	Impractical

How do you MAP into your clients mind with the instinct of loyalty?

    You sell securities.
- ✓ "If I can help you begin to meet your financial goals, will you work with me long-term?"
- ✓ "If I help you succeed will you refer me to the rest of the people in your family and at the office?"
- ✓ "I see you've done well with Fidelity over the years. Do you want to stick with Fidelity Select Funds or would you rather switch to another company?"

You sell advertising.
- ✓ "If I can help you make money will you let me structure your marketing program as well?"
- ✓ "If I write you an ad that pulls will you refer me to your non-competing buddies?"
- ✓ "If I write you an ad that makes money will you give me a list of names I can call to help get the same results?"

Exercise: Consider your product or service and prepare questions, statements and themes about how to specifically sell to people on both sides of the spectrum of loyalty.

Desire for Altruism

No doubt about it, we all have our altruistic moments. Some people live a life of altruism.

Mother Theresa may have been the most well known altruist of our times. People who sacrifice something of themselves for others are often living up to a higher value or spiritual level.

This doesn't mean that altruism isn't rewarded many times over, though.

Altruism is as old as the ancients. Altruism pays off for the individual when the individual believes that their behavior is being seen or felt on another level. At this level they feel as if they are attaining their highest good and that they are truly making a difference.

Self-sacrifice brings self-satisfaction and that is a very good thing indeed!

Of course many people have over-ridden the desire to be altruistic. We call these people realists. Realists tend to be more focused on the self as opposed to others.

This is neither good nor bad but, once again, the realist is either moving away from the group or attempting to move higher up in the group.

The idealistic tend to stay centered in the group.

As you look at the spectrum of behaviors below, where do you find yourself?

Do you find yourself mostly caring, compassionate, self-sacrificing and altruistic? If so you fall on the left side of the spectrum.

If you find yourself more pragmatic, realistic and self focused then you are on the other side of the continuum.

Desire for Idealism and Realism

Idealistic←---→Realistic

Believe themselves to be:

Caring	*Pragmatic*
Selfless	*Practical*
Humanitarian	*Real World*
Giving	*Sensible*
Compassionate	*Looking out for #1*
Visionary	*Realistic*

Believe others to be:

Self centered	*Idealistic*
Heartless	*Dreamer*
Insensitive	*Meddlesome*
Unfeeling	*Unrealistic*

How do you sell someone who has the desire for idealism?

You sell securities.
- ✓ "If you find you make a lot more money than you think would you want me to set up a giving program for you?"
- ✓ "How do you see yourself using your money if you become wealthy beyond your plans?"

You sell direct sales products or services.
- ✓ "A portion of all sales goes towards…"
- ✓ "Would you like us to donate a portion of the proceeds toward…"
- ✓ "Not only would you be purchasing your new X for yourself but you will have made a difference for me and I appreciate that."

You sell business opportunities.
- ✓ "The real nice thing about owning your own business is you can turn around and help other people help themselves."
- ✓ "The great thing about being in business for yourself is that you ultimately decide how you will help people."

Exercise: Consider your product or service and prepare questions, statements and themes about how to specifically sell to people on both sides of the spectrum of altruism.

Desire for Order

Once people collect things, or collect groups of people around themselves, they have a desire to be organized. People like to have "stuff" but they often want to be neat about it!

Being organized is a signpost of control for a lot of people. Being organized means that the person is in charge, and this is a key to motivating others. We want people's behavior to be neat and orderly as well.

We tend to identify organization with intelligence, although there is no evidence to support such a belief.

Some people really enjoy the ability to live without a script. Some people look at a speaker who knows all of his lines as the most boring speaker in the world.

Others appreciate the organized and well-prepared individual. People who are organized like and appreciate processes and algorithms. These people taking direction can feel left off on their own all alone if they don't have the direction.

Having considered the two ends of the spectrum, do you find yourself neat, in control, socialized, orderly, organized, enjoying the process?

On the other hand do you enjoy spontaneity? Do you prefer being flexible instead of having to do things the same way all the time? If so you are on the other side of the continuum.

Desire for Order

Organized←---→ **Flexible**

Believe themselves to be:
Neat   *Flexible*
Tidy   *Natural*
In Control   *Spontaneous*
Socialized   *Unrehearsed*

Believe others to be:
Sloppy   *Too perfect*
Dirty   *Controlling of others*
Out of control   *Concerned with trivia*
Messy   *Neat freaks*
Disorganized   *Rigid*

How do you persuade the organized person?

You sell real estate.
- ✓ "Will this house provide you with the space you need for all of your stuff?"
- ✓ "Where do you see all of your stuff going in this house?"
- ✓ "Will having the den as an office help you keep the rest of the house neater?"

You sell clothing.
- ✓ "How will other people see you in this new coat and tie?"
- ✓ "Does this suit present the image you are looking to project?"
- ✓ "Does this outfit give you that 'take charge and in control' appearance?"

Exercise: Consider your product or service and prepare questions, statements and themes about how to specifically sell to people on both sides of the spectrum of order.

Desire to Save

Nature has always favored that which saves and prepares for the future. The squirrel collects and stores nuts so that it will not go without in the winter. People who save their money are doing the same thing. They simply are using the currency of the 21st century, their money. The individual who saves is fulfilling the drive to preserve their self and their family…and of course that means their genes.

It is rare that a person can go through life without saving and live a fruitful "second half" (the last 30-50 years of life). If this is true what benefits are there of being a "spender" or a "consumer"?

The consumer of products and services is someone who lives in the moment. They fear not for tomorrow and they probably live with more instant gratification. They believe they should enjoy life and they feel they are deserving of the fruits of life.

Very few people can live this lifestyle and have anything left over, but it does make the early years of life more enjoyable. Unfortunately, like the animals that don't save, there will be no quality of life later.

Americans save less than 5% of their annual income. The Japanese save 27% of their annual income. That tells us that saving money can be done and that some societies are wisely preparing for their future. On the other hand, people who live in the United States are having a better life today, if not sacrificing their future for the pleasures of today.

Look at the continuum below. Are you the kind of a person who is storing money for the future when you may be less able to earn it? Do you regularly say "no" to consuming and spending and "yes" to investing and saving? If so, you fall on one side of the continuum.

On the other hand, do you live for today? Do you find yourself living more richly today than others? If so then you are on this side of the spectrum. Now, think about where most of your clients are.

Desire to Save

Saver ←--→ Spender

Believe themselves to be:
Conserving
Frugal   *Enjoying Life*
Thrifty   *Deserving*
Planning Ahead

Believe others to be:
Irresponsible   *Miser*
Imprudent   *Money Grubber*
Living for only today   *Cheap*
Wasteful   *Self Denying*
Extravagant   *Penny Pincher*

How do you persuade the saver?

    You sell securities.
    ✓ "Would you like me to show you how to have an even richer tomorrow?"
    ✓ "Would you like to really have a retirement that is filled with fun and time for what you really want to do?"
    ✓ "How far ahead do you want to prepare for?"

You sell real estate.

    ✓ "You know what the best investment there is, don't you? Your home."
    ✓ "Can you invest too much money in your own home?"
    ✓ "With your own home, every dollar works for you. Either you pay off principal or you get a tax write off."

Exercise: Consider your product or service and prepare questions, statements and themes about how to specifically sell to people on both sides of the spectrum of saving.

Desire for Physical Activity

In ancient times, the inactive and lazy were punished with starvation and attack by animals and enemies. It is a normal drive for people to want to be active. Not too many years ago, humans spent their entire day hunting and gathering. The all day search for food was critical to survival. No activity ultimately meant death.

Today, the United States is the land of the couch potato. The majority of Americans are overweight. Not only is that not attractive, it is a harbinger of early demise.

Within America there is a physical fitness movement. Many cities actually have become known as physically fit. These include cities like Seattle and Minneapolis. People in these cities, among others, seem to have figured it out. If we keep sitting on the couch, we can have all the money we want, but it won't matter. We won't be around to spend it!

Do you find yourself to be full of energy? Do you enjoy vigorous activity? Are you a fitness nut? Would you call yourself athletic? If so, you fall on this side of the spectrum.

On the other hand, maybe you find yourself easy going and low key. If so, you are on the other side of the spectrum.

What about your clients and loved ones? Where do they tend to cluster on the spectrum of the desire for activity?

Desire for Physical Activity

Active ←---→ Inactive

Believe themselves to be:
Energetic   *Self-paced*
Vigorous   *Easy Going*
Fit   *Low Key*
Athletic   *Laid Back*

Believe others to be:
Lazy   *Jocks*
Slow   *Physical*
Sedentary   *Exhausting*
Couch Potato   *Fast Paced*

How do you persuade the person who desires activity?

> You sell securities.
> - ✓ "When you have more money what will you do with your free time?"
> - ✓ "Will you find yourself participating in more fun activities when you see your portfolio build?"

> You sell real estate.
> - ✓ "Are you going to want a room that we can put a Nordic Track or Stairmaster into?"

Exercise: Consider your product or service and prepare questions, statements and themes about how to specifically sell to people on both sides of the spectrum of activity.

Evolutionary Drives

The sixteen desires are all rooted in our instinctual evolutionary drives. These are the drives that shape human behavior.

Some of the drives are obviously more important to tap into, on average than others, in the sales process.

Review these charts regularly so you can be certain that your persuasion messages are feeding into not only the drives but the reaction to the drives (the other side of the spectrum) as well.

Are you **MAPping** into the right drives with the right people? That's ultimately one of the keys to scientifically using covert hypnosis and the master key to success.

An Introduction to Mastering Body Language

Chapter Eleven

It was early in the morning on a cold winter's day. The phone rang. I was still in bed after a hard day's night of writing a chapter in a book. I rolled over and grabbed for the phone.

"Kevin Hogan." Trying to sound like I was awake.

"Is this Doctuh Hogan?" New Jersey accent. No doubt going to sell me something.

"Yes, I am very busy." Almost ready to hang up the phone.

"This is Rita Delfiner with the New Yoke Post." I bet she means New York. Isn't that the tabloid? The National Enquirer of newspapers? I live in Minnesota. She's not trying to sell me something. I sit up.

"Doctuh Hogan, we understand you are a body language expuht." Why don't they have r's in New Jersey?

"Yes, that's right. How can I help you Rita?"

"The President of the United States is going to give a press briefing in a few minutes saying that he didn't have an affair with an office intuhn. We'd like you to watch it and give us your point of view as to whether he is lying or telling the truth."

"O.K. Call me when it's over. I'll turn on CNN now."

Why the heck would Bill Clinton deny an affair? Kennedy had Monroe. That's something you can write home about. If I were married to Hillary Clinton, I mean, the man is only human...but the New York Post...yeah, yeah, yeah...where is my robe. Ah, there it is. CNN. There is Bernie Shaw. Doesn't he ever sleep?

President Clinton appears on the TV screen.

He raises the index finger on his right hand. He is visibly shaken. I would be, too, if I had to deny an affair. It's one of those things that don't matter if you did it or not. You're guilty because some moron says you did.

"...I did not have sexual relations with that woman, Monica Lewinsky."

He rested his hands on the front of the podium, fingers placed over the front. There's Gore in the background. He could be President but who knows if he can even talk. Hillary is over there on the other side. She looks annoyed but supportive. Why did he put those fingers on the front of the podium? He's never done that before. He looks like he has seen a ghost.

RING.

"This is Kevin Hogan."

"Hi Doctuh Hogan, this is Rita Delfiner with the New Yoke Post. Did he do it?"

Did he do it? I just watched the same thing you did for goodness sake. How the heck do I know? I can't read the guys mind, for heaven's sake.

"Rita, I'd like to watch it a few more times and then get back to you." Click.

I rewind my tape in the VCR and push play.

"I did not have sexual relations with that woman, Monica Lewinksy." Rewind. Play.

"I did not have sexual relations with that woman, Monica Lewinsky." Rewind. Play. Rewind. Play. Rewind. Play.

I stand up and I raise my right index finger into the air. I say out loud. "I did not have sex with Monica Lewinsky." Who is Monica Lewinsky, anyway? I stand in the exact same position as Clinton. I am denying that I had sex with Monica.

Then it hit me.

I switch hands. I raise my LEFT index finger and wag it at my TV. "I did not have relations with Monica Lewinsky." Oh my! I did. Holy smokes, I did have sex with Monica. Whoa! Mr. President, you little dickens you. Tell no one, but I couldn't be happier for you.

RING

"City of Bloomington." (It's my wife's voice.)

"Hey, did you just watch the President?"

"No, I'm working." (That's what all government employees are instructed to say when approached about working.)

I want you to raise your left hand, wag your finger at the camera and say, "I did not have sexual relations with that woman, Monica Lewinsky."

"What?"

"Just like Clinton just did."

"I told you I haven't been watching TV."

"Oh." (I explain the events of the morning.)

"...so now, raise your left hand, wag your finger at the camera and say, 'I didn't have sexual relations with that woman, Monica Lewinsky.'"

She does so as I listen.

"Now switch to your right hand. Do the same thing."

She does so as I listen.

"Which hand do you believe?"

"Huh?"

"Which hand is certain it didn't have sex?"

"My right hand."

"Me too."

"But you said Clinton used is his right hand, so he didn't do it, right?"

"Clinton is a southpaw."

Click.

OK. Let's think about this. I rewind the VCR again and push play. I stand and do everything Clinton does. He did it. No wonder he's always smiling. You rascal, Mr. President.

RING.

"Hello this is Rita Delfiner with the New Yoke Post again. What do you think Doctuh Hogan?"

"Rita, you can say, that Kevin Hogan, author of *The Psychology of Persuasion*, says that the President of the United States had some kind of sexual relationship with Monica Lewinsky."

"How did you determine that Doctuh?"

I explain the whole process to her. She asks a few more questions but she has her headline. I'm the first person in the United States to say that Bill Clinton had sexual relations with Monica Lewinsky.

Boy, I hope I'm right….

By the end of the week, I was interviewed by dozens of radio stations all over the United States. Over and over and over. The same questions, the same analysis of the body language and the dead giveaway in impotent denial.

Worst part was, I like the President. Best part, this is going to sell some books. Clinton will understand. That's how you become President.

As a rule, a person's body language should be similar to or congruent with their verbal communication. You should know that I could have been wrong about the President. I've analyzed the former President's body for his entire term in office. I have hours of the President speaking on video. (He happens to be the finest speaker as President we have ever had, and that includes Reagan who was also a brilliant speaker.)

Had Clinton denied his indiscretion with his left hand I would have been less inclined to authoritatively state that he "did it." You can never be absolutely certain about what another person is thinking based upon their body language, but there are definitely clues in the cues that you see. This was a big one.

Now, before we go on, I want you to take your right hand (or your left hand if you are left handed) and say, "I did not have sexual relations with Monica Lewinsky." Now take your other hand/finger and do the same. Do you feel the difference?

Now that you have one specific behavior understood, let's look at some of the critical body language events in meeting with your client.

It's not fair but it's true: Your Physical Appearance Matters

Your body language and your physical appearance will boost you to the top or keep you among the majority of people in the middle and bottom. You have less than 10 seconds and, realistically, closer to four seconds to make a good first impression on those you come into contact with. There is a world of research that clearly indicates that you will be judged professionally and personally in the first few seconds of your meeting someone for the first time. In fact your first impression is recorded and is used as a yardstick for all future communication by those whom you meet. Whatever that first impression is going to be on your part, you want it to be intentional and on purpose.

Before going any further in discussing nonverbal communication, we better take a look at how to really be perceived as attractive with your body language. Most people are completely unaware of just how much their body says and how it often contradicts what the words are saying! There are numerous elements of what we call body language. They include your physical features, both changeable and unchangeable, your gestures and signals that you send to others at the conscious and unconscious level, and the space that you use when communicating with others. In this chapter we will touch on all of these important areas of body language.

What You Look Like Really Talks

Let's begin with our physical appearance. Here are some astounding facts that will give you pause for thought when you consider how important appearance is in attraction.

Your perceived level of attractiveness by other people will be a significant benefit or detriment in your sales career and your life. It isn't fair, but it is true. **People who are attractive learn how to deal with less than perfect physical features and work with what they can.** Before we consider just how to increase your face value in the next chapter, look at the results of some fascinating studies about physical appearance.

The Power of Physical Appearance

Did you know that in university settings, professors who are considered physically attractive by students are considered to be better teachers on the whole than unattractive professors? Attractive professors are also more likely to be asked for help on problems. These same attractive professors also tend to receive positive recommendations from other students to take their classes and also are less likely to receive the blame when a student receives a failing grade! (Romano and Bordieri 1989)

Did you know that marriage and dating decisions are often made with great weight placed on physical attractiveness? A wide variety of research indicates that men will often reject women who are lacking (in their opinion) in positive physical features. Women, on the other hand, place less significance on a man's physical attractiveness in considering him for a date or marriage. (studies by R.E. Baber)

Did you know that in studies done on college campuses, it has been proven that attractive females (attraction as perceived by the professors) receive significantly higher grades than male students or relatively unattractive females? (studies by J.E. Singer)

There is more evidence that shows you must make the most of what you have physically.

Among strangers, individuals perceived as unattractive in physical appearance are generally undesirable for any interpersonal relationship! (studies by D. Byrne, O. London, K. Reeves)

In one significant study of 58 unacquainted men and women in a social setting, we learned that after a first date, 89% of the people who wanted a second date decided to do so because of attractiveness of the partner! (Brislin and Lewis)

In the persuasion process, attractive females are far more convincing than females perceived as unattractive. (Mills and Aronson)

Among American women, the size of a woman's bust is significant to how both American men and women perceive the woman. Women with a "medium" sized bust are considered to be more likable and have greater personal appeal than women with a large or small bust. Women with a small bust are perceived as more intelligent, competent, and moral. Women with a large bust are generally perceived as less intelligent and less competent. (Kleinke, Staneski, 1980)

In yet another study, we find that young men who are obese are generally considered to be slothful and lazy. Both men and women who are obese are generally perceived to have personality characteristics that place them at a disadvantage in social and business settings. (study by Worsley, 1981)

Can You Change Your Appearance?

Study after study reveals that how you look is critical to someone's first impression of you. So what can you do to change how you look? You can't change everything about your physical appearance, but you can definitely make changes that will give you a booster shot.

Research studies tell us that the "exposure principle" increases our "face value." Specifically, the exposure principle says that the more often someone sees you, the more attractive and intelligent you appear to them. If you weren't gifted with a Cindy Crawford or Tom Cruise face, then it's time for you to take advantage of the exposure principle.

If you don't have the advantage of being "seen" time after time by a person or a group, then you must make the most of what you have. In other words you want to look as good as you possibly can on every given day. Because of the significance of body image and weight you must do what you can to keep your body weight down and your body in shape for your overall image to be as good as it can be.

Your teeth will tell a tale as well. If your teeth are yellow and look like you just ate, your face value is obviously greatly reduced. Do everything you can to keep your teeth pearly white and you will be perceived as more attractive. (You've already seen the benefits of the perception of attractiveness.) When you watch the news tonight on TV, look at the teeth of every news anchor, weather person and sports announcer. They all have beautiful white teeth. There's a reason for that, and that is positive impression management.

Where You Sit Can Change How People Look at You!

Standing in someone's office is a problem that will need an immediate solution. As soon as pleasantries are exchanged, you and your client should be seated. If you are both standing for an extended period of time and your client doesn't have the forethought to offer you a chair, then you can ask, "Should we sit down and be comfortable?" Unless you are in a retail environment, sales are not made and deals are not negotiated standing up.

You may have an option of considering where to sit. If so, you are in luck. Scientific research is on your side in telling you exactly where to sit. Seating options normally occur on lunch or dinner dates at a restaurant and in meeting rooms. If you are in a restaurant, quickly search out a location that allows you to sit facing the majority of the people in the restaurant so your client is obligated to sit facing you, away from the clientele and staff of the restaurant. This is ideal for booth seating.

Your client's attention should be on you, not the waitress, bus boy and the dozens of other people in the restaurant. Your seat selection will assure you his attention. Once you have the attention of your client or counterpart only then can you can make your presentation or engage in conversation.

How Do You Select Seating?

Ideally, you can create a seating arrangement that is most likely to facilitate the communication process. Here are the key rules in seating selection.

1) As a rule, if you have already met your client once and you know they are right handed, attempt to sit to his right. If she is left-handed sit to her left.

2) If you are a woman attempting to communicate effectively with another woman, sitting opposite of each other is as good or better than sitting at a right angle.

3) If you are a woman attempting to persuade a man to your way of thinking, the best option is to be at a right angle if at all possible.

4) If you are a man attempting to persuade a man, you should be seated across from each other in the booth setting if possible.

5) If you are a man attempting to communicate well with a female in business or in a social setting, you should be seated across from her at a smaller, more intimate table.

What Do You Do Once You are Seated?

Waiting for the waitress to come in a restaurant can be awkward if you do not know your client very well. If you are meeting your client in her office, you will immediately get down to business after brief pleasantries. (It should be noted that sometimes pleasantries do NOT have to be brief. Many of my biggest and best presentations were made in the last two minutes of meetings that would extend to two hours discussing everything from baseball, to sex to religion. The level of rapport and quality of mutual interests will ultimately be your guide.)

Once seated, keep your hands away from your face and hair. There is nothing good that your fingers can do above your neck while you are meeting with a client. The best people in the world have wonderful and intentional control of their gestures. They know, for example that when their hands are further from their body than their elbows that they are going to be perceived in a more flamboyant manner.

While you are seated, if you are unfamiliar with your client, it is best that you keep both feet on the floor. This helps you maintain control and good body posture. People that are constantly crossing and un-crossing their feet and legs are perceived as less credible and people who keep one foot on their other knee when talking have a tendency to shake the free foot, creating a silly looking distraction. Feet belong on the floor.

Meanwhile, your hands will say a great deal about your comfort level. If you are picking at the fingers of one hand with the other you are pulling negative mindstrings that show fear or discomfort. This is picked up by the unconscious mind of the client and makes her feel uncomfortable. If you don't know what to do with your hands and you are female, cup your right hand face down into your left hand, which is face up. Don't squeeze your hands, simply let them lay together on your lap.

For men, the best thing to do is to keep your hands separate unless you begin to fidget at which point you will follow the advice of your female counterpart, noted above.

How Close is *TOO* Close?

Every four years the two (or three) presidential candidates square off in three debates so Americans can get a clear view of the issues that face the nation. Americans get to see the candidates in a up close and personal way. I've watched for years. The BBC asked me to analyze the body language of then Vice President Al Gore and Governor of Texas George Bush. Specifically, they wanted to know what the candidates' bodies were saying, then as part of a suspenseful ploy, they asked me to predict the election, but we would wait until after the third debate to do so.

The nonverbal communication of the debate revealed a somewhat uncomfortable George Bush. He was usually ill at ease and appeared to be guarding his responses. Al Gore appeared overly confident, arrogant and even a bit "cocky." Gore was completely comfortable, at ease and felt in total control of the first debate. After the first debate, Gore was so overwhelming that his handlers coached Gore to be kinder and gentler in the second debate. After getting "beaten" in the second debate, Gore took off the gloves and came out forceful in the final debate which was a stand up debate in a town meeting type forum.

At the beginning of the first debate, Gore walked toward Bush and into his personal space as Bush was speaking. This threw Bush completely off and Gore appeared to be a lion ready to eat his prey. Unfortunately for Gore, his behavior came off as being rude, arrogant, and too aggressive for someone who was going to be the President of the entire United States and not just those who watch the World Wrestling Federation.

I told the BBC that this ploy on the part of Al Gore, would backfire. Americans don't like jerks and the people on "the fence" would swing to Bush and away from Gore just because of this one 10 second incident on television. It was now apparent to me that George Bush would win the election, though I told the BBC, "Jason, George Bush will win but this election is going to be very, very close." I had no idea how prophetic that would be.

Had I been advising and coaching Al Gore, I never would have let him approach George Bush in any way other than a friendly warm manner. People like friendliness and feel comfortable around people who are kind. Almost all people feel threatened when their space is entered, especially when the perpetrator is physically larger than they are. When you look at the tape of the debate, Bush clearly felt threatened and the viewer feels queasy as we see Bush approached. Gore's intention is uncertain and because of this moment, he lost thousands of votes.

What is the lesson?

Whether seated or standing, you should stay out of your client's "intimate space." Intimate space is normally defined as an 18-inch bubble around the entire body of your client. Entering this space is done so at your own risk. This doesn't mean that you can't share a secret with your client. This doesn't mean you can't touch your client. It does mean that if you enter into "intimate space", you are doing so strategically and with a specific intention. There can be great rewards when entering intimate space but there are also great risks so be thoughtful about your client's "space."

Similarly, if you leave the "casual-personal" space of a client, which is 19 inches to 4 feet, you also stand at risk of losing the focus of attention of the client. Ideally most of your communication with a new client should be at the two to four feet distance, measuring nose to nose. This is appropriate and generally you begin communication at the 4' perimeter of space and slowly move closer as you build rapport with your client.

What is Effective Eye Contact?

Eye contact is critical in any face-to-face meeting. As a rule of thumb, you should maintain eye contact with your client 2/3 of the time. This doesn't mean that you look at her eyes for 20 minutes then away for 10 minutes. It does mean that you keep in touch for about seven seconds then away for about three seconds, or in touch for about 14 seconds and away for about six seconds. Eye contact doesn't mean just gazing into the eyes. Eye contact is considered any contact in the "eye-nose" triangle. If you create a triangle from the two eyes to the nose of the client you create the "eye-nose" triangle. This is the area that you want 65-70% of eye contact.

Should you sense that your client is uncomfortable at this level, reduce your eye contact content. Many people who were born and raised in the eastern countries (Japan, for example) are not accustomed to the eye contact that Americans are.

Eyes are a fascinating part of the human body. When a person finds someone or something very appealing to them, their pupil size (the black part of the eyes) grows significantly larger. This is one of the few parts of body language that is absolutely uncontrollable by the conscious mind. You simply cannot control your pupil size. If you are interested in someone else, your pupil size will grow dramatically. If someone else is interested in you, their pupils will grow larger when looking at you and there is nothing they can do about it.

This is one of the powerful predictors of liking in nonverbal communication.

It should be noted that pupil size will also get larger in situations of extreme fear and when a setting is dark. Pupils expand to let more light in and like a camera, when the setting is very well lit the pupils will contract to the size of a very tiny little dot.

If you follow the tips in this chapter for improving your appearance, being careful about appropriate dress and are careful with your use of space, you will be perceived as more attractive in personal relationships and in business.

There are two other telling behaviors relating to the eyes.

First, if someone is blinking far more rapidly than they normally do, that is usually an indicator of annoying lighting in the setting you are in *or that of anxiety and/or lying* on the part of the person. In 1998 President Clinton gave a short speech offering his reasons for having an illicit affair with Monica Lewinsky. During this speech, his eyes blinked a momentous 120 times per minute. Two days later he gave a speech about a U.S. bombing raid on a terrorist group overseas. In this speech, his eye blinks per minute were about 35 per minute. The difference is extremely important in evaluating the comfort level and honesty of the President in each situation. If someone is blinking far more often than normal (and you do have to know what normal is for each person you meet and adjust for lighting) you know they are very probably extremely anxious and very possibly lying.

When they eyes blink rapidly, they may be anxious or deceiving you.

Second, if you are in conversation with someone and their eyes are easily distracted by the goings on in the environment, this is usually a good indicator that you haven't earned the interest of your listener. In general it is a very wise strategy for you to keep your eyes well trained on your client in distracting environments. To constantly look around at the environment when you are with someone else is perceived as rude. To keep eye contact with another person instead of being distracted by extraneous activity is considered flattering and complimentary, especially by women.

Always sit at a table so the other person is not distracted. The other person should see you and only you.

So, there you have it! You don't have to look perfect and own Trump Towers to be incredibly attractive to the multitudes! However, you want to take advantage of every aspect of your attractiveness that you can and later in this book you will discover specifically what to do to really bring your best you forward!

The Eyes Have It

Did you know that you are able to get a pretty good idea of how someone feels about you by looking at their eyes? You get even more information about how someone feels about you when you put that "look" into the context of their facial expression and their body language.

How you look at someone can be perceived as seductive, frightening, caring, loving, bored, secretive or even condescending. The eyes reveal a great deal about what is going on inside of us. If you can learn how to look and send the right message at the right time with your eyes, you will be perceived as more attractive by more people.

There are six basic emotions in the human experience and the eyes capture them all. There are many more than six different emotions, but most of the emotions we experience are a combination of the **six basic emotions**. By simply looking at a person's eyes we can tell whether they are experiencing.

Six Basic Human Emotions

Happiness
Surprise
Disgust
Fear
Anger
Sadness

Think about that. Across the world, people are the same in this respect. *We all show the six basic emotions in the same fashion.* The eyes are amazing windows to the emotions we all experience. By paying close attention to the eyes, we can learn a great deal about our clients and counterparts and, in particular, those we wish to persuade today.

It is a true statement that most people will judge other people in the first two or three seconds after their first meeting. Therefore, doesn't it make sense to have them hypnotized by your eyes and your understanding of their wants and needs? How do you do this? You use your eyes in simple yet powerful ways to build rapport and create feelings of arousal in the person you are attempting to attract. To do this, you need only to apply the key ideas you will learn in this chapter.

I had laser surgery on my eyes to improve my vision without glasses. In the screening process, I learned that some people shouldn't have the surgery because their pupils dilate (get bigger and blacker!) to a size that is abnormally large.

Everyone's pupils dilate when it is darker in the environment and they contract when it is lighter. When the sun is shining brightly in your eyes, your pupils will be at their smallest. When you walk into a dark room, your pupils will be at their largest. The pupils get larger to gather more light. This helps the eyes see more of what is in the environment.

Your pupils will also get larger when you are terrified. There is an evolutionary response in your body that helps you collect more information about an experience that is frightening. The senses all sharpen in moments of great fear. Your hearing becomes more acute, your sense of touch is enhanced, and you can even taste fear. The pupils in your eyes get larger. This helps bring more light in even if the environment is already well lit. Your brain needs that information to help you escape and to protect you from danger.

Everyone's pupils dilate to a different maximum size and everyone's pupils have a slightly different normal state. However, there is one amazing fact about those eyes: When someone looks at you and their pupils get big and black, they are either scared to death of you, or they like you!

It's almost impossible to control the increase in pupil size that occurs when we see something we like. This expansion is also an evolutionary process that happens to take in more of something that is very dear to the person. Unfortunately for the observing person, it is an uncontrollable response.

Look at their eyes (pupils) and you will know whether they like you or not.

Recent research into pupil dilation has proven quite interesting to attraction. A researcher showing pictures of a baby to women, results in pupil dilation in the majority of women. Women viewing pictures of a baby with the mother elicits an even greater pupil dilation response. These same women viewing a beautiful landscape experience an enlarging pupil size, as well. Interestingly, women viewing a picture of an attractive man, on average, *don't* experience quite the size of pupil dilation noted in the above scenarios! Women can be impressed by a man's appearance but at least at an evolutionary or biological level, physical appearance isn't going to turn on every woman who passes.

These same researchers took the picture of that same beautiful baby and showed it to men. The men's response was a non-event. Their pupils, on average, didn't dilate. When viewing the baby with the mother there was again, a non-event. Generally speaking, nothing happened. When the men were shown pictures of a beautiful landscape, again, nothing happened. As soon as a man was shown a photo of a beautiful woman, the pupils, on average, dilated to a big and black orb. A man, it would appear, is very much turned "on" by the sight of the beautiful woman, even a picture of one.

Pupil dilation by women, when in the presence of real-live men, is another matter. Women typically are not visually aroused by photographs in the same way that men are. Women are very stimulated by some men in some contexts. When women are sitting across from men who arouse them, their pupils do dilate. To the observant witness, it is obvious. Most people are oblivious to the enhanced pupil size and yet it is one of the most telling signals of attraction.

As a public speaker, I have talked to hundreds and hundreds of audiences all over the world. As I speak, I am aware of the women whose eyes are big and black and I always address my presentation to them, making eye contact with those who appear to be aroused or attracted to me. They don't know this is why I selected them to make eye contact with (at least they didn't until now). Part of my job is to excite and inspire an audience when I speak. Therefore I need to gain as much rapport with the audience as I can. By making contact with the people who like me the most, I am able to gain agreement from those people. They nod their heads, lean forward, show interest, smile, and everyone in the audience sees how much fun they are having. In groups, head nods are like a virus. Once one person nods his head almost everyone does!

I receive all of this positive feedback, in part, because I don't just look at faces in an audience. It is because I look at the eyes of dozens of people in the audience and find the biggest pupils I can locate! These searches are like a treasure hunt that always has a pot of gold at the end. If I can do this with an audience of 50 or 100, can you imagine how easy this is to do in a smaller group at a party or in a public place? Start paying attention to the eyes that are looking at you.

You may wonder, "What if you are wrong? What if those eyes are just big because they are among the women whose eyes are normally large? Then aren't you just fooling yourself into believing that all of those women are attracted to you? My response is, "Of course." When you hallucinate, it should always be something that increases your self-esteem and self-confidence! We'll talk about how your beliefs and self-confidence effect your attractiveness elsewhere in this book!

A little while back there was a fascinating study, which revealed that when you show two pictures of the same woman to a man, the man will perceive the picture of the woman with the biggest pupils to be significantly more attractive. Many magazine cover editors know this and actually touch up the cover picture. Obviously, in the bright light of a photographer's studio the subject's pupils would be very small. Because of the importance of pupil size and attraction, the models pupils are enlarged to be much larger than they possibly could be. This makes the final picture irresistible to the magazine purchaser. We simply love people with big eyes!

Men desperately want eye contact with women. Men gauge the interest of a woman by her eye contact. Men are very competitive and territorial when it comes to women looking at other men. They see this as a sign that the woman is

190

no longer interested in them, or that the interest is fading. Therefore, if a woman wants to continue to make a good impression with her male client, the woman needs to maintain steadfast eye contact. A man's self esteem will crumble if a woman begins to observe all the other males in the environment.

On the other hand, we can safely predict that if we have the full attention of the one we are with, they hold us in esteem to some degree. There is no other indicator that is as powerful as eye contact that can show interest in another person. Our eyes unconsciously and automatically move toward that which interests or arouses us. We all know that and we all judge our value in some part by the response we receive from other people. The eye contact we give and receive is just the beginning of the sales process.

It's interesting to note that people with blue eyes are more demanding of eye contact than people with brown eyes. It is quite easy for us to look at a person with blue eyes and see the size of their pupils. When they expand and contract, it is evident. The person with blue eyes is used to people looking at them for an extended amount of time, in part, because of the contrast between their blue eyes and black pupils. The contrast can be striking at an unconscious level.

People with brown eyes, on the other hand, are used to other people looking away more rapidly because at the unconscious level it appears that the person with brown eyes is not as interested in them! The brown eyes present a weaker contrast to the black pupils. It often appears at the unconscious level that those brown eyes are not interested in us! Therefore we tend to look away from the person with brown eyes when in fact they may have been very interested in us!

When the person you are attracted to has brown eyes you must pay more attention to their eyes to see the contrast between the black and the brown. What seemed to be an uninterested person may be someone who is actually quite excited about you!

Confirming our beliefs about the value of eye contact in selling yourself is an attraction study that was done some years ago. People watched films of a couple that communicated with each other in two distinct ways. The first film showed a couple that had eye contact during 80% of their communication. The second film showed a couple that had eye contact 15% of the time. The observers of the films rated the couples that had eye contact 15% of the time as cold, cautious, submissive, evasive, defensive and immature (among others). The observers of the films whose couples had eye contact 80% of the time described the people in the film as mature, friendly, self confident, sincere and natural.

Gazing into someone's eyes is much more than just something special for the two engaging in the eye behavior. It is a clear signal to the rest of the world. These people like each other!

The Eyes Don't Lie

Whenever you are in a situation where attraction takes place, there is plenty of room for deception! People have been known to stretch the truth about their age and income, their intentions and even their degree of love for another. The eyes act as a leading indicator of truth and deception.

In 1997 and 1998 I was heard on hundreds of radio shows talking about the body language of President Clinton, Monica Lewinsky, Kathleen Willey, Hillary Clinton and numerous other key players in the White House scandal that led to the President's impeachment. The interviewers wanted to know who was telling the truth, who was lying and what the facts were based on the body language cues I was reading.

Having carefully watched the President for almost 7 years, I was familiar with his every facial expression and body posture. President Clinton certainly was the most charismatic president since John Kennedy. His ability to excite an audience and win over people who disagreed with him is legendary. He is an outstanding speaker who thrives on being in the limelight. There were, however, two speeches and the famous grand jury testimony where the President was not his usual charismatic self. On these three occasions he was uncomfortable about the deception he needed to partake in. The first was when he shook his right finger at the world and said, "I did not have sex with that woman, Monica Lewinsky." The next was during the grand jury testimony where he was videotaped from the White House. The third was the speech he gave that very evening, after the grand jury testimony, when he offered his regret for being involved in the situation. On these three occasions, his eyes gave him away as being deceptive. The one speech that I want to share information with you about is the speech where he apologized for his behavior.

For 7 years I have watched the President communicate with the country and even though has been called "Slick Willie," his body language has rarely indicated any internal discomfort with what he communicated to the public. In this particular "apology speech" however, his anxiety, fear and deception cues were very high.

When I watch someone to see if they are being deceptive, I look to the eyes for important cues. I want to especially know how many "eye blinks" per minute a person experiences in contrast to when they are telling the truth. For 7 years President Clinton's "eye blink" pattern is that of about 7-12 blinks per minute. That is very normal. During the "apology speech" however his eye blinking was recorded at 70 per minute! What that means is that on some level, the President was being deceptive in his communication.

Once eye irritants like contact lenses and allergies are ruled out, the only internal experience that will cause eyes to blink at that pace is the experience of anxiety normally associated with deception.

You should know that some people have eyes that never blink and a small number of people have eye tics that just won't stop blinking. On average though, a person will blink from 7-15 times per minute. When a person is being deceptive their eyes will blink 5-12 times that pace. Like pupil dilation, controlling eye blinks is very difficult, if not impossible. Take a moment right here and now. Simply try and keep your eyes open for 30 seconds without blinking. It's not easy is it? Now here's another experiment for you to do. Stare at a friend for 30 seconds. No blinking is allowed.

It is very difficult to stop your eyes from blinking! If you are in conversation where someone is telling you about something, and suddenly you notice a big jump in the number of eye blinks per minute, you can safely bet there is some deceptive behavior going on somewhere in what they are saying!

The eyes may or may not be the windows to the soul, but they certainly are strongly linked to the emotions and the entire make up of the brains responses to other people.

Sound Bytes from Scientific Research

- ✓ Generally speaking, the longer the eye contact between two people, the greater the intimacy that is felt inside.
- ✓ Attraction increases as mutual gazing increases.
- ✓ Others rarely interrupt two people engaged in a conversation if they have consistent eye contact.
- ✓ Pupils also enlarge when people are talking about things that bring them joy or happiness. They often contract when discussing issues that bring them sadness.
- ✓ Women are better non-verbal communicators than men. Men can improve though. One reason men aren't as good in reading body language is that men often communicate sitting or standing side by side and don't see as much non-verbal communication as women do.
- ✓ Women engage in more eye contact than men do.
- ✓ Eye contact has been shown to be a significant factor in the persuasion process.
- ✓ When women are engaged in a great degree of eye contact, they tend to be more self-disclosing about personal subjects.
- ✓ When eye contact decreases men tend to disclose more and women tend to disclose less!
- ✓ The longer your eye contact, the more self-esteem you are perceived to have.
- ✓ The more eye contact you can maintain, the higher self-esteem you actually rate your self on!

Simply Irresistible Eyes

Given what we know about the eyes and attraction, we can summarize the experiences of millions of people into a few key ideas for irresistible attraction.

- ✓ Start with your eyes. Are they clear or are they bloodshot? People who look at you will notice and the clearer your eyes the more attractive people will perceive you to be.
- ✓ If you wear sunglasses, get ready to take them off. People want to see what they are getting. They want to see your eyes.
- ✓ If you wear glasses, consider contacts or other alternatives. People need to be able to see your eyes!
- ✓ If you want to be attractive to someone, look at them. Look at them again and again. And smile!
- ✓ Look at a man from head to toe on the initial contact. He will be flattered. Look at the woman from the shoulders up and she will think you have depth and possibilities.
- ✓ Look at the person you are attracted to about 70% of the time when you are communicating with them.
- ✓ Avoid looking at others for any length of time when you are with someone who may be special. Make the person feel as if they are the only one in the room that could possibly catch your eye.

Scary Fact: The Client Often Says "Yes" or "No" Before You Shake Hands and Say Hello

What you wear, your makeup, your jewelry, your watch, your socks, your shoes, your coat, your glasses and everything else about how you look can make or break a sale before you ever open your mouth. Have you ever heard of "love at first sight"? Two sales were made before two people ever spoke. Both people decided that they wanted what they saw, heard, smelled and felt inside. Sales are made and broken every day in the same manner. In this section you will learn how to help your client fall in love with you *and* your products and services, before you even say a word.

Nonverbal communication is almost always unconscious communication. Most people have no idea what is going on at the sub-language level of communication. This section will help you master this most critical process of communication.

Many self-proclaimed experts of influence have mis-quoted a brilliant study by Albert Mehrabian to the effect that 93% of all communication is non-verbal. That wasn't what Mehrabian concluded at all. However, Mehrabian and most of the best psychological researchers do agree that non-verbal communication is between 50 and 80 percent of the impact of a communication. The same is true for the selling climate.

The first element of non-verbal communication you want to learn about is that of space. The space you occupy while in the persuasion process makes a great deal of difference as to the result of the process. Imagine that you are making your "presentation" at a kitchen table. Would it matter if it were yours or your client/counterpart's kitchen? Imagine that you were closing a deal in a restaurant and then contrast that with closing the same deal in a nightclub. Different?

Now imagine that you are in an office setting and that your client is sitting directly across from you. Next, imagine that your client is sitting to the right of you. Imagine you are standing in a retail store next to your client. Now, imagine that you are seated and your client is seated. How are each of these different to you? Each of these images creates different feelings and probabilities of selling your client.

Is Your Scent Making A Statement About You?

If you are going to be spending most of your day meeting with men and you are wearing a cologne or perfume, you have already lost valuable percentage points on your selling probabilities for the day. If you are a woman and are going to be selling to women, you can be lightly scented. Whether you are a man or a woman, if you are seeing men, have no scent but that of a clean body. If you are a man selling to women, you should have no scent.

In general, studies show that colognes and perfumes are a biological turn off to the opposite sex. There are minor exceptions, but there are no scents that you can wear to enhance persuasion compliance.

Scents are powerful in the selling process and if you have clients coming to your office, you should pay special attention. The science of aromachology has revealed that certain scents cause people to spend more money, take more time in stores, relax, feel more erotic and a plethora of behavioral changes from arousal to helping attitudes.

In the persuasion process outside of your home office, you, the sales professional, need to be scentless. If you wear deodorant, buy one that is scentless.

20 Tips to Look Perfect for Your Client

Both female and male sales professionals make many mistakes that cost some people far more than ten thousand dollars in income per year. It is interesting that our research indicates that women will far outsell men of the same skill and knowledge level IF your appearance is perceptually correct. Women make far more mistakes with their appearance than men do for selling.

Physical attractiveness is important to how many sales you make and how much those sales are for. We know that in personal relationships, people tend to choose their spouses based on two factors: One is money or potential income and physical attractiveness. Women value money as the number one characteristic in a spouse and physical attractiveness as second. For men, it is the opposite. Both find physical attractiveness as very important. In persuasion, the same holds true. Physical attractiveness matters.

In order to begin to understand how important physical appearance is, let's look at some research that has been done in the area of interpersonal relationships. Study after study show that physical attractiveness is very important in one person's perception of another person. 89% of all people on their first date decided "yes" or "no" to a second date based on the physical attractiveness of the other person.

People judge others positively or negatively, in large part on their physical attractiveness. Enhance your attractiveness to increase sales..

Numerous studies show that men will reject women based on what they perceive as deficiencies in the woman's appearance. In the realm of interpersonal relations, women are more interested in money than men, showing some practicality but continuing the thread of superficiality!

Many elements of your physical appearance are genetic and are not going to change. You can't grow two more inches and you can't change the shape of your face. There is much you can do to enhance your perceived physical attractiveness. Here are the keys to your appearance for both men and women. Follow these 20 tips and you won't be pulling the negative response Mind Access strings in your client's mind.

1) Women: **Never dress suggestively**. Research shows that you will get a longer interview, but you will make fewer sales. Dressing suggestively pulls out an entirely different set of Mind Access strings to be pulled. Low cut blouses and shirts are out. Mini-skirts are out.

2) Women: If your wedding ring is large and you are going to be seeing women, take it off and put your band on instead. **A large wedding ring reduces sales**. Women outwardly express their excitement about a large wedding ring but it is perceived as a negative for numerous reasons. Your sales will go down if your wedding ring is significantly larger than that of

your client's.

3) Women: If your fingernails are more than 1/2" long, cut them and you will increase your sales. Men and women **perceive long fingernails negatively** in the sales process.

4) Men and Women: If your fingernails look like anything but clean and well rounded fingernails**, get a manicure**. Your fingers are the one area that both men and women can be turned off at. A sales professional has nice looking hands.

5) Men and Women: If you wear glasses, normally smaller glasses are appropriate. You are normally better off making sales presentations **wearing contact lenses** if they do not irritate your eyes too much. Glasses rarely make sales and often break them.

6) Men and Women: **Your weight will make or break sales**. If you are more than 20% over normal, you lose credibility in the sales process. Begin a program of eating right and activity to reduce your waistline. Thinner people sell more. Period.

7) Men: **Facial hair reduces sales** in almost all cases. If you are a man and have a beard, you should cut it now. There are no men with beards in the top 100 sales professionals. If you have a mustache, ask men and women for their opinion. Some men appear to look better with a mustache, but in general, all facial hair reduces sales.

8) Men and Women: **Ear and nose hair can create feelings of disgust** in many of your clients. If you look in the mirror and you see ear or nose hair, cut it and keep it cut.

9) Women: Makeup that is lightly applied is not distracting. **If your make up is heavy, you will lose sales**. The closer to "natural" you appear, the better.

10) Men and Women: Teeth. **Teeth should be white, flossed and clean** before you meet any client. If your teeth are stained, get them cleaned. Yellowed teeth lose sales.

11) Men: Hair Length. **If your hair length goes beyond covering the back of your neck you will lose sales**. Long hair can feel good and even look good, but, it isn't taken seriously. Decide whether you want to make all the sales you want to or whether you need your hair long.

12) Men and Women: Dress like your clients dress... **plus 10%**. If you see conservative clients, dress very conservatively. If you are selling to casual clients, you will dress "dressy casual."

13) Men and Women: When wearing suit coats, **nothing goes in the outer pocket** except a spotless and perfectly fitted handkerchief. No pens, no calculators. Nothing else goes in the suit coat outer pocket.

14) Men and Women: Your **shoes should be shiny** and looking new.

15) Men and Women: **Jewelry**. Men should wear nothing other than a watch and a wedding band. Women should wear nothing more than a watch, a wedding ring or band, a thin necklace and a pin. Earrings that are small for women are acceptable but they should not distract. Earrings for men are always out. No earrings are permissible for men. You will lose sales.

16) Men and Women: You should be **showered** every morning and have your hair conservatively and neatly in place before every sales call.

17) Men: Unless you absolutely must, your **briefcase** should be no larger than a case that will hold two copies of the Encyclopedia Britannica.

18) Women: **A large purse is out**. Never bring a large purse on a sales call with you. If you do, you will look disorganized. Bring a trim purse with whatever essentials you need during the day. Everything else can stay in the car or your desk at the office.

19) Men: **Your suit should fit properly**. With your coat buttoned, take your fist and place it between your belly button and the coat. It should comfortably touch both. If you can't squeeze your fist comfortably between your stomach and your coat, your coat is too small.

20) Men: Your **pants** should touch the "bridge" on your shoes. They should not run on the ground or be raised high up on your socks. They need to touch your shoes or get them altered. Anything unusual costs you sales and that means you lose money.

Saying Hello and Shaking Hands

What should be the most natural thing in the world has become one of the most difficult. How do you say hello to your client?

Walk into the office with excellent posture, taking medium length strides and say, "Hi, I'm Kevin Hogan, the author of the *Psychology of Persuasion*, you're

John, right? Nice to meet you."

On the word John, you shake hands. If you walk into the office and your client takes the lead by introducing himself, simply follow his lead and shake hands as he extends his.

Hold his hands for two or three beats and gently release it. Assuming you

shake hands with your right hands, your left hand should NOT take part in this ritual. Here are the ten keys of shaking hands properly.

Ten Do's and Don'ts of Shaking Hands

- ✓ Always maintain eye contact when shaking hands.
- ✓ Do not use the infamous "two hand" handshake.
- ✓ Do not grab his elbow with your left hand.
- ✓ Do not hold their hand for more than two seconds.
- ✓ Do not squeeze to crush their hand.
- ✓ Do not try to get a better grip than your client.
- ✓ Do not have a limp handshake.
- ✓ Your hand should be firm but under control.
- ✓ Your hands should be dry and warm.

Do I Walk Funny?

Many people do. When I moved from the Chicago area to a small rural town in Minnesota in my senior year of high school, I learned this lesson the hard way. I had won a role in a play called, "The Crucible" as the Reverend Hale. It was a wonderful role for the young person that I was. Unfortunately, I didn't walk "normally" and my posture was terrible. I had a bit of a "swagger" and my shoulders bounced as I walked. It was cute, to some, but it was a sign of bad posture and needed correcting.

The drama's director, John Fogarty, needed his Reverend to walk with an air of confidence and not a "Chicago shuffle." He decided he would tie five-pound weights to each of my ankles. Now that may not seem like a lot of weight but imagine a half of a gallon of milk tied to each of your ankles. It slows you down and straightens you up. I had to wear these weights all day for six weeks. At the end of the six weeks I walked upright and not like the Cro-Magnon man I had become accustomed to.

In life, we all play roles. We play the roles of parents and spouses. We play the roles of volunteers and business people. As a persuader, you play the most important role of all. You play the role of a person who literally helps the world go around.

When you are walking, you should be walking as if a big hand was scooting you along by putting pressure on your butt to go forward. This is an important first step to improved posture. Practice walking around the house as if a big hand was pushing you gently and slowly forward by scooting your butt forward. That will help you with your walk and your posture. The alternative is the weights...and that is a lot of work.

How Do I Make Presentations to Groups?

Everything you have read up until this point still applies, of course. Presentations for groups simply offer a few more challenges and a few greater rewards.

If you are presenting to a group, you already know that you have something important enough to say to get the attention of the group. No one in the group showed up by accident.

Know what you are going to say in advance. You don't have to write out your presentation. In fact, unless you are the President of the United States, no one will listen if you do.

There are a few keys to speaking before groups. One is seat selection. If you are the key speaker and will be speaking from the one and only table, you want to sit on an end or in the middle of one of the two sides.

If you have any known detractors of your product or service, you should have them sit to your immediate left or immediate right. These are the *least* powerful positions on the table. Notice that in presidential press conferences where members of both parties are present at a seated table, President Clinton always had the house Republican leaders seated immediately next to him. These positions have no focal attention and rarely speak with any credibility.

Strategic Movement?

The most powerful nonverbal process you can use with an audience that must determine as a group to "buy" or "not buy" your products or services is that of strategic movement. Other sales trainers call similar strategies spatial anchoring. Both are applicable and here is what strategic movement is all about.

Do you remember Johnny Carson? He was the host of the Tonight Show for almost 30 years before Jay Leno took over in the 1990's. Each night that Johnny came out, he stood on a small star, which marked exactly where he was supposed to stand. It was the best spot on the entire stage for camera angles, connecting with the audience and because of the curtain back drop, we knew without seeing Johnny's face that he was there and not a guest host, who would stand on a different star.

The only thing Johnny ever did from this specific location was make people laugh. He didn't wander around the stage and tell his jokes. He stood right there and made people laugh. There were many nights when Johnny literally could just stand on his star and people would laugh. That is spatial anchoring. Audience laughter was anchored (conditioned to) Johnny's standing on his star.

When I first visited NBC in 1984, I thought it was fascinating that only Johnny stood on that star. At the time I thought it was an ego trip or some bit of arrogance on the part of Carson. How wrong I was. I knew nothing at that time of spatial anchoring and strategic movement.

When you are called on to make your sales presentation in front of a group, you are on stage. You are the star. You will want to select three specific points on the stage, or in the meeting room from which to speak. Each of these points is a specific location and not an approximate area. Point "A" is your podium. Teachers and preachers use podiums and lecterns. Therefore, *the podium (point "A") will always be used only to relay factual information to your audience.*

You will choose a point to your left about four feet from your podium that you will deliver all of the bad news discussed in your presentation. (You can't make many sales without painting a vivid picture about how bad things will get if the corporation doesn't hire you.) The bad news point, is point "B" and you will only talk about problems and anything that is going to be perceived as "bad" by your audience. *Point "B" will be approximately four feet to the left of the podium.*

Point "C" will be approximately two and one half feet to the right of the podium and you will always paint uplifting, positive, exciting, motivating pictures from this location. Everything we want the audience to agree with will be discussed from this point after we establish this as the "good news" point.

Imagine that you are giving your presentation for this group and you need to be very persuasive. My favorite example here is that of fund raising for a charity. Your job? Get a big check for your favorite charity.

You place your folder or notes on the podium and immediately walk to "B" point. You tell a story about a hurting child or a suffering individual. You then explain how this one incidence is far from isolated. You move to the podium. You expound the facts and figures about the devastation of the problem that you are asking the group to help solve by making a big donation.

Now you move to point "C" where you will become excited about how the charitable organization is currently solving the problems and helping the suffering you talked about at "B." Everything that is good and wonderful you will "anchor" into point "C."

As you conclude your speech, you will have a path that you have laid. You have moved from A to B to C to B to A, several times. *You conclude on point "C" because it is the good news and offers each person to participate in healing the wounds you opened at "B."*

The truly unique tactic in strategic movement is the ability to subtly answer questions at the unconscious level without saying anything significant on the conscious level. Imagine that the audience is given the opportunity for questions and answers with you. An individual in the audience asks you about the group's considerations of donating to a competing charitable organization.

"Well, of course, you know that charity is a good charity and there would be nothing wrong with that...of course...(walking to point "C") by taking advantage of the plan that we have, we can accomplish all of the goals that you want to have accomplished in the community. I'm sure you realize it is up to you to make it happen. We can only help those who need it if you make a decision tonight."

Discussing the other charity in a neutral or slightly positive manner from point "B", allows you to unconsciously associate all of the negative feelings to your "competitor" and you solve the problem as you move to the "C" point. *If you find this manipulative then you are working for the wrong charity. If anyone else is more qualified to help a group, sells a better product or offers a better service, you should be working for them!*

There is no more powerful manner of utilizing space than that of spatial anchoring and then using strategic movement. The next time you watch a great speaker, notice how he or she utilizes strategic movement. If they stay at the podium, notice how all the good news is given while gesturing with hand "A" and all the bad news is discussed when gesturing with the other hand. The greatest speakers are masters of spatial anchoring and strategic movement.

To finish off this chapter, check out the 29 Body Language Points below.

Body Language:
29 Points to Make Persuasion Soar

- ✓ The **right** side is where you make the best impression.
- ✓ Pupils dilate when they are interested in what they see.
- ✓ Rapid eye blinks often mean anxiety and deception.
- ✓ Forward **leaning** is a sign of liking.
- ✓ Eye contact when it isn't necessary is almost always a good sign.
- ✓ 70% eye contact is just about right in the USA.
- ✓ Your body weight sends a message.
- ✓ Your hairstyle speaks volumes.
- ✓ Hairpieces usually indicate insecurity.
- ✓ Rapport begins by matching physiology.
- ✓ Women feel comfortable when men are just a bit **below** eye level.
- ✓ Women feel comfortable when you are straight across from them.
- ✓ Men feel comfortable when you are at a **90-degree angle** from them.
- ✓ Touch is a sign of liking.
- ✓ Nod your head. It unconsciously affirms your client.
- ✓ Look out for leakage: A sure sign of nervousness.
- ✓ The nose usually engorges when the person is deceptive.
- ✓ Dressing to the situation is appropriate.
- ✓ Radical dress means the person is making a **statement**. What?
- ✓ Spatial anchoring is a powerful non-verbal communication tool.
- ✓ The people who sit in "Mom and Dad's chairs" are looked to for assurance.
- ✓ The person sitting next to the person standing up has no **power**.
- ✓ People in rapport tend to synchronize together.
- ✓ Physical attractiveness means more than we wish it would.
- ✓ Blue-eyed people expect to be looked at more than others.
- ✓ Scents of vanilla are considered positive in the USA.
- ✓ Our face value goes up with each **exposure**!
- ✓ Negative emotions are usually triggered on the right side of the brain.
- ✓ **Smile**. It's tough to resist a sincere smile.

The Psychology of Covert Hypnosis
The Ten Unconscious
Laws of Unconscious Communication

Chapter Twelve

You drive down the street. You have to stop at stop signs, yield to oncoming traffic and even slow to 55 (at least when you see a highway patrolman!). These are all simple laws. Laws created by society for the safety and betterment of the masses aren't necessarily perfect, nor are the absolutes. Laws of society don't always work.

On the other hand, universal laws like the law of gravity always work. If you drop 10,000 baseballs off the top of the Sears Tower in Chicago, the balls will all drop to the street below, probably doing major damage. None of the balls will rise up toward the atmosphere as you drop them off the Sears Tower. These are universal laws that never change. If you try to break a universal law...normally you won't get a second chance to make things right!

Legislated laws are different. If you follow them, you will probably live longer and pay fewer traffic tickets. The laws of persuasion aren't quite like the laws of society or the laws of the universe. In fact, most people aren't even aware of the laws of persuasion...*they simply tend to act in accordance with the laws at a completely unconscious level.* There are major prices to pay when the laws of persuasion are broken. The problem is that most people aren't aware of the laws in the first place. If people unconsciously follow the rules, they will be happier and communicate well with others. If people don't follow the rules, they will run into lots of problems, broken relationships, less income, be more readily downsized in corporations that are cutting back and well...you get the idea.

There is nothing that you do that is more important than communication with others. There are very specific laws that govern not only the communication process. It's interesting because, sometimes when you drive past the highway patrolman at 75, you don't get a ticket. Sometimes you don't yield to oncoming traffic and you don't get in a car accident. Every now and then you run the stop sign and you don't hit a pedestrian. The laws exist, though, and when they are followed they tend to work in the favor of the law-abiding citizens. When they are broken, the chances that something will go wrong are dramatically increased. The same is true of the laws of persuasion, which are only slightly different from the laws of persuasion.

As our species has evolved for millions of years we have discovered that we tend to need the cooperation of others to succeed. Gaining the cooperation and compliance of other people is absolutely critical to the persuasion process and the continuance of society as we know it.

This chapter will deal with the 10 Unconscious Laws of Persuasion. Following each of these laws is important in gaining compliance from others. In most situations on most days of your life, if you follow each law, you will find Covert Hypnosis to be a fairly simple experience. What's better? If you utilize these 10 laws in all of your communication you will find that your life is fun, sometimes challenging and always rewarding.

Law of Reciprocity - *When someone gives you something of perceived value, you immediately respond with the desire to give something back.*

It's December 24 and the mail has just arrived. You open a Christmas card from someone who you had taken off of your Christmas list! This is a crisis! "Honey, are there any more Christmas cards left?"

"Yeah, in the drawer."

"Thank god." You go to the drawer and sure enough there is a card there but there are no envelopes to fit the card into! You search and search, finally deciding to use an envelope that isn't quite large enough...but you have to use something!

You sign the card and yes, you personalize it! (You write something special just for the sender!) You stuff the card into the envelope that is still too small...you slide a picture of the family in and you even find a left over "family newsletter" that tells everyone what your family has been up to all year.

"I'll be back in awhile, I have to go to the post office and mail this letter."

Why do you have to go to the post office?

You have to go because the letter must be mailed with a postmark before Christmas! December 24 will show that you cared. December 26 will show that these people were an afterthought in your mind...not worthy of sending before Christmas. You race off to the post office and you have just discovered...the power of reciprocity.

You were taught to share your toys and your snacks and your space and your time with you all those around you. You were scolded when you were selfish and you were rewarded with kind smiles and pats on the head when you shared. The law of reciprocity was installed at a very early age.

The world's greatest people and marketing mavens give something to their clients and I don't mean a business card.

- ✓ Have you ever received a bar of soap in the mail?
- ✓ Have you ever received a box of cereal in the mail?
- ✓ Have you ever received return address labels from a charity in the mail?
- ✓ Have you ever received a handful of greeting cards from a charity in the mail?
- ✓ Have you ever received a sample size shampoo bottle in the mail?

These are all examples of what we call "inducing reciprocity." The practice is very simple, yet absolutely brilliant. If your product is top quality and it is something that everyone can use, send everyone a small sample of it and they will be more likely to buy it the next time they go to the store for two reasons.

1) We will recognize it as something we have used. The brain picks up on what is familiar. (Have you ever noticed how many cars there are like yours on the road? What happened to all the rest?!)

2) Reciprocity has been induced when someone gives you something and you give them something back. Reciprocity has also been induced when someone gives you something and you feel compelled to give something back. *Kellogg's* was nice enough to send us their free box of cereal and because it tasted good, we should at least buy their cereal this one time. We return the favor.

Reciprocity, based on scientific research, appears to be the single most powerful law of persuasion there is, but is there a problem?

- ✓ If you sell life insurance, you can't give away $10,000 of free coverage.
- ✓ If you sell real estate, you can't give away bathrooms.
- ✓ If you sell speaking services you can't give away free speeches.
- ✓ If you are a stockbroker you can't give away 100 shares of Microsoft.

What do you do if you don't have sample size products and services? How do you take advantage of this powerful law of share and share alike?

Give away something of perceived value to someone and others will feel compelled to do likewise.

You do not have to give away free samples to utilize reciprocity. You MUST give away something that has perceived value. My favorite method of inducing reciprocity **is taking someone to lunch** or **sharing a valuable tip** related to building their business or income in some way. (I like these approaches because they are measurable and the person knows that you really helped them when they follow through on your suggestion.) Taking someone to lunch is usually an inexpensive way to induce reciprocity and you have the added benefit of meeting one of your client's 16 basic desires. (The desire to eat.) Sharing helpful secrets that are truly specialized knowledge is also an elegant way to induce reciprocity. One simple idea can often help someone earn hundreds or thousands of dollars per year more in income.

Here are a few creative ideas for people to use as inexpensive give away items to your clients/counterparts.

Law of Time - *Changing someone's time perspective helps them to make different decisions. When people change their time perspective, they change how they feel about something and the decisions they make in regard to it.*

Time is the subtle equalizer in life. No matter how rich or poor you are, time is the one commodity that is the same for everyone. What happens in this moment is normally not a matter of conscious choice or thought.

Quite often when you walk into a client's office or you contact them in some other way, they will immediately equate you, at the unconscious level, with all of the other people they have ever met. In all probability they probably have more negative experiences than positive experiences with people.

Two things need to happen. You must distinguish yourself from all the other people they've known and you need to move their time filter from the past to the present or future. People have emotional responses that are attached to various stimuli. You are a stimulus. You trigger positive and negative experiences in all of your clients' minds whether or not each client knows it. What's more interesting is that this response isn't necessarily linked to YOU!

Imagine you were a salesperson. Most people would see you as a SALESMAN and they have a negative emotional response to ALL people. Therefore, in most cases, you are a BAD SALESMAN when you walk in the door. You haven't opened your mouth or asked any questions, and you are already a BAD SALESMAN. Ready for more?

In this situation, when you walk out the door, your client is going to think differently of you, but by the next time you talk with your client, his brain will be back in BAD SALESMAN mode for two reasons. First, he will confront many other IDIOTS posing as persuaders between now and then. Second, his past emotional memories are not going to be wiped away by a fun one hour meeting with you!

Therefore, you must *become an expert at altering time.* You MUST become a master of moving people through time so that they are not effected by their past programming and emotions. You must be able to get them to look at your product and service from a completely different perspective! And you can.

Time plays a big role in people's decision-making process. There are three fundamental ways that people experience time. Past, present and future.

Past: Some people live in the past or use the past as their guidepost for all decisions they will make in the present and future. These people are often cynical and depressed. They also make fewer bad decisions than other people. Their guard is up and they will make fewer errors because of this. They will also miss out on opportunities because of their experiences. You will need to remember this!

- ✓ I was ripped off once before doing this.
- ✓ I ate at a place like this once and it was terrible.
- ✓ I got conned the last time I bought a car.
- ✓ I never get a good deal.
- ✓ The stock market always goes down when I invest.

These are all common experiences for people who process all information through "filters" of the past.

Present: Some people live in the present moment. These people tend to have much less stress and tend to give little thought to the past or future. They tend to be lousy planners and seek instant gratification. Usually their credit cards are maxed out because they have sacrificed a future they cannot see for the pleasure of the moment. They think like this:

- ✓ I know it's right when I feel it.
- ✓ I do what feels good.
- ✓ I just wanted to have fun.
- ✓ It looks fun, so I'm going to do it.
- ✓ I never thought I'd get pregnant.
- ✓ Who'd have thought I'd lose all that money?

Future: Some people filter most of their thoughts by the future. They tend to live in the future, delay instant gratification and have determined that the past, for better or worse, isn't that relevant for them. People who live in the future are constantly planning, organizing, preparing and sacrificing. They sacrifice the moment for a brighter tomorrow. They think like this:

- ✓ I could buy a car now but that money is better off invested.
- ✓ I'll wait for retirement.
- ✓ I could buy that now but I'd like to watch that money build up over time.

✓   I better not do that because I might get pregnant.

Once you know how a person generally filters their information, you can have them look at different events in the past, present or future OR you can change their perspective from which they are looking.

You can change someone's time perspective with some linguistic maneuvers that rival the martial arts.

To get the other person out of the mistakes of the past, get her to see things from a future perspective.

Client: "Look what happened to the market this last year. It went to hell. Dropped by 50%. Why would I want to invest in your mutual funds?"
Salesperson: "You might *not* want to. But the next time the market doubles or triples, wouldn't you want just a little piece of that for your future?"
Client: "My experience is that I listen to a salesperson and I get ripped off."
Salesperson: "When you go out 10 years into the future and look back, what do you do right to correct that?"
Client: "Last time three times I bought a big yellow page ad, I lost my butt."
Salesperson: "Understand. If we can create an ad that will pull in the future will you be up for that?"
Client: "I tried hypnosis before and it doesn't work."
Salesperson: "So you had someone who didn't know what they were doing. If you were to work with someone who was adept at his art that knew how to help you would you be willing to do that?"

Law of Contrast - *When two things, people or places that are relatively different from each other, are placed near to each other in time, space or in thought, we will see them as more different and easier to distinguish which one we want most.*

There is a wonderful piece of television history from the archives of the Tonight Show with Johnny Carson. Carson hosted the Tonight Show for almost 30 years before Jay Leno became the host.

One night, Johnny had the number one Girl Scout cookie salesperson in the country on. He asked her the secret of her success. She said, "I just went to everyone's house and said, 'Can I have a $30,000 donation for the girl scouts?' When they said 'no,' I said, 'Would you at least buy a box of girl scout cookies?'"

The audience couldn't stop laughing and neither could Johnny. The little girl had mastered the contrast principle, at age eight.

Have you ever walked through a grocery store and watched people, especially women, take two competing products and put one of them in each hand then look at them side by side, literally weighing which one they should buy? The principle that guides people in this product choice is called the Law of Contrast.

Psychological studies have shown that people can use the Law of Contrast in a very specific and pre-designed fashion. If you can show your expensive product or service first, then show what you would like to sell (what you think creates the best win-win with your client) second, the client is very likely to purchase the *second* item.

When you were a child you would go into a store with one of your parents, and as Mom shopped, so did you. You may have picked up two or three items to propose to your mother for possible purchase. Time after time your Mom programmed into you either one of two themes:

1) It's too expensive, you can't have either of them.
2) You can have the little (cheapest) one.

You soon learned that the best method of selling Mom was to note how little the item cost. "Mom, it's only a dollar," your voice would resonate in a pleading fashion. With the proper eye contact and pitiful face, the strategy regularly worked.

The Law Of Contrast doesn't say that you will always sell the least expensive of two products. It does say that if you put two products or services close together in space, in time or in a person's mind, the person will begin to clearly see the differences and their programming will help them choose "which" instead of "whether or not to."

Price was the most common programming installed into children as a child, but there definitely were many parents who programmed the theme, "it's junk, don't buy garbage," into their children. These adult clients now buy higher quality items when possible. The Law of Contrast acts within each of us to help us choose which of a number of items to buy.

Give people the best option LAST. Give an inferior option first. (Exception? People who are in a happy mood tend to agree to the first suggestion.)

> *Let people agree to something NECESSARY first, and then much smaller options second.*

A useful rule to remember in any persuasive situation is that when someone mentions that your product or service is "too expensive"" or "costs too much" you respond with a gentle, *"Compared to what?"*

"Compared to What"? is a question that puts your client's thoughts into perspective and allows them to re-think their apparent "no" response. If your client was heading toward a "no" response, "compared to what?" may often bring them back to the "yes" response.

Law of Friends - *When someone asks you to do something and you perceive that the person has your best interests in mind, and/or you would like him/her to have your best interests in mind, you are strongly motivated to fulfill the request.*

How many times have you experienced someone knocking on your front door asking you to donate money for some cause? Compare the number of times you donated to the cause when you knew the person who asked you to donate in contrast to how often you donated when you didn't know the person who asked you to donate.

If you are like most people, you donated more often when your neighbor came to the door asking you to donate. You felt empathy for the person you know who is possibly being "put out" by this charitable request. The people who solicited from you less regularly received donations because they didn't have that same empathy or trust. We tend to say "yes" when we know someone or perceive they are your friend.

In a similar context, most people would never go to a meeting for multi-level marketing if their friend or acquaintance didn't ask them to look at this business opportunity. The greatest strategy a multi-level marketing corporation can utilize is the "listing of friends and family" strategy as the first contacts in the MLM'ers early days in his new business. These friends and family are the most likely to say, "yes" to actually going to a meeting. (Don't ask if they will invite you to Christmas if things don't work out!)

As people develop relationships with their clients, they become friends. Friendships grow and become special and future sales are all but assured with the ongoing relationship.

> **Help people see you as their friend and someone who cares about them and you will dramatically increase the probability of their compliance.**

An extremely powerful persuasion tool that few, if any, people ever use is that of *pointing out the negative aspects of you, your products and services*.

Psychological research backs up this assertion. One of the most effective ways to influence people is to argue against your own point of view or argue against your own self-interest so that it appears that you are being unbiased in your proposals.

One group of researchers had a heroin addict tell people that there should be stricter courts and more severe sentences. The researchers found the heroin addict to be more credible than others presenting similar points of view. This was one of the few instances when people believed someone who was not perceived as physically attractive. When the message conflicts with the expectations of your buyer, you'll be perceived as more serious. This is a powerful Mind Access Point and when you utilize it with a careful skill, you will regularly bring out any minor negative aspects of your products and services.

> Be eager to point out any negative aspects of you, your proposal/suggestion. This accomplishes two important things. First it makes you appear far more **trustworthy** and second it allows the other person to be set **at ease** as you are doing his job of finding the drawbacks of the proposal.

Law of Expectancy - *When someone you respect and/or believe in expects you to perform a task or produce a certain result, you will tend to fulfill his expectation, whether positive or negative.*

There is a famous study from the 1970's by psychologist, Dr. Rosenthal, that reveals that the expectation of one person can radically alter, both positively and negatively, the actual results of how people will perform.

The study dealt with dividing students into what teachers were told were bright and dull groups of students. The students were told nothing. In the group that was made up of supposed high IQ students, they performed at an average of an "A" level after 8 months. The group that was made up of supposed low IQ students, performed at an average of a "D" level after 8 months in their school work. In reality, there was no difference in the IQ's of the students. They had been randomly divided into the groups and the only variable in the study, which was immediately discontinued because of the ramifications to the students, was the expectation of the teachers involved.

> **The behaviors you expect of yourself and others are more likely to be manifested in reality. If you believe that your client will most certainly buy you or from you, they probably will.**

In psychology, the placebo effect is a well documented and scientifically measurable response on the part of the body to be healthier (or in the case of a nocebo, to be sicker) based upon expectancy, suggestion and belief.

In the Korean War, there were thousands of casualties and not enough morphine to relieve the pain of the suffering soldiers. Medics and doctors were forced to give sugar pills and the suggestion that the soldiers would shortly be out of pain. Approximately 25% of all soldiers taking the placebo had their severe pain relieved.

This same level of expectancy is necessary as a belief in yourself about your abilities to be successful and also about your influential ability with your clients to win them to your products and services.

Exercise: How can you utilize the Law of Expectancy when selling your products or services?

Law of Association - *We tend to like products, services, or ideas that are endorsed by other people we like or respect.*

Tell me, what is it that Michael Jordan knows about underwear that I don't? Didn't Michael sign a $40,000,000 deal with Calvin Klein to do a few commercials about underwear? Now, it's my opinion that I know as much about underwear as Michael Jordan and I would have shot those commercials for HALF what he got! BUT Kevin Hogan is a name known in the field of persuasion. Michael Jordan is a name known throughout the world. Michael Jordan was really paid 2 cents for every person on earth that knew his name. If I were paid two cents for every person that knew my name, I'd get paid about $7,000. That is why Michael Jordan got paid $40,000,000.

Calvin Klein paid $40,000,000 to link one of the world's most loved and best known people to their product. Underwear. That is what the law of association is all about.

When your products and your services are linked to credible, likable, positive-image people, your client will tend to like the products or services.

For years, authors have known that the best way to sell a book is to get people to write favorable back matter and front matter for the book. This adds credibility to the book because we respect the person who wrote the quotes.

The power of a testimonial or of someone famous using your products or services can be the key that turns the locks of the doors to the unconscious mind. If you do not have the ability to have the famous endorse your products or service, ask other people who are using your services to write you a short letter testifying to the fact that your product or service has helped them change their life, their business, or made some significant difference that they didn't have before.

The testimonial speaks volumes about you *so you don't have to.*

Allow people to see you and your products or services linked to the respected, the famous, the experienced - and your probability of the "yes" response is heightened dramatically.

Exercise: How can you utilize the Law of Association in selling your products and services?

Law of Consistency - *When an individual announces in writing (or verbally to a lesser degree) that he is taking a position on any issue or point of view, he will strongly tend to defend that belief regardless of its accuracy even in the face of overwhelming evidence to the contrary.*

The people you want to persuade have HISTORY. Their past decisions and public proclamations dramatically influence their beliefs and attitudes. Once a person has publicly said, "I'll never X," they normally never do. Many people make public statements that they have not thought out that often turn into beliefs and permanent attitudes. The reason is simple. We are taught that our word is our bond. When we say something, you can count on us.

Former President Bill Clinton has been on both sides of this law. In 1994, his continual changing of his publicly stated positions cost the House and Senate seats, creating a republican majority in both houses of congress for the first time in decades. In 1998, his adamant stand against talking about the Monica Lewinsky case for ethical reasons helped him build the highest popularity rating by a President in years. By consistently stating, "I'm going to just do my job," the country began to believe in Bill Clinton again and stood behind him as their president.

Did you know that 70% of all people are the same religion they were when they were raised as children? This is the law of consistency in real life action! The following graphic will illustrate the power of various religious sects to hold members over a lifetime. Maintaining consistency is at the core of loyalty.

214

Percent of Current Members Raised in Same Faith

Source: Adapted from American Demographics Research.

Fundamentalists	52%
Southern Baptists	86%
Misc. Protestants	40%
Other Baptists	77%
Lutherans	75%
Methodists	72%
Inter/non-denom.	27%
Liberals	49%
Presbyterians	59%
Episcopalians	54%
Catholics	89%
Jewish	83%

All Religions	70%

Americans respect consistency and predictability.

A recent research study had subjects make decisions among various choices.

Group A was asked to "remember their decision."

Group B was asked to "write their decisions on a magic slate and then pull the sheet up, 'erasing' their decision."

Group C was asked to write down their decisions on paper with ink and hand them in to the researchers.

Which group stuck with their decisions? Right. Group C stuck with their decisions over 3/4 of the time. Group B kept their decisions half the time and Group A tended to change their minds.

The lesson is to get your client to **write things down** as he participates in the sales process. He could write down anything from goals for the coming year to what he would really like in a car, a house, a stock portfolio or a vacation time share package.

In persuading and *even first encounters, the key is to get a pen in the other person's hand and have her write!*

Never ask a question which will pin someone down to a permanent "no" response.

Exercise: How can you utilize the Law of Consistency in selling "you"?

Law of Scarcity - *When a person perceives that something he might want is limited in quantity, he believes the value of what he might want to be greater than if it were available in abundance.*

What the public finds valuable never ceases to amaze us. Remember the Christmas season of 1996? This was when advertisers promoted Tickle Me Elmo dolls to children and then, to drive the price up, simply refused to produce the dolls in quantity. The prices of the dolls grew outrageous. Stores sold out of the dolls after creating huge demand and over-pricing them. Within weeks, the Minneapolis Star Tribune printed six and seven *columns of classified ads* offering to sell their Tickle Me Elmo's for anywhere from $300 all the way up to $695!

Imagine this: A child goes into the store when the dolls first come out and Mom buys her child a doll for $30. Eventually the media promotes these dolls to the point where stores and shopping centers are flooded with people trying to find Tickle Me Elmo's being forced to settle for all the other products in the store for their children's Christmas presents. The marketing campaign was a bonanza for Tickle Me Elmo, radio station giveaways, retailers and it was all induced by intentional marketing scarcity.

Which of the following should you use as an indication of scarcity?

1. Act now!
2. Limited Supplies!
3. One Day Only!

All of those are common themes in advertising and marketing. Which works best? "Act now" is third most effective. "One Day Only!" is an effective theme but doesn't even compare to "Limited Supplies." If you can show that there are only a few of your products or services available, that is going to increase your products perceived value!

The limited supply frame almost always goes back to your client's childhood. There was one or two pieces of cake left and when your client was four years old, he knew that if someone else got that piece of cake there would be none for her. It was imperative to attempt to get one of the last pieces of cake.

Scarcity was installed at an early age and has been reinforced throughout our adult life. The strings wound into scarcity are very powerful indeed and you should begin to devise methods to use the principle of scarcity in your daily meetings.

The other person must be made aware that something about you or your services, or your product is scarce. (Scarcity can include quantity of product, the time you have to spend with someone or a number of specific products at a special low price.)

What is it that your client loses if he doesn't "buy" from you? That is your scarcity point.

What does the girl LOSE if she doesn't get to go out with you?

Law of Conformity - *Most people tend to agree to proposals, products, or services that will be perceived as acceptable by the majority of other people or a majority of the individual's peer groups.*

Everyone wants to be accepted. "What will people think," is something that we all wonder about at the unconscious level. We all want to be liked and we all want people to look at what we buy and do with respect and admiration. When your client thinks about how his peers will view his purchase, the sale can be made or broken without going any further.

Therefore it is important to assure your client, at the unconscious level, that his buying your product and service is an outstanding idea.

Conformity is related to consistency in some ways. Conformity is being consistent with your peer group's acceptance. Consistency is being perceived as predictable and ethical within your peer group and even within yourself.

Non-Conformists and "rebels" even tend to conform to their groups that are known to be rebellious against society. Consider that Greenpeace activists are very much non-conformists in the eyes of the public, but among their own group, they conform to the non-conformist standard.

Jehovah's Witnesses and Latter Day Saints are both Christian sects who are considered apart from Christianity by other denominations. They are non-conformists and are proud and honored to be. However, within their own groups, they have clear-cut and definite standards that must be conformed to. Your understanding of your client's conforming standards can make or break your sales.

Allow the other person to see their future after saying "yes" to you as one where his peers and family not only approve, but are excited about their decision.

"Imagine how your wife will respond when she sees that you have gone out and bought her and really your whole family a brand new car..."

"Imagine how your husband will feel when you show him that you took the initiative to invest in your retirement so his life will be easier...essentially not having to work until he is 77."

Law of Power - *People have power over other people to the degree that they are perceived as having greater authority, strength, or expertise in contrast to others.*

Power comes with authority and charisma. Power is the ability to change. Power is both real and a perception. Your clients will perceive you as more powerful if you act with confidence but not conceit, comfort but not disregard, and certainty but not knowing it all.

Power is something that exists within you and must be brought out. Once people perceive you as competent, caring, knowledgeable, confident and certain, then their confidence level in you goes up.

If you attempt to use power *over* other people, instead of *with* other people, then you will lose sales and lose friends. Power with people is perceived by most as strength and is often called "charisma." Power over others is normally resented and people are less likely to conform if they think you are trying to control them.

One recent study that discussed power and authority revealed that 95% of all nurses were willing to dispense drugs to patients, after being authorized by physicians, that they knew would indeed likely kill the patient. That's power.

When you are selling a product, it is assumed you are the expert. If you know everything there is to know about your product, you become the go-to guy. Subtly make sure your client knows you are the best or among the best in your company. People *like to deal with the guy at the top*.

Auto mechanics may not have a high recognition value for power, but when your car breaks down, they become the most powerful people in the world, don't they? They have the solution to your problem. If they made the solution appear easy, they would have no power. The simple fact that most people are ignorant of how to utilize power is why most people are perceived as beggars or nuisances.

Exercise: What are three subtle ways you can let your client know you are among the top people as far as knowledge, client service and/or sales in the company?

218

The Secret Ingredients of Covert Hypnosis

Chapter Thirteen

"It's only words..."

The following conversation happened so often to all of us in childhood that we all recognize it immediately before coming to the "punch line."

Child: "Mom can I go to the neighbors?"

Mom: "No, honey."

Child: "C'mon, Mom, can I go to the neighbors to play?"

Mom: "I said, NO."

Child: "But why?"

Mom: "**Because**, I said so.

The word *"because"* is the first "Word MAP" you can use every day with every client you meet. This simple word is the perfect example of a MAP (a stimulus/response mechanism) that was installed early in your client's life. Early in childhood, the word "because" was conditioned as the absolute answer and reason for questions that we asked Mom and Dad.

Today, we respond the same way to the word "because" as we did when we were children. "Because" is typical of a MAP easily entered. Like magic, you utter the word and people comply.

> **Use the word "because" as part of your verbal reasoning, for almost any question asked of you, and you will find your clients begging to comply with your requests.**

Does this sound too amazing to be true? Is unconscious communication really this simple? Does just uttering the word "because" in a sentence really cause an instant reaction for compliance in your clients? What evidence exists for such a claim?

Dr. Ellen Langer, a Harvard social psychologist, and editor of *Psychology Today* magazine wanted to know the answer as well. In a study where Dr. Langer was considering the impact of asking for "favors", she contrasted the use of inquiries with the word "because" (a reason for having something done) and without the word "because." The study, which is now almost a part of persuasion folklore, went like this:

People were waiting in line to use a copy machine in the school library. Someone would ask one of three questions.

A) "Excuse me, I have five pages. May I use the Xerox machine because I have to make some copies."

B) "Excuse me, I have five pages. May I use the Xerox machine because I'm in a rush."

C) "Excuse me, I have five pages. May I use the Xerox machine?"

Before going any further, take a moment and imagine the scenarios and predict what the results were.

Ready?

When option (C) was used, an amazing 60% of people agreed to let the person make copies, just for asking.

When option (B) was used, an astounding 94% of people agreed to let the person make the copies.

Finally, option (A) which was used as a control to contrast with option (B), found that 93% of the people complied with the requests.

At least one and maybe two MAPs are immediately displayed in this simple but brilliant study:

> **Asking for a favor can be an effective tool in gaining compliance.**

The second point is to remember that the word "because" is a MAP. It is a stimulus-response mechanism in most people.

Use the word "because" in response to "why?" questions because it triggers compliance at over 50% the normal response rate in many situations.

There are a number of words and phrases that are MAPs that are easy to enter. For now, you can easily understand how simply and innocently word-strings are programmed into our thinking.

In the *Psychology of Persuasion*, I wrote about seven of the most powerful words in the English language and how to use them in communication. I have decided to publish the complete master list of magic words. These are the words we use when we sell and write. In the next few pages you will find the magical building blocks of selling: The words you use. First, we have listed the magic words of selling. These are 150 of the most attention commanding words in the English language. When you prepare your message for your clients, make sure that these words are peppered throughout! These words seem to have equal effectiveness in interpersonal communication and in text.

Begin practicing today so you develop the nuts and bolts skills of persuasion. Nothing you read here can take the place of actually writing out sentences and headlines for your services. Nothing you read here can take the place of adopting these words into your vocabulary.

Acclaimed
Advancement
Amazing
Announcing
Appealing
At last
Attention
Authentic
Aware
Bargain
Because
Boosts
Breakthrough
Challenge
Change

Choice
Classic
Comfortable
Compare
Complete
Convenient
Delivers
Deserve
Discount
Discover
Discovery
Distinguished
Easy (ily)
Effective
Energy
Exceptional
Exciting
Exclusive
Experience (d)
Expert
Extraordinary
Fast
Free
Fresh
Fun
Guarantee
Heal
Help
Honest
How to
Hurry
Imagine
Important
Improved
Indispensable
Incredible
Informative
Instantly

Intimate
Introducing
Irresistible
Last chance
Love
Luxurious
Magic
Miracle
Money
Money-making
Money saving
Natural (ly)
New
Now
Offer
Original
Overcome
Peace of mind
Perfect
Please
Pleasure
Plus
Popular
Power (ful)
Practical
Prevents
Price Reduction
Profitable
Promise
Proven
Quickly
Realize
Recommended
Refreshing
Relax
Reliable
Relief (ve)
Remarkable

Research
Results
Risk free
Revolutionary
Romantic
Safety
Sale
Satisfaction
Save
Scientific
Secret
Security
Sensational
Service
Simplifies
Soothe
Special offer
Status
Stop
Stimulating
Striking
Stylish
Superior
Sure fire
Surprising
Thank You
Timely
The truth about
Traditional
Trusted
Ultimate
Unlimited
Unusual
Useful
Valuable
Wanted
Warning
You

Yours

Exercise: Create at least 25 sentences using this instruction: Utilize two or more of the magic words in sentences that pertain to your product or service. If possible, create several possible uses for the magic words and weave them into phrases and sentences that will help you persuade.

Reading this book will help you persuade. Utilizing the tools in this book will ensure you persuasion success.

(Example: *The Science of Influence: Triggering Compliance* is a scientifically proven CD program that includes three **easy** to use techniques that will **change** your life forever. http://www.store.kevinhogan.com.)

The Master's Formula to Find Your Magic Words

What are the most powerful phrases in your specific industry? Is there a way to know what words are changing minds for your competitors? Here's the formula that will allow you to finally get the inside information.

1. Find the most successful products in your category. For example, if you sell aspirin to retail stores, you will select Advil, Tylenol, Bayer, etc.

2. Rank the products first by total gross sales. Assign the best selling a product value of 10. The next best a value of 9 and so on. You will weigh each word based upon the value assigned to it. A company's advertising that sold 10 bottles of aspirin doesn't receive as much weight as a company that sold 1,000,000 bottles.

3. Write out each word that appears on the label of the product on a sheet of paper. (Ignore ingredients and consumer warnings, in this specific case.) In the case of Tylenol, there are several hundred words on the label of the box I'm holding. Here are some of the words that are in the biggest and boldest fonts.

A)   Easy
B)   Swallow
C)   Extra
D)   Strength
E)   Pain
F)   Reliever
G)   Fever
H)   Reducer

I)   Geltabs
J)   Exclusive
K)   Gelkote
L)   Process

(Of course, no one cares about the "Gelkote process" but the marketing big shots at Johnson and Johnson will figure this out and replace those words at a later date. Aside from this error, the people who make Tylenol are using the magic words and hitting all the hot buttons.)

4. After all of the words have been cataloged, move to your next competitor and write down all of the words on their packaging.

5. Put a check mark on a master sheet that lists all the words on all the packages of all of your competitors by each word so you can count the frequency of the word in all of your top competitors. For example: If Gelkote is listed on all of your top competitors' packaging, you know that it belongs on yours. However, it's not there, so don't put it on yours! Instead, I bet you will be using PAIN, RELIEVER, FEVER, REDUCER, EXTRA, PRESCRIPTION, and STRENGTH. These are the words that are going to be on all the top products in the analgesic group.

6. Therefore you will model the success of the 10, 9, 8 and 7's in your industry! It could have taken you MILLIONS of dollars to find out this information in test marketing, however you are getting it for the price of two hours work.

But what if you don't sell a product? What if you sell a service or own a restaurant or you sell mutual funds? Find the advertising from all of your top competitors, the boys at the top of the totem pole and do the exact same process. Find out the frequency of words and phrases that all the companies at the top are using. These then become the words and phrases you want to model for your written communication with your clients.

Of course, knowing that these are the words that got your clients to buy your competitors' products gives you some pretty amazing advanced intelligence doesn't it?!

Knowing In Advance What They Will Do

Chapter Fourteen

Buying Profiles for You and Your Clients

If the "eliciting values" exercise earlier in this book was the only exercise of self discovery you have ever partaken in, then you learned a great deal about yourself...but there is much more. You learned how to create a hierarchy for your values and how to elicit the most important values from your customers.

Now it is time to focus your laser beam and uncover your *buying profile*.

Discover your buying profile by answering just a couple of quick questions in this section. Buying profiles are based on the VALS2 research developed at SRI Consulting. Buying profiles are critical to the persuader because they help us understand why people buy what they buy. Learning your buying profile assists you in gaining personal insights into your own personality and buying "programs."

Learning how to easily decode other people's profiles is one of the keys to making more sales per contact. In addition to the greater short-term profits this brings you, you build relationships, which create long-term success in the selling business.

Once you know why people buy, pulling Mind Access strings is quick and easy.

SRI Consulting's brilliant work has helped the field of psychographics explode. This book cannot hope to reproduce the powerful survey methods of VALS2, so we will simplify the process from 40 questions to 2 questions. For the face-to-face salesperson, a 40-question survey is not practical. Two questions don't offer us the precision we would need for market analysis, but it does offer us a predictable and useful model for understanding what causes people to buy from you. The two key elements are **why people buy things** and **what means they have to buy them** with. First consider the "why."

Principle-oriented people do things because taking action meets with their code of ethics, their values and beliefs. A fundamentalist Christian and fundamentalist Muslim are both likely to be principle-oriented. Both have very different evidence for what is right or wrong but both are principle-oriented. Principle-oriented people are guided by ideas that in their mind appear to be etched in stone. They see little gray and view the world in terms of "right" and "wrong."

Principle-oriented people may invest in socially responsible mutual funds because they don't buy tobacco stocks. They tend to buy things because it is the right thing to do. They tend to buy products and services that make a statement about their beliefs. They will buy to rebel against what is wrong. The principle-oriented person will buy to destroy evil. They may be interested in ecology and the environment. They are likely to find education as very important.

Status-oriented people do things to impress others. They buy things that make it obvious to others that they have a certain status with their peers. Adults that are status-oriented will buy to impress their peers. Teenagers will do the same thing but it may not appear that way to adults. Young people may dress in a particular style of dress or have a specific kind of appearance, which may not be typical of what might be considered "high status," but they are status-oriented regardless.

Status-oriented people want to look better or worse in society. They want to fit into a group by appearance if not reality. (Clubs, gangs, churches.)

Experience-oriented people do things because they are fun, adventurous, exciting, enticing, challenging, etc. They want to take part in something. They are interested in physical or social activity.

They will do something for the pleasure of doing it or the avoidance of pain.

When you buy most of the things you buy, is it for the status it brings you, the experience you get from buying/using it or the principle behind buying it? Before you answer the question below, a few more examples will help you know which of the three categories most applies to you.

Example: If you buy an automobile to impress others because "it looks good," write down status. If you bought it because it is American made, write down "principle."

If you bought it because it is fun to drive regardless of what it looks like, write down "experience."

Example: If you bought your house or a certain type of house to impress others, write down "status." If you bought a home because it is the right thing to do for your family, write down "principle." If you bought your home because you wanted a space for you to really dwell in and love as part of yourself, write down, "experience."

Example: Is most of your expendable money (not bills and payments, but "fun money" spent on things that will be visually impressive to others (status), functional for you or your family (experience), or things that are in the best interests or beliefs of yourself and/or your family (principle).

Write down what you sincerely believe your major buying value to be in the space below. (status, experience or principle)

_____

What are Your Means?

The second key element in determining your customers' (or your own) buying profile is to identify what your "means" are. Your means include your income, your education, your potential, your credit line, and your willingness to spend money now regardless of when you have to pay for what you buy.

Most people will buy if they perceive some benefit of pleasure or some reduction in pain as long as they value the benefit more than money.

Because we do not have the ability to judge all the means of any one individual without a survey, we are obligated to predict based upon environmental clues as to what another person's means are. For you, we will utilize your household gross income, which is a predictor, but not the only element of your means, as we have just noted.

In the space below, write down your household's gross income for the previous year. This is an *approximate* **measure of your "means."** It doesn't include your future potential, your education, your credit, your net worth, your ability to leverage and other estimates of your "means" but it does give a rough estimation in helping create a psychographic profile of yourself.

_____

If you wrote a number higher than $75,000, write the letter "A" by your income figure. If you wrote a number between $40,000 and $75,000, write the letter "B" by your income figure. If you wrote a number between $18,000 and $40,000, write the letter "C" by your income figure. If you wrote a number below $18,000, write the letter "D" by your income figure. If your figure was within $7,000 of a higher or lower income figure, write both letters.

We will now use this information to create a basic profile of your buying typology.

There are eight categories of buying profiles that SRI Consulting has identified. Our categories, while given the same names, are not identical to those noted by SRI simply because our typologies are more predictive in nature as we have far less data about each person we meet to determine specifically which category an individual will most represent his type.

By combining your means measure with your buying value, you can see for yourself which profile fits most closely to you.

There are eight profiles including:

- Actualizer
- Fulfilled
- Achiever
- Experiencer
- Believer
- Striver
- Maker
- Struggler

Each of these profiles will now be discussed along with typical questions that help open the keys to the mind of the person of each profile.

Select your profile category from below and then read about yourself to determine if you have accurately predicted your buying profile.

The high means profiles are Actualizers, Achievers, Fulfilleds and Experiencers.

The low means profiles are the Strivers, Makers, Believers and lastly the Strugglers.

The experience profiles are the Experiencers and the Makers.

The status profiles are the Achievers and the Strivers.

The principle profiles are the Fulfilleds and the Believers.

The Eight Buyer Profiles and How To Pull Their Mind Strings

Actualizers

Actualizers, according to SRI, make up approximately 10% of the population. This group makes up the smallest percentage of the population. Actualizers are set apart from the rest of the population by the fact that *neither status, principle or experience seems to be a driving force in their buying profile.*

It is their means, their resources, that allow Actualizers to express themselves by taking advantage of their resources.

Actualizers tend to have many assets, greater education and knowledge and even greater health, all resources that they use as "means" for self-expression.

Actualizers have certain experiences and habits that are far different than the normal American.

They are five times more likely to read publications like Conde Naste Traveler and Scientific American. They are four times more likely to read Audubon, Tennis, Sky Magazine, Barron's, New Yorker, Travel and Leisure and the NY Times Daily Edition than the normal American.

The Actualizer is three times as likely to listen to Traditional Jazz, Folk and Broadway Soundtracks. They are twice as likely to listen to Beautiful Music, Contemporary Jazz, and Pop from the 40's, 50's and 60's.

The Actualizer is four times as likely to have a membership in an Arts Association. They are three times as likely to be a cross-country skier and three times as likely to visit an art museum.

The Actualizer is twice as likely to own a cappuccino maker, give dinner parties once each month, travel abroad, vacation on a cruise ship, swim 20 days per year and own a foreign car when compared to the average American.

Actualizers tend *not to* own a motorcycle or watch wrestling on TV. They are less likely to use cinnamon toothpaste!

The most common zip code for Actualizers is interestingly enough, 90210!

Given this detailed information about Actualizers, we now have enough raw data to know specifically how to pull their Mind Access strings .

Appeal to the Actualizer's sense of independence, taste and character. Show the Actualizer how they can express themselves by utilizing their resources.

The Actualizer is an independent and take-charge type of person. When dealing with an Actualizer, utilize that sense of independence and power to facilitate communication. You learned a great deal about the power of a few well-designed questions earlier in this book when we discussed values.

Here are some examples of questions that will help you pull the strings of the Actualizer.

(Business Machine Sales) "Doesn't it make sense for you to *own the finest equipment available?*"

(Travel Agent) "Isn't a trip to Eastern Europe metaphorical of the freedom *you have found in life?*"

(Multi-Level Marketers) "Owning your own business is the final *expression of your independence,* don't you think?"

(Life Insurance) "By allowing your family to be *financially independent* after you are gone is really the icing on the cake for your ability to *control the destiny and security* of their life."

Key Points for pulling Actualizer Mind Access strings : Appeal to independence, character, self-reliance, and taste by utilizing their resources.

Fulfilleds

Fulfilleds, according to SRI, make up about 11% of the population. The Fulfilled, like the Actualizer, tends to have a higher income and more resources and assets than the norm. They differ from the Actualizer in that they buy not to live through their assets and resources, but to express their principles.

The Fulfilled personality does things because they believe it is the right thing to do. You may find the fulfilled person to be a literalist or a fundamentalist whether Christian, Jew or Muslim. They tend to be responsible, mature and family oriented. They tend to be satisfied with life and seem to be pleased with the level of success they have achieved. Fulfilleds are homebodies. They don't need to travel a great deal to find fulfillment. Trend analyst and futurist, Faith Popcorn, might call these people "Cocooners." These people appear calm, self-assured and have self-confidence.

They have some respect for authority but are open to social change for improvement of society or self. The sensible Fulfilled tends to shop for value and not lean toward the extravagant. They buy quality and products that will last. In contradiction to the "cocooning," they will tend to travel internationally more than the norm. Interestingly, this person of great means is also much more likely to own a station wagon than the norm. The Fulfilled is twice as likely to have a swimming pool in their backyard than the norm. Fulfilleds are much more likely to have a piano in the house, than the norm.

The Fulfilled isn't likely to wear cowboy boots and probably doesn't enjoy drag racing.

Appeal to the Fulfilled's sense of what is right, the right thing to do, principles and their sense of what is right and wrong.

The Fulfilled is probably a happy and content person. They have found the right religion, are happy with their family and content with life. Appeal to their values and beliefs, which they know are right.

Here are some examples of questions and statements that will assist you in pulling the strings of the Fulfilled.

(Satellite Dish Sales) "The best aspect of the new satellite dish system is that it offers *something for everyone in the family.*"

(Car Sales) "What is great about the Saturn is that it *maintains 61% of its value* after five years."

(Real Estate) "This home will allow you and your *family to live together* in the way that will bring you the most *happiness.*"

(Life Insurance) "Do you already see how taking care of your family's future after you are gone is *the right thing to do?*"

Key Points: Focus on their rules of right and wrong. These rules could be the Ten Commandments or the principles that have guided their lives. The rules will be different for everyone, of course. Focus on their happiness and continued happiness. Remember that family is normally a driving factor for the Fulfilled.

Achievers

<u>Achievers,</u> according to SRI, make up about 16% of the population. They are

status-oriented people with means. In general they like to be in control and they are proud of the fact that they are in control of their work and lives. They pride themselves in their work. Many are workaholics. They seek and like consensus, predictability, agreement and stability. They shy away from risk, intimacy and self-discovery. The New Age Movement is not something that interests the Achiever.

Work provides the achiever his prestige. They tend to be committed and dedicated to their work and families. Their social lives include church, family and business relationships. They are conservatives, respect authority and accept the status quo.

"Image is everything?" Not quite, but *achievers like to look good to their peers.*

The Achiever reads magazines like Parenting and Entertainment Weekly almost twice as much as the average person. Achievers about 50% more often than the norm read Golf Magazine, Country Home and the Wall Street Journal.

Here are some examples of questions and statements that allow you to pull the strings of the Achiever.

To access the strings of the Achiever, appeal to the low risk, tried, true, and tested. Appeal to the Achiever's need to look good to his peers.

(Financial Products) "What is best about this mutual fund is that it has a *proven track record* and a *very low risk* compared to the S&P."

(Real Estate) "This home shows the world that you have made it."

(Auto Sales) "Is this the car that is going to make you look good?"

(Seminar Sales) "You won't be subjected to a lot of that self-improvement-*new-age nonsense*. This is a *nuts and bolts program that is tried and true in the real world.*"

Key Points: Focus on the fact that your product or service will make you look good. Remember the key themes of tried, tested, and true.

Experiencers

Experiencers, according to SRI make up about 12% of the population.

The action-packed person with means to take action is the Experiencer. This often younger, rebellious person is the person who is vital, enthusiastic, risk taking and impulsive in nature. They like variety as the spice of life. They like what is new, different, bizarre, offbeat.

They are quick to take on new start up projects and just as quick to let them fall apart. The good starter and often-poor finisher makes them easy to involve in new things. Their politics and beliefs are not extremely important to them. They tend to be "uncommitted." Experiencers do not like to conform.

They are covetous of the wealth of others and also want prestige and power.

Experiencers spend a lot of money on consumer goods like fast food, music, movies and videos.

The Experiencer is three times as likely to read GQ as the average person. Hot Rod, Rolling Stone, Inside Sports, Seventeen, EW, Glamour, Vogue and Penthouse are also read over two times more often than the normal person.

Rap, Heavy Rock, New Wave Rock, Contemporary Rock and Contemporary Black music genres are popular with Experiencers. So is dance music.

The Experiencer will play pool once per month at least two times more often than the norm. They go to concerts more often than the norm. They are twice as likely to own a speakerphone and go horseback riding than the norm. They often buy weight-training equipment and are 77% more likely to own a foreign sports car than the norm.

Experiencers do NOT buy small dogs, rarely own pianos or radial saws compared to the norm. They won't see the ophthalmologist much compared to the norm. They will almost never own bonds.

Appeal to the Experiencer's right and desire to have more than they do. Appeal to the Experiencer's need to participate, have fun, and to their rebelliousness.

Here are some examples of questions and statements that will allow you to pull the Experiencer's strings.

(In general) "If you're sick of doing things the way everyone wants you to do them, then you should really sign on with our company..."

(Selling Clothes) "If you really want to be on the cutting-edge of fashion, this dress/suit/outfit is for you..."

(Insurance Sales) "If you're sick of the government stealing your money, then you can fight back by owning a tax free annuity..."

(Auto Sales) "Do you want a car that you can easily work on and make a statement with?"

Key Points: Remember to appeal to the fact that Experiencers tend to be on the rebellious side. How is your product or service going to help them rebel? Appeal to their spontaneous nature.

Believers

Believers, make up about 17% of the population according to SRI Consulting.

The Believers tend to be principle-oriented people without the means of the Fulfilled. The Believers tend to be conventional and conservative people who often have church as a focal point in their life. The believer is a person who has certain and specific beliefs. What they believe is traditional, family, church, patriotic, etc. Many believers have moral codes that are deeply rooted and literally interpreted.

The Believers follow routines and rituals and are organized around the home, family, social and/or religious institutions. Believers buy American-made products, may be conservative Democrats, and prefer established brands. Their income, education and means are moderate but sufficient to meet the needs of life.

Believers read Organic Gardening, Weight Watchers, and the National Examiner about 50% more than the norm. Prevention, Readers Digest, Woman's Day and the Ladies Home Journal are read about 30% more than the norm.

Appeal to the Believer's specific beliefs by revealing a knowledge and appreciation for their beliefs. Appeal to family, tradition and moral behavior.

Here are some questions and statements that allow you to open the doors to the Believer's minds.

(Product Sales) "There is nothing more important than supporting our own people and that is why we want you to consider our American-made products..."

(In General) "How important are your religious beliefs in deciding whether to....?"

(Real Estate) "How close do you want to be to your church when you decide what home to buy?"

(Financial Products) "Do you want to invest in funds that are primarily invested in socially responsible stocks?"

(In General) "Are values important to you in making decisions about...?"

Key Points: Remember to appeal to their beliefs, their specific beliefs. Remember that Believers make up the largest buying profile in the USA and Canada.

Strivers

Strivers, make up about 14% of the population, according to SRI.

Strivers want to and feel they deserve to ""make it." They want motivation and incentive. The Striver's life often revolves around planting roots and finding security. They are low on the economic totem pole and often have social and psychological difficulties.

Strivers need and appreciate a pat on the back and a great deal of positive feedback.

The Striver will buy something if they think it will help them make more money. Money is a central and revolving theme in the Striver's life. They feel they have been ripped off and have had bad luck in life. Strivers are impulsive and get bored rather easily. Strivers may dress beyond their means. They probably buy more products per person on credit than most other people. They want to have nice things and probably don't think about the long-term consequences of their actions when they plunk down their credit card.

Strivers read Jet, Penthouse and Essence over 50% more than the rest of the population. Other magazines that are read by Strivers almost half again as often as the rest of the population: Playboy, Ebony, Motor Trend, Rolling Stone, Sporting News, Inside Sports, Muscle and Fitness. Strivers listen to Contemporary Black and Rap about 25% more often than the norm.

Strivers are 31% more likely to buy a lottery ticket than the norm. They are 74% more likely to visit a CircleK Store and 60% more likely than the norm to buy an Instant Developing Camera.

Strivers are very unlikely to work for a political party, contribute to public TV, or be enrolled in Frequent Flyer programs. They are half as likely as the norm to attend adult ed classes as the norm. They are only 2/3 as likely to buy golf irons, and PC's as the norm.

> *Appeal to the Striver by noting how he has been given a raw deal in life and deserves better. This is an active theme in his life. Appeal to his beaten down ego by giving positive ego strokes.*

Here are some examples of statements and questions that open the mind of the Striver so you can pull their strings.

(In General) "You deserve to have the things that everyone else does, don't you?"

(In General) "Up until now, life has truly given you a bad deal. Now you have a chance to take back control..."

(Financial Products) "If you really want to be like (name a wealthy or famous person), do what they did and invest your money now so you have what you deserve when you retire."

(Real Estate) "Is this the kind of home that your friends and family will like?"

Key Points: The Strivers have little income and low self-esteem. They will buy on credit and extended payment plans. Appeal to the fact that life has given them a bad hand of cards and that you are going to do what you can to change that!

Makers

Makers, according to SRI, make up about 11% of the population.

Makers work with their hands. They may be construction workers, homebuilders or work in any field where they can use their building skills. They place a high value on being self-sufficient. What they can't afford to buy, they

236

make or fix. Their lives are family, work and physical activity. (See the magazines they read below.) Though certainly in the lower half of the income earners, they make the most of what they do have with their handyman like skills.

The Maker tends to be politically conservative, sometimes conservative Democrats. They are skeptical of what is new, whether products, services or ideas. They respect the government, but take personally government intrusion into their personal lives.

They are un-moved by the possessions and appearances of wealth by others.

Makers read Hunting, Field & Stream, Guns and Ammo, Outdoor Life, Hot Rod, Sports Afield, Popular Mechanics more than twice as often as the norm.

Appeal to the Maker's skill at working hard and his practical points of view. If your product or service can help him do his work better, or allow him time for physical recreation, you have found his Mind Access string.

Questions and statements that allow you to pull their Mind Access strings more effectively are noted below. Notice the common themes.

(In general) "You want to have this X because it will help you do Y in a more efficient manner."

(In general) "Sensible people with a practical bent appreciate owning X because it is useful...."

(Financial Products) "With your ability to do so many things that others have to buy or pay for in services, the opportunity for you is that you can secure your future by investing in a good mutual fund portfolio..."

(Automobile Sales) "This car is easy to fix and is big enough for your entire family and all of your camping gear."

(Retail Sales) "Sure, you may not have enough for a huge down payment, but you can fix it up, and re-finance at a lower interest rate, later, which will save you money. Even adding a bathroom will up the value of the house to where you will quickly build equity."

Strugglers

Strugglers, according to SRI, make up almost 11% of the population.

The Struggler is living in poverty or is surviving on a very close to poverty level income. He or she, probably has a poor education and very few marketable skills. They are most concerned with issues of security and stability. They probably aren't even living paycheck to paycheck. They are likely to be behind on their bills and have difficulty in all related areas of finance.

Strugglers read True Story, Soap Opera Digest, The National Examiner, Star,

Jet, and the National Enquirer more than the norm, but not much. Lack of money simply prohibits this category of people from being anyone can sell to other than products that Ed McMahon represents....

Key Points: The Struggler only needs to buy products that are going to solve short-term problems and should not be the focus of marketing and sales campaigns.

The Changing Face of America

The echo boomers are familiar with family break-ups, tragedies of drugs, gun, violence and gangs. For the most part, they really have not rebelled against their parents.

The echo boomers in general are likely to be comfortable with the technology all around them and lead America and the world into the rapid changing techno-world. As your customers change as people and we change as a society, we will need to know more than the two basic components of a buying profile that we examined in this chapter.

We will need to learn more about the unconscious basis of personality and how to pull all of the right strings all of the time. In this section we looked at how a customer's means will effect his buying profile and who he is as a person.

Then we looked at how a person's reason for buying whether it is status, principle or activity and experience affected the buying profile. Those are two unconscious filters that everyone has but we rarely think about. They affect whether your customers are buying or not buying every day.

In the next section, you will learn about many more of these unconscious filters of our experience called metaprograms.

The ability to see a client's metaprograms, the unconscious filters of experience, is almost like being able to read his mind.

Once you know a person's metaprograms, you don't need to be able to read a person's mind, because you can easily change it, if you want.

238

Software of the Mind

Chapter Fifteen

Inside the Mind: How Your Client Decides

Your customer buys what she wants and not necessarily what she needs. That is a fact. If you sell your product only to your client's apparent needs, then you are losing sales and thousands of dollars per year in income.

Your customer buys all products and services based on the result of awareness, desire, opportunity and the final interaction of numerous metaprograms.

> *Persuasive messages that only include what people need are not as likely to be acted upon as those that focus on building wants and moving the person toward those wants.*

Once the person decides they want something, they merely need to justify the purchase of the product or service...or idea. How we can help them justify the purchase is where understanding and utilizing their metaprograms comes into play.

METAPROGRAMS

Meta programs are unconscious filters and directions of experience and behavior. (We often alter this definition slightly for the convenience of utilizing similar software-like programs that are running in your customer's head but are as yet uncategorized.)

A metaprogram is a personality trait that a person is unaware of in most communications, at the conscious level. Each personality trait is so powerful that if you could alter it even modestly it would change the future of your customer (or even yourself!).

Carl Jung discovered metaprograms in the 20th century and called them temperaments. He believed that people were different from each other in fundamental ways. He used terms like "function types" or "personality types" to describe these differences. While noting the differences Jung also agreed that within each person is the same multitude of instincts that drive them that we all have.

In the 1950's Isabel and Kathryn Myers (daughter and mother) synthesized Jung's typing themes into the famous Myers-Briggs Type Indicator. (Their book, *The Myers-Briggs Type Indicator Manual*, along with Keirsey and Bates', *Please Understand Me* are required reading if you are going to be working with customers. The MBTI helps you analyze where your customer fits into each of the temperaments discovered much earlier by Hippocrates, Adickes, Kretshmer, Spranger and Adler.)

It is believed by many that the four metaprograms (or temperaments) measured by the MBTI are inborn, genetic and are only relatively changeable throughout a person's life. There do appear to be some context related differences within some people. (Some people are very extroverted in work and introverted at home, for example.)

Here are the four metaprograms that have been utilized in developing the 16-type MBTI, and how to utilize them to pull Mind Access strings. *The key words that pull Mind Access strings for each person's sorting pattern are listed below that trait. These are the words that pull the strings of the people viewing life through each specific program. Utilize these words and the themes behind the words in your sales presentations.* Refer to *Please Understand Me*, by Keirsey and Bates for far greater detail into the four Jungian metaprograms.

World Experience Program

1. Extrovert...Introvert

sociable	territorial
breadth	depth
external	internal
interaction	concentration
many relationships	limited relationships

The **extrovert** is a person who is more likely to be outgoing and socially adept. They like to go out to places and mingle. They are focused on what is going on in the outside world.

The **introvert** is more interested with intrapersonal communication. They are interested in what lies within. The introvert is interested in ideas. Introverts tend to be territorial. Notice that the .... above indicate that these traits or characteristics lie on a continuum and that the continuum can be context dependent. A person who is 51% introverted will act and experience life much differently than a person who is 99% introverted, won't they?

About 75% of the English speaking population describe themselves as extroverted.

Judgment Program

2. Thinking...Feeling

objective	subjective
principles	values
policy	social values
laws	circumstances
criteria	intimacy
firmness	persuasion
justice	humane
categories	harmony
standards	good or bad
critique	appreciate
analysis	sympathy
allocation	devotion

The thinker is someone who analyzes information in the decision making process. The thinker aims toward the objective and "real" result.

The feeler is someone who is more inclined to go with his gut level instincts. The feeler is someone who is likely to move toward the subjective result. Both groups seem to have the same emotional intensity, but the feelers are more likely to let their emotions "show."

About 60% of men are thinkers and about 60% of women are feelers.

Closure Program

3. Judgment...Perceiving

settled	pending
decided	gather more data
fixed	flexible
plan ahead	adapt as you go
run one's life	let life happen
closure	keep options open
decision-making	"treasure hunting"
planned	open-ended
completed	emergent
decisive	tentative
"wrap it up"	something will turn up

The judger is someone who deals with the outer world in a more black or white fashion.

The perceiver sees the outer world and accepts it, more or less, for what it is. When judging begins, perception ends.

The two attitudes do not occur simultaneously, as in some other metaprograms. A person will perceive discussion or debate until a specific point and then a judgment is made. Similarly, a person will suspend judgment until he has enough perceived information. The distinction in this continuum is what is the person more comfortable with. Do they prefer to come to judgment or do they prefer to consider and perceive. Judgers put order into their lives, perceivers simply live their lives.

The English speaking population seems to be divided into about a 50-50 split as to which tendency each person is likely to fall into.

Perception Program

4. Intuition..Sensation

hunches	perspiration
future	past
speculative	realistic
inspiration	actual
fantasy	down to earth
possible	no-nonsense
fiction	fact
ingenious	practical
imaginative	sensible

How does your customer perceive the world? His life? You? That will depend upon his perception program. This program helps us see that some people are exploring what is possible while others are more interested in what "is."

The intuitive person is directed by the unconscious mind to a far greater degree than the person who is a sensor. The sensor is guided by his five senses and his specific and verifiable experiences.

The intuitive person may have difficulty putting their hunches into words, but they are just as certain about the veracity of their knowledge as the sensor is.

The sensors tend not to worry about the past or the future. The intuitive may often seem unaware of all that is going on around him. Intuitive people love metaphors and imagery and are excellent prospects when you have a wonderful story to tell.

Approximately 75% of the English speaking population are sensors.

The New Metaprograms

There is a definite quality of overlapping programs within each of us. If you watch the NBC news and flip to the CBS news, some of the stories are the same and some are unique to each channel. Metaprograms are similar to this experience. In this section, you will learn some of the "new metaprograms" that are critical to pulling Mind Access strings in the sales process.

You may feel that there are relationships between two metaprograms and that is a sign that you are becoming consciously aware of the programs that are running your mind, and a good sign of understanding this method of understanding and utilizing personality traits in Mind Strings.

Metaprograms are among the deepest filters of perception. These internal sorting patterns unconsciously help us decide what we pay attention to. Metaprograms are, generally speaking, "content free but context dependent."

Like a computer software program, the sum of your client's metaprograms do not actually store information, but determine what drives him. His state (of mind) is affected by his metaprograms and they play a significant role in creating his internal representations (his pictures of how he views the world at the conscious and unconscious level).

In order to use a computer program effectively you must understand how use it. In order to communicate with and sell your products and services to your customers in an efficient manner you must understand what metaprograms they use. Because metaprograms are deletion and distortion filters that adjust our generalizations (beliefs), we can predict the states of mind of our customers if we know their metaprograms. If you can predict your client's internal states, you can easily influence your customer's decisions and actions.

There are about 50 metaprograms that have been identified as sorting patterns, types, traits and functions for individuals. You will now learn the "new" metaprograms that most affect the sales process. Remember that all metaprograms exist on a continuum and are not either/or representations of personality!

As previously noted some people are *very* extroverted and other people may be just a little extroverted. The behavioral distinctions between someone who is extroverted and someone who is *very* extroverted can be described as analogical to a good conversationalist compared to someone who never stops talking to listen.

We have already discussed the four core metaprograms that Jung, Myers, Briggs, Keirsey, and Bates have so brilliantly educated us about. The first of the new metaprograms we want to examine is that of the pain/pleasure sorting pattern. This metaprogram is probably the most important metaprogram in making or losing sales.

Pleasure/Pain Program

A. **Experience Pleasure**.................................**Avoid Pain**

bright future	sick of the way things are
feel great	stop getting hurt
move toward	away from
make new friends	stop being lonely
obtain	get rid of

Decades of scientific research clearly show that people are more motivated by avoiding pain than by pleasure.

What this means is that you not only will paint a picture of a vivid wonderful future for your customer, but you must also find their current wounds (pain) and heal them.

In fact, this one Mind Access Point drives over a hundred other Mind Access Points. The foundational string is that people will do almost anything to avoid significant pain.

People are motivated to move toward pleasure and away from pain. Of the two drivers, most people are programmed to move away from pain more than moving toward pleasure.

When your customer was a child, he was regularly threatened with pain (a spanking, a slap in the face, loss of privileges) when he behaved in a bad way. This developed very thick and powerful Mind Access Points, which many other Mind Access strings are attached to. A smaller number of your customer's parents regularly motivated them as children by offering rewards for good behavior. Most parents use threats of punishment in order to gain compliance. Your customer continues to want to do anything he can to avoid pain. If that means complying with you, that is what he will do.

The Amway Corporation has built one of the largest privately held corporations in the world by pulling the Mind Access Points of those with an entrepreneurial spirit and focusing on the pleasure end of the pain pleasure metaprogram. They help their distributors build dreams and create vivid and lush futures. They move their distributors toward pleasure, as a rule of thumb.

In contrast, hundreds of the world's largest corporations have built their fortunes by pulling the Mind Access Points of the populace on the pain side of the pain/pleasure metaprogram. History and scientific research has shown that people are very averse to pain. As mentioned above, most people will do far more to avoid pain than experience pleasure. The experience of pain is the driving force of billions of dollars in the advertising industry. How many of these slogans and commercial themes sound familiar to you?

> "Aren't you hungry for Burger King, now?"
> "Do you suffer from headache pain?"
> "Do you feel achy?"
> "Can't sleep at night?"

When you are talking with your client, your job, in part, is to show how your product or service will create great pleasure if they buy from you and also act as a way to avoid pain. If they fail to hire you, you show them how their wound will grow and create pain for them in the future. If they hire you, you will help them heal their wound.

Anthony Robbins, the world's most powerful motivational speaker, got to that apex by being able to clearly create vivid pictures of what would happen to people if they didn't allow him to help them. You can utilize the power of the pain/pleasure metaprogram just like Robbins has done.

If you have elicited your client's metaprograms, then you can focus on the context specific information you have elicited instead of relying on the general rules we have discussed here. In marketing, we must rely on the norms. In the direct sales situation we have a marked advantage of knowing exactly what motivates each specific client.

One effective language pattern that helps the client experience the pain of not working with you, is for you to say a variation of the wound opening, "If you don't act on this now, then won't things simply get worse?"

The more the customer fears and moves away from pain, the more likely she is to act now. It is our job to paint a picture of the consequences of failing to hire you. Experiencing pain must be more than an idea, it must be real to the customer.

If we fail to sell our customer the services that they need, then they still associate too much pain to change and you have not done your job. No amount of "closing techniques" will get a person to change their point of view or buy a product if they are still unconvinced. You must help the person see the obvious and clear benefits, emotional and logical to accepting your products and services.

Your job is often to paint the status quo as miserable. Most people have a fear of change. It is pre-programmed within them. Therefore, when painting the status quo, it must hurt to experience it. You must bring out the pain of not changing and make it vivid. Someone who associates no drawbacks or very little pain in the status quo will not accept your proposal. They will say, "no."

The more someone moves away from pain and experiences fear, the more likely they are to act on a decision, now.

The Amway Corporation has utilized a wonderful tool for helping potential distributors feel the pain of failing to become Amway entrepreneurs. For just a moment, remember when you were first presented with the opportunity to become involved as a distributor. One of the dark pictures the speaker painted for your future was this: If you don't become a distributor, how else are you going to become, financially independent? Do you really want to work at that the same job and forever? Are you really going to be happy with $35,000 per year, every year for the rest of your life?

Does Amway or *any company or salesperson,* have a right to pull at these Mind Access strings? You bet they do, because they are making the world go around. Multilevel marketing may or may not be an outstanding entrepreneurial opportunity for any individual, but just for a moment, realize how Amway has become so vast: *Amway utilizes the pain/pleasure metaprogram better than any private organization in the world.*

This Exercise Is Worth $100,000, Do It Now.

Use the space below to write down 20 painful futures that your customers could experience if they don't own your product or use your service. Then write down 20 bright futures that your customers will experience if they do use your product or service. The next time you meet with a client, you will have a vast array of futures to offer your customer. It is the quality of the images that you help your customer see that will make you thousands of dollars per year in additional sales.

_____

_____

_____

_____

_____

_____

_____

_____

_____

_____

_____

_____

_____

_____

_____

_____

Cost/Convenience Program

B. Cost.. Convenience

At some point in the sales interview, you will need to determine whether your client is more concerned and with speed and convenience or cost.

Many people will take a quick trip to the local convenience store to pick up a few items even though they cost far more than the grocery store charges, for the simple reason that the convenience store is right on the corner and it only takes a minute to get there. It is convenient. The convenience of the store's proximity is considered by most to be more important than the increased cost of the goods at the store.

If you are selling financial products, then you'll need to find out whether your client really has the time to closely follow the daily stock reports and make day-to-day decisions about his investments. Would he be happier if you took care of this for him? Is it worth the small cost involved for you to handle his finances in exchange for the incredible burden it lightens within him?

If you sell real estate, does your buyer really want to commute an extra 30 minutes per day to save ten thousand dollars on the price of a house? You need to find out whether the person is more motivated by cost or convenience before the buying process begins.

Relationship Program

C. Match...Match/Mismatch...Mismatch/Match...Polarity

same as	same except	completely different
in common	more	totally changed
like before	progress	one of a kind

Take three coins and place them on the table in front of you. Describe the relationship between those three coins.

If you said that the three coins are *all money* or that they are *all coins* or that they are *all heads* off or *all* made of metal, then you are what is known as "matcher."

If you said that they are all somehow similar but there are also differences in some way, then you would be typed as a "matcher with a mismatch."

If you said something to the effect of, "they're all different but they do have this in common," then you are a "mis-matcher with a match."

If you found that all three coins were *distinctly different from each other with nothing in common* then you are what is known as a "polarity" responder.

In the real world, you may or may not be able to utilize such a tool. In your sales interview, if you needed to instantly know your client's relationship program, you would ask, "What is the relationship between your job (or something similar) this year and last year?"

Convincer Program

D. Internal..**External**

I think	She thinks
I feel	They tell me
My instincts tell me	Research shows

How does your customer know if he should buy your products or services? You can ask him how he was convinced the last time he *successfully* made a major purchase like yours. You don't want to know how he was convinced of making a big mistake, you want to know how he was convinced of making a good decision.

"Are you glad you bought your current home?"

"Sure it's been great."

"What convinced you to buy this home?"

Your client will now tell you a story. That story will largely revolve around people and data helping him make his decision or around his gut level intuition, his feelings. Once you know whether your client is convinced of good decisions by either Internal or External sources of information, you can then pace and match that source of information.

"I just had a feeling that it was the right place."

"I want you to tell me if you get that feeling again when we look at the next home we are going to visit."

or

"It matched all of the criteria we set up. It had three bedrooms upstairs, an office and a swimming pool."

"You mentioned that you are now looking for a larger home earlier with a fireplace and the same nice qualities of your current home. When we come across your next home, let me know right away."

Convincer-# of Times Program

E. Assumed....Once....Many Times.....Regularly....Always

Some customers won't buy from you the first time you propose something to them. Some people will need to look at your program numerous times before they decide to buy. This being the case, we can elicit their metaprogram for how many times it takes them to see something of quality before they actually purchase it.

"I'm curious, the last time you bought your life insurance, how many times did your agent have to come and show you the benefits of insurance before you actually said, OK?"

"We talked about it after the first time he came out, then he called back and we told him to stop back out the next week. He did and we signed up then."

"Gotcha, so you and Mrs. Johnson appreciate someone who gives you the night to make sure you are doing what is in your best interest then have me come back out tomorrow, is that right?"

or

."..well frankly we had a pretty hard time deciding whether or not to buy insurance from our guy or not. It was such a great expenditure. I think he was out here three or four times..."

"Makes sense to me. I can easily see how difficult it is to make important decisions carefully. What I'd like to do is leave you with several print outs (proposals), you look them over and I'll stop back tomorrow. Then if you feel you still want to move carefully, I'll stop back next week. OK?"

Picture Size Program

F. General/Big	Specific/Detail
Overall	Exactly
The important thing is	precisely
Generally speaking	to be exact

Have you ever noticed that many customers you have get bored to tears when you start going over the details and nuances of your products and services? These people are what we call "big picture" people. Other people will feel that you are trying to cheat them if you just give them a few broad strokes of information. They want all the details. Anything short of a full disclaimer and a detailed future amortization puts you in their doghouse and they won't buy from you. These people are "detail" buyers.

People who are rushed for time generally need you to put your proposal into a four-minute sound byte commercial. If they want more information, they will ask for it as you then become a priority in their day. This may or may not mean that you literally talk faster. **It does mean that regardless of what you sell, you should be able to discuss your product intelligently for 20 seconds, 20 minutes or two hours.** You will meet people who will buy a car in 20 seconds and a house in 20 minutes. You will also meet people who won't buy anything until they have had hours, days, weeks, or months to consider it. Be aware of their Picture Size Program and you will enhance your probability of making the sale.

"When you bought your last car, how long did you actually have to think about it before you told the salesman, yes? Did he give you all the specs on the vehicle or did you just see it and say, 'Hey, that's a nice car, I'll take it.'"

Possibility/Necessity Program

G. Possibility...Necessity
    Opportunity   Must
    Chance   If need be
    Could happen   only if

Does your client buy your financial products because he *needs* a nest egg at retirement or because it expands the *possibilities* of how he can live his retirement years? The distinction can be very important.

You must propose your products and services through the same filters as your client's metaprograms for instant compliance. If your client invests in mutual funds because it will afford him the *opportunity* to travel abroad and have freedom, then he is a possibility investment buyer. Another salesperson attempting to sell him because he'll need the money to replace social security will fail to make the sale because he has not utilized the filter.

A useful question to find out whether the person tends to be possibility or necessity thinking is,

"Why are you in the business you are in?"

Your client either had to get the job they have or start the business they own, or, they saw this job or business and opportunity or possibility for some brighter future. Once you know which end of the spectrum your client is on, you operate through that filter as well. As with all metaprograms, if you pace the client's metaprogram and work within their filters, you will gain rapid compliance.

What are the similarities and differences between the Possibility/Necessity metaprogram and the Pleasure/Pain metaprogram? What differences do you notice?

Change/Status Quo Program

H. Change..**Status Quo**

Different	Consistent
Evolve	Stable
Alter	Steady
Switch	Same

Does your client like things to stay the way they are? Does he like to see his business or himself evolve? Grow? Does he like to change? Does he need to keep things status quo?

If you know the buyer's Change/Status Metaprogram you have a grand opportunity to create security in the status quo or excitement in change.

People who like change rarely keep jobs for a long period of time. They tend to get bored easily and they are constantly trying new things. People who like the status quo will tend to stay in the same jobs and do the same things day after day, month after month, year after year.

Accept Readily/Skeptical-Closed Program

I. Accepting.................Cautious.........Skeptical..........Closed

Accepting	Cautious	Skeptical	Closed
understand	careful	beware	never
unconditional	consider	can't	
always	sometimes	makes no sense	
friendly	nervous	afraid not	

You will discover that your customers fall on a continuum from open acceptance to critical skepticism of new ideas, products and services.

The program has some similarities to that of Change/Status Quo. However, they are not the same. People who are accepting are willing to listen.

Those who are closed are usually closed because of some event(s) that have transpired in his life.

Interestingly, people who are closed to opinions often got that way because they were once vulnerable and got hurt or taken advantage of. These are the people that put up "No Soliciting" signs. As every salesperson knows, they are among the easiest people to gain compliance with.

Psychobiology of Covert Hypnosis
Easy to Understand
Mind Access Points that Tap Your Clients DNA

Chapter Sixteen

Covert Hypnosis for the Genes?

There are a few multi-billion dollar corporations that know how to reach the inborn genetic programming within each of us so we will be inclined to purchase their products. You are going to now learn a few of the secrets of these multi-billion dollar international successes.

The world's best advertising is not geared at just our behavior but at something that is next to impossible to change: our DNA. We aren't going to take you through a scientific explanation of how each of these Mind Access Points work. That would take a set of encyclopedias. What you are going to learn is how to apply the research that we have done in the persuasion situation so that it is easy for you to utilize.

All people need food, clothing and shelter in our society. Those are inborn programs. We must eat to survive. We must have clothing to survive the cold winters. We must have some kind of shelter for inborn needs of security and territorial ownership. Beyond this, there are very few inborn needs, but there are many inborn tendencies that drive human behavior as your customer grows and becomes an adult.

Your Appeal Should be to the Many, not Just the One

Our genes do not simply generate the tendency for us to survive and care for the self, but they virtually command and carry out a powerful compulsion to care for the larger groups that we are part of. In fact, almost all of our genetic make-ups are so designed that we will help the larger groups we are part of survive before they will save themselves.

Have you ever seen a news story where a man raced into a burning building to save a young child? Not only is that an altruistic act, it is part of most people's genetic programming. The compulsion to care for others in our group is very powerful.

Almost all people are pre-programmed to act in the best interests of the following:

- Themselves
- The Family
- The Group
- Society
- God

The big mistake that persuaders make is that they only appeal to the customer's/counterpart's best interest when they should be appealing to the customer's interest in how your product will help his family, his employees, his civic groups and church organization, society as a whole and even God. It was only in 1998 that there was discovered a portion of the brain that is activated when communicating with the divine.

There is an old McDonald's commercial that illustrates how to appeal to the greater genetic needs. The theme song, "You deserve a break today, so get up and get away, to McDonalds..." plays in the background. The image is that of a man who has had a long day at work and the theme initially plays to his deserving a break. The genetic motivator however is not self-satisfaction. The motivator is when you see Dad and Mom and the kids all driving off to McDonald's together.

> *What a person may not be able to justify for himself can often be justified if it becomes obvious that it benefits our family, or society, or the group with which we belong.*

Exercise:
We learned that in order to motivate a person, you often must widen the context for the emotional reasoning to engage. Describe how you can you do this for

your product(s) and/or services?

Competition is a Driving Genetic Force of Survival

The field of evolutionary psychology has taught us that competition between individuals and groups is what naturally selects winners and losers in society.

When you are appealing to your customer to purchase your products and services, appeal subtly to the fact that owning your products or services will give him an advantage in society, within the group or against his competitors. The make up of the individual is to survive competitively.

The world's greatest competitors are those who become the wealthiest individuals. Bill Gates, Ted Turner, Warren Buffet. All of these men are very good people yet brilliant competitors. Bill Gates doesn't seek to own a share of the market with Microsoft, he seeks to dominate the market with Microsoft and does so by providing outstanding products at reasonable prices. Microsoft seeks to dominate with great products and services. You can do the same by appealing to the competitive nature in your customers. Do so quietly and with careful subtlety. *It is a genetic fact that those who opt out of competition reduce their level of prestige on the societal ladder.*

Success, survival and failure in all levels of animal and human society are wrapped up in the ability to compete and dominate.

Exercise: Realizing that competition is one genetic component of what creates success and failure in society, take your time and carefully answer the following three questions.

1. How can competing to dominate your market with great service and great products help you and your family ascend the ladder of success?

2. How can you sell more of your products and services by appealing to the need in our customers to be at or near the top of the success ladder?

3. How does being competitive enhance the quality of your life?

Persuading Groups is Far Easier Than Individuals

It is a known fact that madness is the exception in individuals and far more common in groups. Most normal humans would never throw ice balls at unprotected innocent people walking down the street. Watching a football game in season would never convince you of this truth as referees are constantly on the look out for spectators who they know can generate great harm. Fans watching soccer games have been seen on numerous occasions to literally kill people at soccer games because of the intensity generated during the competitiveness of the game.

Every public speaker knows that persuading most of the people in a large group of people is far easier than persuading one individual in a one-on-one setting. There is an almost evident IQ deficiency in groups. Groupthink takes over and people will follow the vocal proponents of a proposition. Most people are like sheep waiting for the shepherds.

Scientific research clearly shows that the more people are in a group, the more likely that the vast majority of the group will comply with whatever the leader is proposing. The fascinating caveat is that there is a very common fear of speaking and presenting before groups. This gives the master salesperson that is adept in Covert Hypnosis a powerful edge against all others in the persuasion process.

People act like animals in groups and are easily herded. Even the master of Covert Hypnosis cannot expect or even consider having 100% assenting opinions in group settings. In all groups there are individuals who rise above group think. When facing their objections, always honor and respect their point of view and continue on with your presentation. The vast majority will always rule and you will nearly always succeed in group selling situations if you follow all the key elements and pull all the right Mind Strings.

Remember the truism from the 19th century: The larger the lynch mob, the more brutal the lynching. Those in an emotional frenzy lose all sense of ethics. Think of experiences that you have had that make this fact clear to you.

Those in group settings tend to be led by the unconscious minds of the rest of the group. The average intelligence of the unconscious mind is about that of a six year old. This doesn't mean that there isn't a vast array of information stored in the unconscious mind, indeed there is. It does mean that the unconscious mind is far more reactive and emotional than the analytical conscious mind. The conscious mind rests in group settings making an easy target for the ethical salesperson or the unethical swindler.

It is encoded in people's genetic make up to find safety in groups. Once in a group, the normal person's defenses are dropped as there is a feeling of safety in almost all of the group.

Appealing to the Genetic Quest for Affiliation

All humans need to feel wanted. Science and medical research clearly reveals that feeling un-wanted stunts all forms of human growth and development. Physical, psychological, and emotional growth all are influenced by a person's perception of feeling wanted.

In fact, people who say they don't need to feel wanted are literally lying or psychotic. The need is pre-programmed.

You need to make it clear to your customers that you are interested in them as more than a customer. People can literally sense a true sense of interest and when they do, they are likely to develop the long-term relationships with you that will create win-win selling situations.

One recent medical study concluded that, "a lack of warmth and meaningful relationships" is a significant cause of heart attacks in many people. What does this tell us about needs pre-programmed into our behavior? We are physically influenced by love, compassion and relationships.

> *It is imperative that your customer perceives you as someone who truly cares about him. He must feel a sense of compassion and interest in him by you before you can predictably make sales at will.*

Dr. Dean Ornish published a wealth of material in 1998 about the fact that closeness can literally heal people and separation from loved ones can kill. Understanding this biological fact helps us influence others in a powerful way, doesn't it?

Exercise: Name and explain how numerous products and services are utilizing and/or exploiting this information. (Dating services, 900 lines, Psychic Friends, Chat Rooms, etc. etc.)

Is She Happy in Her Work?

Did you discover that your client/counterpart doesn't like her current job? Does she think that her work is important? (This would likely have come up during the values elicitation in the persuasion process.)

> *If people do not believe their work is important, use this fact as leverage for them to buy you, your product or service, saving them from physical illness.*

Did you know that if a person doesn't think what they are doing is important, that they are extremely likely to become ill and experience numerous and lengthy illnesses? With the knowledge that this has been pre-programmed into our thinking, this allows the persuader powerful control in any process.

Exercise: Explain how you can utilize the fact that perceived importance of a person's work is directly linked to illness as a Mind String Point.

He Seems So Confident

There are no self confident and supremely confident people. In fact, research shows that although we may feel secure, we do not feel extremely self-confident.

Exercise: How do the world's leading corporate marketers utilize this absolutely critical to sales Mind Access Point? List numerous examples. Include examples of selling cosmetics, clothing, and automobiles. Isolate the buttons that they push.

Positive Attitude? Here's the Truth for Persuaders

Projecting a positive attitude is not nearly as helpful to the self when contrasted with the great degree that it encourages others. When your customer sees your positive attitude, it gives them optimism and encouragement that you are a good person to be with and buy from. Generating a "positive attitude" is very important to persuasive success, because it improves the relationship you have with others.

Your Customer Likes some People...
...But not as many as You Might Think

Your customer doesn't like many others in his group. He tolerates them. If your customer is a franchise owner, he probably has a few friends in the same franchise, but not many.

Remember this as you are pacing your customer. Just because he owns a McDonald's doesn't mean he likes all the other franchise owners.

He probably will be hard pressed to admit this, but just knowing this genetic pre-disposition on your part is enough to save sales for you. Within the group there are various cliques of people. The fact that everyone is in the same high school doesn't mean they will like each other. It means they will all be happy to be rivals against another school but it doesn't in any way imply there will be friendliness within the school.

People tend to form cliques within their own larger groups. They tend to like the people in their clique. They are less interested in other people in the larger whole and they are likely to strongly dislike those in competing groups.

What is even more interesting is how much your customer doesn't like those outside his group. If you are selling insurance to the First Church of God, you will not build rapport by noting how well the First Church of Christ liked you. In fact, you are likely to lose the sale. They are not in the same group.

The more intricately they play a role within their own group, the less likely they are to like or even tolerate those in another competing group.

Exercise:
For your product or service, specifically list marketing and sales strategies using only the Mind Access Point listed in this section. How would you sell to a political or religious group? How would you sell to an individual with strong group affiliation?

How the Enemy Makes A Sale for You

When it seems that there is no competitive edge to your product or service, you can utilize a genetic predisposition that was alluded to in the Mind Access Point discussed above. You can assist in creating an enemy to bind people together.

The Internal Revenue Service is an enemy that has been able to bind the thoughts of the public together. Our elected officials have done this so we will vote for them. The enemy can be "good" or "evil." Appearances of good and evil are in the eyes of the beholder, of course. McDonald's doesn't like Burger King. Microsoft doesn't like Apple.

> *Create or identify an enemy that needs to be fought and then define how you, your product or service will help in the fight against the common enemy. An enemy can be a person, a group, a nation, or a non-living thing, like drugs, cigarettes, associations, churches, newspapers, etc.*

How do you utilize this principle of genetics in your favor?

President Clinton, in the wake of the Paula Jones/Monica Lewinsky hearings was able to take focus off of himself by finding a common enemy of almost all Americans, Saddam Hussein.

The strategy of "talking war" was brilliant as it bound the nation as it did seven years earlier in the Bush administration. The real threat of biological weapons in the hands of Iraq was enough to take Clinton/Lewinsky off of the front page of the newspaper and put Hussein, UN Inspectors and talk of war on the front pages. This created a new perspective in the public's thinking about the significance of the Jones/Lewinsky scandals.

Creating or identifying a common enemy is an excellent tool for building rapport and increasing compliance. If you can assist your customer to become frustrated with the status quo, his likely future, the success of his competitors, he is more likely to act in a positive manner on your request for his compliance.

The concept of using anger, disgust, fear, hatred and negative emotions in effective selling and marketing is as old as monetary exchange. For years we have seen commercials about how disgusting roaches are to have in the house. We spend billions on security systems every year in America, but only once the customer has experienced through future pacing or in actual case history of his security being violated. People will purchase products to relieve pain, reduce anxiety, be less depressed...and these products go far beyond medications! Some people buy magazines, books, CD's, computer games, Internet services, cars, houses, groceries, all to reduce negative emotions.

Exercise:

Discuss numerous examples of how you can utilize this powerful Mind Access Point with your sales campaigning.

The Have's and The Have Not's

"Money doesn't bring you happiness."
"People care too much about money."
"Money isn't important."
"I don't need things."
"I don't like being around all those control freaks."
"All I need to be happy is..."

When you are selling, you pace the client's actions and beliefs, but, also realize that he is only human and therefore programmed like most other humans. Your customer will often state something that he really doesn't believe because he wishes that what he was saying was true.

What are the facts about control, having, and happiness? How do these biological truths relate to your selling your products and services?

> *Control: The more you have, the healthier you are. Control is what keeps you focused and aware. People who experience a great deal of control in their lives tend to be healthier. When people feel in control or they feel your product or service will put them in control they are likely to buy from you now.*

If your customer is to succeed in life and move up the ladder of success and survival, he needs problems, the ability to solve them and the victories that come from defeating his problems. Control is analogous to personal power. Personal power is the ability to take action and achieve. The ability to meet life's challenges head on and win is not only useful in raising self-esteem and self-efficacy but also the general health of your client or counterpart!

If your product or service will give them more control in her life and she realizes it, then she will buy you or your product. PERIOD. Without control, people become hopeless. When people become hopeless you are once again able to help your customer. If your product or service can generate hope, you give new life to your customer...literally. If your customer sincerely believes that your product or service can help him, then you can literally help him change his life.

We need a significant amount of control for happiness. If you can paint a clear picture of how you can help the other person regain control in some area of his life or business, he will buy anything from you.

Exercise:
Hope and control are necessary to the immune system. Assuming the mind/body "knows" this, explain the utter usefulness of this information to the salesperson, the husband, father, and friend...

Who Your Customer Wants to Be Like

In all species, including humankind, the masses are compelled to be like the leader of the group(s). Your appeal to your customer therefore, should in part be one of installing the desire to be like the leaders in his or her field.

This could mean being a better parent, a better employee, and a better supervisor. Your job is to show how your products and services help your customer be more like the leader(s) of the group(s) he is most intimately linked to. In general, we imitate our leader's behavior. As a sales person, we therefore want to show how using our products will make the customer more like the leaders.

A Key Male Mind Access Point

Men who are rich in testosterone often find themselves in great trouble or achieving great success.

Testosterone inspires confidence and aggression. Most entrepreneurial types tend to be high in testosterone and tend to be confident of their ability to achieve in business and life. Knowing this allows you to pull a useful Mind Access Point. Appealing to the core urges of a man in some manner is useful in awakening his confidence and "go for it" attitudes.

> *Help him re-experience past victories in any aspect of life and you will probably succeed in creating a testosterone rush. Linking you or your product to this rush will enhance the probability of compliance.*

Testosterone is tied to "winning" in men.

An excellent manner of instilling a testosterone rush into men is to have them recount a story of a time when they overcame the odds and won. This normally creates a testosterone surge in men and builds confidence. By successfully linking this internal state to your product or service you almost assure yourself of making a sale.

Exercise:

Describe at least five methods of subtly linking your products or services to a man's past successes to enhance your probability of making the sale.

See You at the Top

One of my all time favorite self-development books is *See You at the Top* by Zig Ziglar. When Zig wrote this book he had little if any idea that the book would go on to sell 1.5 million copies. Zig could have predicted such an outcome had he known the genetic draw of humans to gravitate toward leaders in a group. Not only do we want to be like the leader in a group, we want to be *liked* by the leader in a group.

The higher up the ladder a person climbs, the more "friends" a person has. Now, it should be noted that these friends may be "fair weather friends," but clearly those who wish to consider themselves friends of the leaders in groups are far greater than those who dwell near the bottom of the societal ladders.

Therefore you have an opportunity to appeal to an individual's pre-programmed desire to first be at the top of the ladder and second, to be friends of the person at the top of the (or "a") ladder.

You may have the opportunity to share with your customer that if he moves up the ladder in his group that his health will improve. Recent research shows that those who are higher up the "ladder" have less hypertension. Health benefits are going to be a good justification for any action in the 21st century and this is one that is truly worth noting when it ties in with your products and services.

> *People want to either be at the top, be seen with the people on top or be given hope that they may be able to make it to the top. You, your product or service should somehow be able to help the other person up the ladder.*

Genuinely "Nice"

There are a great number of truly nice people in this world. We have all met a true altruist. This person is willing to give you the shirt off his back and he would literally feel blessed to do so. However, you may be surprised to know that gestures of compassion are not always the result of altruism. In fact, such is not the case, in the majority of situations.

Compassionate gestures help us feel superior, often causing people to look down on benefactors. In fact, not only are those who give doing so for a heightened sense of importance but those on the receiving end rarely gain long term appreciation of those who helped them. Resentment, oddly, is often the result.

The greatest example of this Mind Access Point occurs on a macro level. Over the last several decades America has given or loaned numerous countries billions upon billions of dollars. What is the normal attitude of the countries that have been the beneficiaries of these loans and donations? They hate America passionately.

> *When appropriate you may find it useful to appeal to the feelings of strength a person gets from doing "a good thing" in addition to the feeling of "goodness" a person experiences upon helping others.*

The Best of Times...The Worst of Times

When times are relatively good, on average, we are biologically programmed to venture out and increase risk and adventure in our lives. When times are bad, on average, we are likely to play our cards closer to the vest and be much more conservative.

When participating in the sales process it is very useful to know whether your client is going through good times or bad. If she is going through good times you can appeal to her desire to experiment, her need to expand her horizons and explore. If she is going through bad times, you need show how your products will allow her to meet her conservative needs.

The emotional appeal of your product is very important in determining whether you will make the sale or not. People will justify their purchase logically, but first need to fit the product into their emotional filters.

> *Appeal to their need to take risks and participate in adventure in good times. When experiencing bad times, appeal to your their needs of security and safety.*

The Enhanced Covert Hypnosis Model

As you approach the end of this book, you realize that you have gained a greater understanding of your customer, what he needs to be happy and successful, and how he thinks. This provides you the opportunity to begin to integrate all of the points in this book, into your thinking. You are going to soon find the ability to facilitate change in others' thinking and sell you, your product or service virtually at will.

In order to accomplish the ability to sell at will, you must be able to develop strategies for selling in 10 key areas of the selling process.

You must develop specific strategies (patterns of behavior) in order to achieve rapport, develop relationships, pull their Mind Access strings, change "no's" into "yes's" and close sales. In the next chapter you will learn the key areas that you will fine-tune in your skills.

Ten Powerful Covert Hypnosis Strategies...

Chapter Seventeen

These are destined to be the ten keys to persuasion success in your journey to persuading at will.

1. Managing Your State of Mind in All Situations

Your state of mind is one element of the sales process that you have a great deal of control over. Your "state" is generally considered to be made up of three elements, two of which you can control and one of which is difficult to control.

A) *Your Internal Representations*

There is no question that the pictures, words and emotions you experience in your mind, are in large part under your control. If your internal representations are sabotaging you, then you need to take back control of your mind. You must begin to paint new pictures for yourself. Begin to see your life as more likely to succeed. Begin to see yourself as becoming competent in understanding the behavior, actions, and thinking of other people. Realize that as you become effective in understanding the workings of others you become more in control of yourself.

Your Internal Representations include what you say to yourself when you talk. These representations include the tone of voice when you talk to yourself. *If you don't like what is going on in your brain, change it now.* You can change the tone of your voice when you talk to you from one that implies, "You Dummy" to one that commands, "You ARE going to Make it BIG!"

When you experience pictures that create a sense of hopelessness immediately change the picture to a struggle that ends with your success instead of failure. Taking an active role in your self-management is very important to your success as a highly effective salesperson.

B) Physiology

Managing your mind is inextricably linked to managing your body. If you are finding yourself to be obese, suffering from aches and pains that can be attended to and notice that your day to day posture and "carrying of yourself" is impotent you must take action to change now.

Overweight? Start a weight reduction program immediately. Your body image directly affects your self-esteem and that means it affects your sales. *Become active and get your body image in line so you are proud of the way you like. How you see yourself impacts your perceived attractiveness by others.*

Do you suffer from pains, aches, and other somatics that can be treated or helped with therapy? Do it! Pain and other somatics reduce your effectiveness and drain you of necessary energy that you need to give to your customers.

Is your posture lousy? Start sitting up straight and walking as if someone has a huge hand pushing your buttocks forward. This will improve your posture dramatically. The way you carry yourself will change many "no's" into "yes's" because many people perceive that a hunched over appearance is indicative of low self confidence. When people think you are not confident it drains their confidence in you as a salesperson and reduces your sales volume.

C) Genetic Factors Can Be Helped Too!

If you suffer from depression, anxiety, panic disorder, and other emotional challenges, talk to your medical doctor and find appropriate medications to help yourself. There is no shame in utilizing anti-depressants and anti-anxiety medications to make up for inefficient neuro-biology. It is very difficult to change your "brain chemistry" in a predictable manner with cognitive techniques alone. Take advantage of the laser beam like medications that are available to help you. Consult your physician. There is ALWAYS something you can do.

2. Managing Your Customer or Counterpart's State of Mind

You can begin to manage other people's minds once you have your own state managed. Managing your customer's state is accomplished in the same manner that you manage your states of mind. The only difference is that you must pull your customer's Mind Access strings instead of pulling your own.

A. Internal Representations

If your client needs to experience a brief dose of status quo misery to help him change to a brighter future, then you are obligated to paint a vivid picture of both what he must move away from and what he must move toward. Make the voices he is going to hear in his mind clear and loud. Help him feel the pain of stasis and the pleasure of change if he can't do it for himself.

B. Physiology

Sometimes it is necessary to get your client to move to create internal change in his state of mind. Hand him something. Give him a book and have him turn the pages. Ask your client to participate in some activity with you. DO SOMETHING with your client. You are not obligated to always sit face to face, across the table from each other.

If the other person is in a "stuck state" the sale is going to be lost if you don't change his state. Sometimes it is appropriate to get up and go or at least move somewhere else. Changing their physiology will change his internal state.

C. Appeal to You Client's Genetic Makeup

You have learned in this book dozens of genetic traits and pre-programmed tendencies. Utilize this information by practicing the strategies necessary to pull the genetic Mind Access strings that you have learned about.

3. Gather, Manage and Implement Intelligence

Eliciting values, beliefs, and feelings, is a method of gathering vital intelligence about your customer. The best salespeople gather intelligence about their customers before they meet, if possible. In this book you have learned about personality and buying types and who buys based upon what metaprograms are running inside them. That is intelligence. There is more to be learned, however.

If you are selling to corporations, you can uncover everything from corporate earnings to corporate strategy by simply making phone calls to the company and asking before you go on your visit. Learn what you can about the needs, interests and wants of the company.

Secretaries are a fountain of knowledge. One of my favorite selling strategies is to not try and bypass the secretary but instead, make friends with her.

"Hi Jane, this is Kevin Hogan, the author of *The Psychology of Persuasion*. Does your boss decide what speakers to bring into your corporation or is that someone else I should talk to?"

"Once I get him on the phone, what does he look for in a good speaker?"

"Does he really go for motivational speakers or those who present more practical applications in sales and marketing?"

"What was your favorite speaker in the last year or two?"

"What was his favorite speaker in the last couple years?"

This gathering of intelligence is powerful. In this example you are speaking with the secretary who is indeed the gatekeeper in the corporate world. Instead of passing by the gatekeeper you have made friends by asking for her opinions and building a sense of respect for her and her knowledge about what her company likes. This is how you want to gather intelligence beyond the more general buying profiles we discussed earlier in the book.

4. Networking Your Way to Success

Networking only works if you have at least one of three things. You are the best in your business, you have great products and/or you have great services. If you can meet someone's needs time and again, then you can network your way to sales success.

One rule that is constructive to keep in mind is to do something to help someone else's career every day. If you can help others with their families, businesses, careers, you will eventually reap the rewards of what you have sown.

Networking is more than keeping a fat Rolodex. Networking is the ability to recommend someone who can solve someone else's problem. People appreciate you when you help them and have nothing to gain in return.

Assist people every day with random or intentional acts of kindness and you will build a network of friends and people who will help you in your future. It is almost impossible to help people every day and not experience the rewards of networking down the line.

Networking also demands that you have the courage to call the people who can make a difference in your career. Many people will not call on the right person to buy or even for advice simply because they believe the celebrity won't talk to a humble salesperson. This is nonsense. 10-20% of celebrities, CEO's, and

272

even political leaders are attainable. If what you have to offer is useful enough, you can get your minutes with the biggest decision makers.

Be willing to be bold and occasionally embarrassed in exchange for the benefits of being known by the "right people."

5. Be a Hunter

The world's most successful people don't simply sit back and wait for business to come to them. The world's greatest become adept at hunting for those who will buy your products and services. Business *is always* good for someone. Business can almost always be good *for you.*

One distinction between those who have great success and those who are work-a-day people is the hunter mentality. The hunter is always looking for people he can help. The hunter is relentless in the pursuit of the right groups and markets for his products and services. The hunter doesn't rely on lead sources from inside the company. The hunter is constantly developing his own contacts.

People who succeed in multi-level marketing are those who see opportunity for almost everyone they meet. This doesn't mean the hunter is pushy or involves people in a project that won't be in the individual's best interest. It does mean that a hunter will always be aware of people's needs and desires.

The hunter always goes the extra mile. When you go the extra mile you always have more opportunities for success than the average salesperson. Going the extra mile can mean asking for referrals or better, asking who else will definitely benefit from an outstanding product or service. The hunter is always bending over backwards to help others. The hunter is generally thought of as "lucky" because they seem to regularly be meeting opportunity with preparation, one definition of luck.

6. Building Credibility with People

When communicating with others, is it apparent that you have their best interests in mind? If you have any doubt that you are not selling a great product or a great service you must choose a product or service that is great to sell. If you are selling yourself as a consultant, then you must be the best. You must constantly go the extra mile to make yourself part of the top 20%. This is where credibility begins.

An excellent manner of establishing credibility is that of being able to bring out the key drawback of your product or service and make certain that your customer sees that one flaw. Once you have done this you have not only established credibility but you have already dealt with what is normally the only objection to your making the sale, except money issues, which may or may not be easily solved.

Remember the call letters: WII-FM. They stand for "What's in it for me?" If you can put yourself in your customer's shoes and answer that question with a laundry list of benefits, you will begin making more sales, higher volume sales and a higher percentage of sales.

How do you appear less than credible on occasion?

Sometimes we get nervous in the persuasion process that our product may not be the best for our client and we continue to sell anyway. It is at this point that you must ask your customer, "If this product could only help you to this certain degree at this price, is it something that would be really useful to you?"

If they say "yes," you can allow the pangs of nervousness to leave. If they say "no," then forget making the sale. You could still choose to pull all the right Mind Access strings, walk away with a check, but you will have created a Win-Lose, and that means your career will take a step backward. *Never, ever, enter into any sales transaction where one party loses.*

Creating beliefs (i.e.. levels of certainty) is critical. If you expect to fail you probably will. If you expect to succeed you probably will. What you say to yourself in private is what you become. Begin to see yourself as a provider, a helper, a caretaker, and a creator of value. If this isn't possible, you are selling the wrong product.

You will have a difficult time selling a particular make of cars if you don't believe that they are the best cars, for the money in the country. Believe it or move to a different dealership. Refuse to sell what is second best. Never compromise your integrity. People will talk about you and believe in you if you are the best, selling products that have great value. Once you are selling something you believe in, your enthusiasm will be contagious.

Your potential and that of all of your competitors is correlated to beliefs. These beliefs fall into two distinct categories. In selling, ethical selling demands that you believe in your idea, product, service, etc. Second, it must be evident that you KNOW that you are creating value by partaking in the sales process. If you feel tainted by selling then consider how your customers will feel if they are buying someone else's products and services. Are your customers going to be buying second best if someone else goes to see them? Don't let it happen.

Being believable is about being congruent. Remember when Kathleen Willey appeared on 60 Minutes in 1998 and clearly but emotionally told of her encounter with President Clinton at the White House? Americans believed her because she was congruent. She was perceived as congruent because what she said matched with how she said it. Her verbal communication matched her non-verbal communication. She was believable.

Keypoint: Once you reach the point that you are congruent with what you are persuading another, you will be unstoppable.

Exercise:

Name some congruent people. Describe specifically why you believe these people to be congruent. Name some incongruent people. Describe specifically why you believe these people to be incongruent. What can you do so you stay in the category of congruent people? If you are not perceived as congruent and believable you will not make the sale. If you are perceived as believable and you sell excellent products and services, you will be on the road to success in selling. Your enthusiasm about the home you are selling, the stocks you are touting, the automobiles your customers are going to drive away in, is all going to be transferred to your customer like a mind virus. (A meme.) Your level of certainty, combined with pure rapport, and meeting their true wants and needs, allows you to sell at will.

7. Develop a Sense of Fascination

Decide that you will learn everything about your customer that she is willing to comfortably share with you. Develop a sense of fascination about the work and livelihood about others. What is grand about your customer? What is great about their job? What is fascinating about their philosophy of life? Allow yourself to become curious and excited about learning about other people and their interests.

Remember that what is interesting to you is likely to be boring to most other people. What is interesting to your customer, on the other hand, is something he can talk about for hours on end. Your customer's interests become your new areas of fascination and curiosity.

8. Change the Frame

Everyone looks at "things" from their own point of view, from their own perspective. Key number eight, will help you learn how to alter the way someone is looking at something so you can alter how they feel about that self same "thing."

Framing is analogous to what light you are going to place a communication in. What may seem to be a disaster for a client, can be re-framed as being an opportunity for change and growth. What may be seen as the end of a long sad marriage could be re-framed into the beginning of a new happy life.

Reframing

Reframing is taking lemons and then upon further review, you make lemonade out of the lemons you have been given. Reframing allows you to help someone see something they perceive as a problem that really may be an opportunity in disguise. Read the examples below then write out common objections to your products and services and "reframe" them so you never have to think about doing this on the spot.

Example: If you are working with "big picture people," you will now see the value of framing (creating an areas of focus) things in a manner where they are small and barely worth consideration or where they are large and life changing.

"You know John, I realize that $197 per year for life insurance doesn't seem to be much to think about, but, it really is important that you do this now, because of the un-predictability of life and death."

or

"You know John, I realize that $18 per month can be seen as quite a bit of money, yet, that is why you MUST decide to do this. If anything happens to your wife will have a check for $100,000 waiting for her to take care of your kids. What greater gift can you give?"

Obviously, frames help us see an issue from a different point of view than the one we just saw. Frames are used in Hypnotherapy and NLP to enhance and control the communication process. (Erickson, Rossi, Bandler, Grinder, Robbins, et. al.)

Here are a few different kinds of frames and how to utilize them in putting your products and services, and, yourself in the best light possible with your clients.

The "As If" Frame

Have you ever had a client that said, "I don't know what will happen if..." It may be that you have heard something like, "I don't know what my wife would say if I..."

When you face these unknowns the most effective strategy is to utilize the "As If" Frame. You can utilize this them by asking one or more of these three pattern questions.

If you did this X, what would happen?

Imagine that we were successful at X, then what would happen?

If you did decide to do "this" (agree to "this") what was it that would have changed your mind?

These patterns are so powerful that normally the customer's objection or worry will be drained right from his mind as he answers the question.

Preframing

You will recall that pointing out a minor flaw in your product or company can be a very useful tool in the sales process. It gives you immense credibility. Always, always, handle the problem that is likely to come up, in advance of the problem (objection/perceived, argument, obvious other point of view). Deal with any challenge early in the persuasive meeting while the significance of any issue will be considered to be very small and seemingly irrelevant.

Persuasion and Influence is in large part an issue of controlling the frame of communication. You must realize that unless a person dismisses you out of hand, that they see something they like about your offer. Therefore control that frame, that focus of attention and key in on this area. Therefore in any disagreement, argument, objection you must change the focus of attention of the other person or people.

Example: "Covert Hypnosis may not be the ideal weekend sales and persuasion course for you. It is possible that you will consider the price tag of $2,000 too great an investment in return for control of your life and a dramatic near term increase in income. Covert Hypnosis is about people who want to be happy, in charge of their lives and their communication. Covert Hypnosis is for people who want to be influential because they offer something unique to the world. If this isn't you, then simply don't come."

Deframing

Jim Pickens, the author of the most powerful sales book in history, *Closers*, calls deframing the "take away close." Once you are skilled in Covert Hypnosis techniques you will have the confidence and ability to prudently utilize deframing.

Deframing is a linguistic tool that can only be effectively implemented when you know a person's match/mis-match meta program, or, when you know the person definitely wants your service, product or offer. In a nutshell, you give the customer one opportunity to purchase your product or hire you. If they don't, you make it explicitly clear that you will move on and allow others to take advantage of your services.

This is the basic deframing pattern:

"It makes no difference to me whether you buy this X or not. You have until tomorrow to make a decision and reserve your X or not. If I don't hear from you by noon, I'll know you didn't want it. No pressure. Bye."

9. Uncover Conditions to Confirmation

Even the greatest product in the world may not be able to help a person with a condition. You may be able to sell a $300,000 home at half price to an owner occupant, which is a bargain anyone is unlikely to ever experience. But if your client doesn't have the money for the down payment and hasn't got the income, resources or ability to sign the loan for other reasons, you have a condition and you should never ask a person to enter into an agreement where he will lose. Value is very important but it is not the only element in deciding whether to make a sale or not. If the client cannot do something, don't ask them to. A condition exists in some selling situations, which means a sale won't be made, and when they do exist, you won't let that sale happen. It's a Win-Lose.

If you sense your customer has a condition, simply ask, "Is there something I'm missing, that I should know about that is causing you to wonder about this product?" If they respond with a concern, address their concern and let them own your product. If they respond with a condition, don't let them buy your product. There will be another day for both of you.

10. Develop a Series of Logical Reasoning

People will buy your products and services based upon their desires in most cases. You need to develop a step-by-step process that will assist your client to bridge the gap between emotion and logical reasoning to purchase your product. You should have several series of thought processes that you have prepared for your client to consider.

If you are selling a home and your client has the requirements met to buy the home, you have a potential sale. If your client falls in love with the home you have an emotional sale. Your job is now to move your client from emotional thought to logical justification for purchasing this home.

How can you go from logical to emotional?

First you can ask if this is a home they would really love to live in. An affirmative response leads you to your next thought, which is,

"Are you aware that every dollar you spend on your monthly house payment works for you in one way or another? Either it goes toward the principle which means the *money comes back to you* or you can use the rest of the payment as a tax deduction which means *some of the money comes back to you.* When you pay rent, all of the money goes away from you, down the toilet, flushed into the sanitation system forever. The question is, do you want to own a home or do you want to make someone else wealthy, instead of developing your own wealth, for the rest of your life?"

You move from an emotional response to a logical rationale to an integration of emotions and logic. This is ethical, it is honest and it is in the best interest of your client if no conditions exist.

11. Know When to "Close" and When to Leave

Most people believe that you "close" the sale after the sales presentation is over. That is not correct. You close the sale the moment the customer wants to buy and not a second later.

When the customer is ready, you let them agree to buy your product. You have them sign the papers, take ownership and shortly thereafter, you leave. If the customer asks you for a lunch date, that is one thing. If they are busy and have a schedule to keep, make the sale happen and then politely but with efficiency wrap up your business. In many cases, I have made the sale, had the client write a check, put it away in my briefcase and then had lunch with the client. In situations such as this you do not discuss your business, you continue to develop the long-term friendship by focusing on the client and his loves and interests.

In general, when your client is non-verbally or verbally telling you they want to hire you or they want your product, let them buy it now. Then, after you have taken care of business, take care of any post-closing activities and thank your new customer.

Conclusion

I've used hundreds of examples from the fields of therapy and selling to illustrate how to utilize Cover Hypnosis. Always change the CONTENT to your specific situation whether you want the girl to go out with you or you want the kids to listen, or whatever the specific context is for YOU.

Covert Hypnosis continues to be the most powerful material for persuasion to date...

It's my hope that this massive volume on persuasion, covert hypnosis and subtle influence will be used with ethical intent. These are the secrets of unconscious communication and they will change your life.

Kevin Hogan

Bibliography

Allesandra, Tony and Michael J. O'Connor. The Platinum Rule: Do Unto Others As They'd Like Done Unto Them. New York, NY: Warner Books, Inc., 1996.

Anastasi, Tom. Personality Selling, Selling the Way Clients Want to Buy. New York, NY: Sterling Publications, 1992.

Andreas, Steve and Charles Faulkner. NLP: The New Technology of Achievement. New York, NY: William Morrow and Company, 1994.

Aronson, Elliott. The Social Animal. New York, NY: W. H. Freeman and Company, 1995.

Bagley, Dan and Edward J. Reese. Beyond Selling: How To Maximize Your Personal Influence. Cupertino, CA: Meta Publications, 1988.

Bandler, Richard & John LaValle. Persuasion Engineering. Capitola, CA: Meta Publications, 1996.

Bethel, William. 10 Steps to Connecting With Your Client: Communication Skills for Selling Your Products, Services, and Ideas. Chicago, IL: The Dartnell Corporation, 1995.

Bloom, Howard. The Lucifer Principle: A Scientific Expedition Into the Forces of History. NY. Atlantic Monthly Press, 1995.

Brodie, Richard. Virus of The Mind: The New Science of the Meme. Integral Press. 1996.

Brooks, Michael. Instant Rapport: The NLP Program the Creates Intimacy, Persuasiveness, Power! New York, NY: Warner Books, Inc., 1989.

Brooks, Michael. The Power of Business Rapport: Use NLP Technology to Make More Money, Sell Yourself and Your Product, and Move Ahead in Business. New York, NY: Harper-Collins Publishers, 1991.

Buzan, Tony and Richard Israel. Brain Sell. Brookfield, VT: Gower, 1995.

Cialdini, Robert B. Influence: The New Psychology of Persuasion. New York, NY: Morrow, 1993.

Cohen, Allan R. and David L. Bradford. Influence Without Authority. New York, NY: John Wiley & Sons, 1991.

Dalet, Kevin with Emmett Wolfe. Socratic Selling: How to Ask the Questions that Get the Sale. Chicago, IL: Irwin Professional Publishing, 1996.

Dayton, Doug. Selling Microsoft, Sales Secrets from Inside the World's Most Successful Company. Holbrook, Mass. Dayton, 1997.

Dawson, Roger. Secrets of Power Persuasion: Everything You'll Ever Need to Get Anything You'll Ever Want. Englewood Cliffs, NJ: Prentice-Hall, Inc., 1992.

Decker, Bert. You've Got To Be Believed To Be Heard: Reach the First Brain to Communicate in Business and in Life. New York, NY: St. Martin's Press, 1992.

Elgin, Suzette Haden. Success with the Gentle Art of Verbal Self-Defense. Englewood Cliffs, NJ: Prentice-Hall, Inc., 1989.

Farber, Barry J. and Joyce Wycoff. Breakthrough Selling: Client-Building Strategies from the Best in the Business. Englewood Cliffs, NJ: Prentice-Hall, Inc., 1992.

Gitomer, Jeffrey. The Sales Bible: The Ultimate Sales Resource. New York, NY: William Morrow, 1994.

Grinder, John. The Structure of Magic, Vol 1. Palo Alto, CA: Science and Behavior Books, 1976.

Hamer, Dean. Living With Our Genes: Why They Matter More Than You Think. NY. Doubleday, 1998.

Hogan, Kevin. (Audio Program) Mind Access: Beyond the Psychology of Persuasion. Network 3000 Publishing, Eagan, MN: 1997.

Hogan, Kevin. (Video Program) Persuasion Mastery Course, Network 3000 Publishing, Eagan, MN: 1997

Hogan, Kevin. Life By Design: Your Handbook for Transformational Living. Network 3000 Publishing, Eagan, MN. 1995

Hogan, Kevin. The Psychology of Persuasion: How to Persuade Others to Your Way of Thinking. Gretna, LA: Pelican Publishing Company, 1996.

Hogan, Kevin. Through the Open Door: Secrets of Self Hypnosis. Gretna, LA: Pelican Publishing Company, 2000.

Johnson, Kerry L. Sales Magic: Revolutionary New Techniques That Will Double Your Sales Volume in 21 Days. New York, NY: William Morrow and Company, Inc., 1994.

Johnson, Kerry L. Subliminal Selling Skills. New York, NY: AMACOM, 1988.

Keirsey. David and Marilyn Bates. Please Understand Me: Character & Temperament Types. Del Mar, CA: Prometheus Nemesis Book Company, 1984.

Kennedy, Daniel S. The Ultimate Sales Letter. Holbrook, MA: Bob Adams, Inc., 1990.

Kent, Robert Warren. The Art of Persuasion. Surfside, FL: Lee Institute, 1963.

Knapp, Mark and Judy Hall. Nonverbal Communication in Human Interaction. 3rd Ed. Fort Worth, TX: Harcourt Brace College Publications, 1992.

Knight, Sue. NLP at Work: The Difference That Makes A Difference in Business. Sonoma, CA: Nicholas Brealey Publishing, 1995.

Kostere, Kim. Get the Results You Want: A Systematic Approach to NLP. Portland, OR: Metamorphous Press, 1989.

Lavington, Camille with Stephanie Losee. You've Only Got Three Seconds: How to Make the Right Impression in your Business and Social Life. New York, NY: Doubleday, 1997.

Lewis, David. The Secret Language of Success: Using Body Language to Get What You Want. New York, NY: Carroll & Graf, 1990.

Linden, Anne with Kathrin Perutz. Mindworks: Unlock the Promise Within — NLP Tools for Building a Better Life. Kansas City, MO: Andrews McMeel Publishing, 1997.

Mehrabian, Albert. Silent Messages: Implicit Communication of Emotions and Attitudes. Belmost, CA: Wadsworth, 1981.

Moine, Donald J. and John H. Herd. Modern Persuasion Strategies: The Hidden Advantage in Selling. Englewood Cliffs, NJ: Prentice-Hall, Inc., 1984.

Moine, Donald J. and Kenneth Lloyd. Unlimited Selling Power: How to Master Hypnotic Selling Skills. Englewood Cliffs, NJ: Prentice-Hall, Inc., 1990.

Nicholas, Ted. Magic Words That Bring You Riches. Indian Rocks Beach, FL: Nicholas Direct, 1996.

Overstreet, H. A. Influencing Human Behavior. New York, NY: Norton, 1925.

Patton, Forrest H. Force of Persuasion: Dynamic Techniques for Influencing People. Englewood Cliffs, NJ: Prentice-Hall, Inc., 1986.

Piirto, Rebecca. Beyond Mind Games: The Marketing Power of Psychographics. Ithaca, NY: American Demographic Books, 1991.

Peoples, David. Selling To The Top. New York, NY: John Wiley & Sons, Inc., 1993.

Qubein, Nido. Professional Selling Techniques: Strategies and Tactics to Boost Your Selling Skills and Build Your Career. Rockville Centre, NY: Farnsworth

Publishing Co., Inc., 1983.

Richardson, Jerry. The Magic of Rapport. Capitola, CA: Meta Publications, 1988.

Robbins, Anthony. Unlimited Power. New York, NY: Fawcett, 1987.

Robertson, James E. Sales the Mind's Eye: What They Didn't Teach You In Sales Training. Portland, OR: Metamorphous Press, 1990.

Sadovsky, Marvin C. and Jon Caswell. Selling the Way Your Client Buys: Understand Your Persons' Unspoken Needs & Close Every Sale. New York, NY: AMACOM, 1996.

Solderholm, Craig E. How 10% of the People Get 90% of the Pie: Get Your Share Using Subliminal Persuasion Techniques. New York, NY: St. Martin's Press, 1997.

Stiles, William H. Hypno-Salesmanship: The Suggestive Art That Helps People Buy. New Castle, PA: Bill Stiles Associates, 1996.

Thompson, George J. and Jerry B. Jenkins. Verbal Judo: The Gentle Art of Persuasion. New York, NY: William Morrow and Company, Inc., 1993.

Tracy, Brian. Advanced Selling Strategies: The Proven System of Sales Ideas, Methods, and Techniques Used By Top people Everywhere. New York, NY: Fireside, 1995.

Vitale, Joe. Cyber Writing: How to Promote Your Product or Service Online. New York, NY: AMACOM, 1997.

Vitale, Joe. The Seven Lost Secrets of Success. Houston: VistaTron, 1994.

Willingham, Ron. The Best Seller: The New Psychology of Selling and Persuading People. Englewood Cliffs, NJ: Prentice-Hall, Inc., 1984.

Kevin Hogan is the author of nineteen books. He is best known for his international best selling book, *The Psychology of Persuasion: How to Persuade Others to Your Way of Thinking.*

In the past decade he has become the Body Language Expert and Unconscious Influence Expert to ABC, Fox, The BBC, *The New York Times*, *The New York Post* and dozens of popular magazines like *Forbes*, *Investors Business Daily*, *InTouch*, *First for Women*, *Success!*, and *Cosmopolitan*. He has become the go-to resource for analyzing key White House figures for various media.

Hogan has taught Persuasion and Influence at the University of St. Thomas Management Center and is a frequent media guest. Articles by and about him have appeared in *Success!*, *Redbook*, *Office Pro*, *Selling Power*, *Cosmopolitan*, *Maxim*, *Playboy* and numerous other publications. He was recently featured in a half dozen magazines (including *wProst*) in Poland.

Kevin is a dynamic, well-known international public speaker, consultant and corporate trainer. He has trained persuasion, sales and marketing skills to leaders in the government of Poland, employees from Mutual of Omaha, Boeing, Microsoft, Starbucks, Cargill, Pillsbury, Carlson Companies, Fortis Insurance, Great Clips, the State of Minnesota, 3M, The United States Postal Service and numerous other Fortune 500 companies. He recently spoke to The Inner Circle and at the Million Dollar Roundtable (MDRT) convention in Las Vegas.

His keynotes, seminars and workshops help companies sell, market and communicate more effectively. His cutting edge research into the mind and keen understanding of consumer behavior create a unique distillation of information never before released to the public. Each customized program he leads is fit specifically to the needs of the group or organization. Kevin will give your people new and easy to implement ideas to achieve excellence.

Some of the other books by Kevin Hogan:

The 168 Hour Week: Living Life Your Way 24/7
12 Factors of Business Success
The Secret Language of Business
Selling: Powerful New Strategies for Sales Success
Covert Persuasion
The Science of Influence
The Psychology of Persuasion: How to Persuade Others to Your Way of Thinking
Irresistible Attraction: Secrets of Personal Magnetism

Want to learn more about the science of influence?

For More Information

Get gift that keeps giving, a one year subscription to *Coffee with Kevin Hogan,* the e-zine that everyone reads about influence, selling, body language and personal development every Monday morning. Go to http://www.kevinhogan.com/bonus.htm today!

And as a bonus gift, get Kevin's 179 page e-book, **Breaking Through the 8 Barriers of Communication**. You'll discover the 8 ways to avoid turning people off and instead, build powerful LASTING rapport. A full length book!

Lightning Source UK Ltd.
Milton Keynes UK
UKOW040713201011

180636UK00001B/1/P